A Stakeholder Approach
to Corporate Governance

iii

Recent Titles from Quorum Books

A
STAKEHOLDER APPROACH
TO
CORPORATE GOVERNANCE

Managing in a
Dynamic Environment

ABBASS F. ALKHAFAJI

QUORUM BOOKS

NEW YORK
WESTPORT, CONNECTICUT
LONDON

Library of Congress Cataloging-in-Publication Data

Alkhafaji, Abbass F.
  A stakeholder approach to corporate governance.

  Bibliography: p.
  Includes index.
  1. Corporate governance.   2. Industrial management.
I. Title.
HD38.A38   1989   658.4   88–32489
ISBN 0–89930–447–8 (lib. bdg. : alk. paper)

British Library Cataloguing in Publication Data is available.

Library of Congress Catalog Card Number: 88–32489
ISBN: 0–89930–447–8

First published in 1989 by Quorum Books

Greenwood Press, Inc.
88 Post Road West, Westport, Connecticut 06881

Printed in the United States of America

The paper used in this book complies with the
Permanent Paper Standard issued by the National
Information Standards Organization (Z39.48–1984).

10 9 8 7 6 5 4 3 2 1

Contents

Tables, Figures, and Models

TABLES

FIGURES

MODELS

Preface

This book presents the fundamental concepts of corporate governance in a logical, concise, and simple manner. It provides a foundation that concentrates on clarifying issues and increasing understanding in a new approach to corporate governance—the stakeholder approach.

The term *corporate governance* in this text refers to the mode of structure, the power that determines the rights and responsibilities of the various groups involved in running the organization. Also included in this definition is the legitimacy expectation of the business, the method of operating, and the overall accountability of management and the board of directors. The term stakeholder refers to those groups who have *direct* interest in the survival of the organization, and, without their support, the organization would cease to exist.

There are many issues in the area of corporate governance, some of which are (1) the feeling that many of the directors often place their interests above those of the corporation, (2) questions about excessive social costs caused by corporations operating solely in their own economic interests, and (3) the fear of the abuse of power concentrated in the hands of top-level management and the board of directors.

In terms of corporate governance, many have been critical of the legitimacy of the governance procedures and have supported reforms that could have a monumental impact on the way large corporations are governed. In the past this governing process was rather easy because very few participants were involved. Businesses were being managed by their owners. As the companies grew they consequently went public with stock offerings and the governance process became highly complicated. Today, society and government are concerned about the abuse of power by those who manage the corporation. Issues such as illegal campaign contributions, secret payments to pay off foreign officials, and lack of health and safety concerns for workers are common in the current business environment.

Over the past several years, a new approach to management has arisen in the area of public issues. Consequently these issues have brought forth many changes in both the structure and operation of business, making the job of management much more complex.

Previously, business was only concerned with economic essentials such as producing goods and services for their markets, rewarding shareholders, providing employment, and maintaining growth in their company. During this era, if these particular objectives were satisfied, the business community felt they were fulfilling their obligation to society and satisfying social needs. However, during the past two decades things have changed drastically. These changes stem from new issues such as safety in the workplace, pollution control, concern for equal opportunity, and the quality and safety of consumer products. These issues came to be referred to as public issues due to their impact on people and the government regulations they created.

The firm was concerned only with a small number of external factors such as quantity of output, price, product quality, choice of employees, and use of resources. This has all changed and today's business firm must consider a host of other issues involving values, ethics, the media, shortages, and instability in the marketplace. Furthermore, social attitudes toward business have changed and they must now consider government regulation, public interest groups, and more importantly, the shareholders of the firm, all of which came to be seen as threats to their economic mission. Decision making of the firm of the past was performed internally with the company's self-interest in mind; social and political issues were not very significant.

The new business environment and its external environment are not clearly separated as the past has shown. Many social issues of two decades ago are today's government regulations and current decision makers must consider these social, political, and economic influences. More recent issues are concerned with the cleanliness of the environment, equality among people, and health and safety factors, all of which are implemented in business operations creating a more complex management function.

Other important issues involve ethical behavior, and because of social concern government has enacted laws and regulations to address this area. Modern corporate business is under constant observation not only from the social arena but from the media as well, who are concerned with ethical and economic performance.

With these underlying problems, the initial role of corporate strategy has found itself concerned with defining major goals and objectives of the organization and designs policies and plans to achieve these goals. These aspects are all designed to respond to the changing environmental conditions of business and individuals. Management must be responsive to these public issues because they can create changes in operations or the overall structure of the business. The main idea has been to integrate environmental concerns into the regular business operation. This brings public policy issues into the decision-making process.

This book is an attempt to discuss these and many other issues that are facing society in general and business in particular. The book is organized into five parts; each part is carefully designed to be the foundation for the others and is then divided into chapters.

Part 1 deals with the trend of business development. It discusses the concept of the company, legally and conceptually. The changing environment and society's expectations, along with the development of business law in the United States, are addressed. The significance of large corporations, corporate accountability, and regulation are given attention here, as well as the difference between public, private, and subsidiary organizations and a comparison of the different forms of business organization.

Part 2 deals specifically with corporate governance. It presents the issues, the traditional model, European model, stakeholder model, effectiveness of the board, board liability, the reforms of corporate governance, and the stakeholder approach, respectively. Each main issue ends with the results of an empirical study included to generate comparisons with the academic view of corporate governance.

Part 3 is concerned with the implications of corporate governance with respect to corporate social responsibility, business ethics, and business–government relations. Also included are cases of insider trading, the Foreign Corrupt Practices Act, and deregulation.

Part 4 discusses the reconstruction of U.S. business in recent years. It examines mergers, takeovers, leveraged buyouts, management buyouts, employee stock ownership plans, and international acquisitions.

Finally Part 5 emphasizes corporate governance and strategic management.

Acknowledgments

This book would have been impossible without the help of numerous friends, colleagues, and students. Among the friends who gave timely encouragement and insightful advice are Dr. Rogene Buchholz, Dr. Raymond Lutz, Dr. Mike Ross, Dr. Glenn Robinson, Dr. Abbas Ali, Dr. Matt Gibbs, Dr. Richard Judy, Dr. Rauf Khan, Dr. Mohammad Alhadi, Dr. Abo Habib, Dr. Daniel Twomey, Dr. Wagdy Abdallah, and Mr. Galal Elhagrasy.

I am grateful to several students who reviewed some of the chapters and provided valuable comments. Some also provided valuable support in the form of typing (Julie Immesoete, Andrea Neeves, Laurie Dominick, Betty Boyer), interviewing (Audrey Griffin, David Thompson, Jill Chess, Jody Kind), and editorial assistance (David Straite, David Messner, Chris Thompson, Paul Ashley, Brian Berube, Bruce Bittler, Andy Boldy, Eric Carros, Alex Chatman, Mary Christy, Chris Getner, Ron Hackett, Jim Henderson, Jim Leddon, Juanita McClymonds, Marcia Miller, Lisa Moore, Matt Piroch, Joe Price, Tracey Ramsey, Marge Sherman, Randi Smith, Scott Stull, Randy Giangiuli, Edward Opalko, Susan Ellis).

I extend my thanks to all of my students in my management seminars and administrative policy courses for their continuous support. Special thanks to Dr. Frank Mastrianna and all my colleagues in the Department of Management and Marketing at Slippery Rock University (Calhoun, Crawford, Houston, Krishnakumar, Lorentz, Manocha, Tompkins, and Vaughan) for their encouragement and support in this endeavor. Of course, the responsibility for any errors or omissions lies only with the author.

My special thanks and appreciation to my loving family for their support and for giving me the inspiration and strength to write this book. This book is dedicated to my dearest father and mother and my beautiful daughters Alliah and Sheamah whom I love and I miss very much.

PART ONE

Business Development

1

Corporate Governance and the Changing Environment

INTRODUCTION

This book presents an overview of corporate governance issues, models, debates, and the impact they have on a number of other controversial issues, such as business ethics, corporate social responsibility, business–government relationships, and the reconstruction of U.S. businesses. This book is devised to aid today's professional managers in managing social issues as effectively as they would manage other parts of the business. Business people, both present and future, must be aware of and be able to effectively deal with these issues in order for their business to survive and prosper.

Corporate social responsibility is a relatively new area. Where the corporation was once an economic entity, it must now respond to those issues of importance to the society in which it operates. No longer can the corporation function merely for maximizing profits the most efficient way, ignoring the environment and its occupants, but must take these constraints, as well as others, into consideration. Profits must be seen as a long-term objective. Measurement of this objective must be calculated on a social scale as well as a monetary scale.

The managers of today have to know, and understand how their actions can be beneficial or harmful to society. Actions must be carried out in a way that is beneficial to the public as a whole. Due to the power of society and the strong interests the public has in social issues, the corporation cannot afford to act in a detrimental way. For if it does, the corporation will surely perish.

Ethics is also another important area of concern to businesses today. An unethical act or procedure committed by the corporation results in lost credibility on the part of the organization. The ethics of the company should be communicated through the chain of command, so that these ethics, as well as the penalties for noncompliance, are common knowledge to all employees. Education in the area of ethics is a must for future managers, to insure that such ethical concerns are dealt with more effectively.

Business–government relations are a more concrete area of discussion, due to the fact that actual laws and regulations have been implemented. Management, both present and future, must realize that the impact of the government looms large in all our lives and cannot be avoided in the business arena. Issues such as compliance, public policy formation, costs, and the benefits of regulation must be dealt with by managers. A knowledge of these areas is essential for business survival and the success of the manager in the business world. The international aspect of most of these issues is equally important. One of the most significant developments in the last three decades has been the rapid growth of international business. Though many firms have been operating internationally for years, it is only recently that cultural interaction has created an atmosphere conducive to a decrease of environmental constraints. The author believes that a thorough understanding of corporate governance is the key to all business problems. This book uses an integrated approach to create a comprehensive model of corporate governance. A number of studies are included to present a practical perspective on different issues discussed in this book.

THE ISSUE OF CORPORATE GOVERNANCE

Corporate governance has become one of the most widely discussed issues in corporate circles and society as a whole. Many previously accepted or unquestioned aspects of corporate performance have become unacceptable to large segments of society. These aspects involving legal and ethical behavior, the impact of technology, and the size and complexity of the organization, have resulted in important, far-reaching changes in business management practice. Many studies have shown that the management of large corporations is not accountable to the board of directors (which the traditional model suggests).

According to traditional theory, the board of directors is supposed to represent the interests of stockholders—the owners of the corporation. The board's main role is to oversee and evaluate the performance of management in running the business. If that performance is not satisfactory, it is the board's responsibility to initiate changes in the performance of management.

The board's responsibility is to evaluate management performance, especially that of the chief executive, and to compensate or remove management as the board sees fit. That is what is supposed to happen, but such action usually does not take place.

The board of directors is increasingly remote and improperly informed about the operations they are supposed to direct. This represents a violation of the traditional theory which will be discussed in depth in later chapters.

The level of criticism for the corporate system has increased tremendously in recent years. The conduct and performance of business and the power and privileges associated with large corporations have been called into question. Some critics have alleged that the present system of control has failed to hold management and the board of directors accountable for their use or misuse of corporate power. Some have even gone further by suggesting the implementation of external controls on the system. Harold S. Geneen urges radical reforms—even if the government has to enforce them.[1]

Lewis Solomon states that the problem of corporate reform is too complex and intractable to respond to so simple a solution as the reform of corporate boards: "Our efforts to review the Boards of Directors are simply anachronistic—*new methods must be devised* if we are to make corporate management genuinely accountable."[2] Many other people think that corporate governance issues are clouded by more confusion today than ever before.[3]

The purpose of this book is to clarify as much as possible the basic issues of corporate governance. An extensive review of the debates on how to improve the process will be presented. In addition, an empirical study showing management's view of the three models of corporate governance will be included. The result of the study will be used to compare and contrast what has been stated as theory and what is the real practice in corporate governance. Interviews with a number of management personnel in different organizations will also be included.

The book also presents the stakeholder approach and why it might be an appropriate answer to a number of governance problems. Despite the importance of stakeholder interest in corporate decision making, there is no comprehensive, constructive study (to the best of my knowledge) showing who is necessary for corporate governance, as viewed by various levels of management, and the importance of stakeholder participation in corporate policy making.

THE FRAMEWORK

The framework of this book can be divided into three parts:

1. *Management perceptions* of corporate governance, which represent the real world and how management feels about corporate policy and who should have a voice in it.

2. *Corporate laws, Securities and Exchange Commission (SEC), and New York Stock Exchange (NYSE),* which determine the basis of who should have ultimate control of corporate policy, who finally terminates upper-level management, and who finally rewards CEO (upper-level management).

Model 1.1
Factors Influencing Corporate Governance

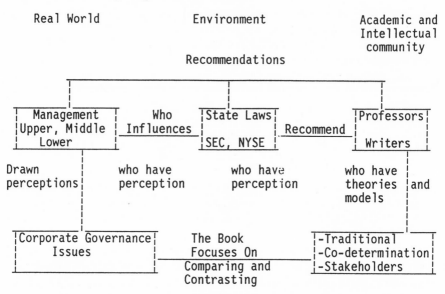

Real World   Environment   Academic and
                                    Intellectual
                  Recommendations   community

3. *Academic community*, professors, writers, and others who have theories and models of who should be making or have a voice in corporate policy. (See model 1.1)

The study, as indicated in model 1.1, focuses on management perceptions alone, such as their statements indicating what they perceive to be their present opinions. Those opinions are compared with the models of the academic community.

It will be demonstrated that establishing internal social controls over the way corporations treat their stakeholders is desirable in and of itself. These actions may also reduce government involvement and narrow the existing gap between corporate performance and society's expectations. Many people have questioned the nondemocratic way in which large corporations are run and the nonparticipation in major decision making by people who are most affected by corporate actions. The conscious awareness of the social and political consequences of economic actions has also spawned the rise of consumer, environmental, civic, and other interests of "stakeholder" groups that press for corporate action on particular issues.

In this book the term *corporate governance* refers to the mode of structure and the power that determines the rights and responsibilities of the various groups involved in running the organization. It involves the legitimacy expectation of the business, the method of operating, and the overall accountability of management and the board of directors. By having a thorough understanding of corporate governance, issues previously mentioned can be dealt with more effectively. This understanding will also increase the importance of each group's contribution to corporate behavior.

NOTES

1. Harold S. Geneen, "Why Directors Can't Protect the Shareholders," *Fortune* (September 17, 1984): 28.

2. Lewis Solomon, "Restructuring the Corporate Board of Directors: Fond Hope—Faint Promise?" *Michigan Law Review* (1978): 581–83.

3. A. A. Sommer, "Corporate Governance: Its Impact on the Profession," *Journal of Accountancy* 149 (July 1980): 52.

2

Business Trends

The earliest form of business was the simple trade of one type of good for another. Historically, individuals have depended upon the exchange of food, clothing, and other such commodities for their survival. Although the activity of trading has been around for centuries, no one knows the exact date when the concept of the company came into existence.

The idea of a business organization with multiple owners and an extended life can be traced back as early as the twelfth century. During this period, people were entering into and forming partnerships. One partner, the "tractator," would undertake the management of the enterprise. His duties included the purchase, transportation, and sale of goods, along with responsibility to creditors. The other partner, the "commendator," provided the capital but assumed no further obligations or liability.[1]

As trade continued to grow, so did the complexity of the business organization. The evolution of the company can best be observed in England. With the discovery of the Americas and the growth of commercial activity, Britain became an important center of trade. Companies were formed in hopes of monopolizing a given trading area. The companies formed at this time were of two kinds: regulated and joint stock. The regulated company was an association of men who ran their own business and made their own profits according to the regulations of the company. The joint stock company was an association of capital through individual shareholders who chose officers to administer the fund.[2] Joint stock companies were the mainstream of corporate development.

The corporate form of business came into being in the United States with the Industrial Revolution. Before the Industrial Revolution, the traditional firm was a single-unit enterprise, owned by an individual or a small number

Figure 2.1
Corporate Linkage

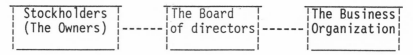

of persons, producing a single product, and located in one geographic location.[3] The process of governing these single-unit enterprises was relatively simple. All decisions were based on the personal interests of the owner(s) and were purely economic in nature. As the need for large amounts of capital and decreased individual risk surfaced, so did a more complex form of business, one that required separation of ownership and control.

THE CONCEPT OF THE COMPANY

A company as defined by Webster's dictionary is a number of persons united or incorporated for joint action, especially for business. A company can be viewed as a single person or as an assemblance of people who turn inputs into outputs. The term *company* has evolved so that it now represents various forms of organization. (This will be discussed in more detail in chapter 3.)

The company is defined legally as an entity created by law that exists separately and distinctly from the individuals whose contributions of initiative, property, and control enable it to function.[4] Figure 2.1 represents the link between the owners, the board of directors, and the business enterprise.

Legally the company or corporation is an artificial person. Although the members of a corporation may change, the corporation itself can continue for a long time. One of the main characteristics of the company is that it provides continuity. It does not stop with the death of one owner or manager. The corporation also gives limited liability. The debts of the corporation are the responsibility of the separate legal person, the corporation. Therefore, the individual members are not legally responsible under ordinary circumstances.[5]

Corporations grew in size and number as the need for capital increased. Corporations began to issue more stock and stockholdings became more and more distributed throughout society.

The corporation's status as a legal entity stems from a charter, a document issued by a state authorizing the formation of a corporation. The owners are called shareholders, or stockholders. Once a year they vote for a board of directors, which serves as their representative. The directors elect the necessary officers, who are responsible for the day-to-day operation of the corporation and report periodically to the board of directors. The charter is a three-way contract between the corporation, the stockholders, and the state, and all parties are bound by it. A corporation not only exists but also must follow special laws. Since a corporation is an entity which is created by the state of residence, it must abide by federal law and special state law/regulation through which the corporation's existence is possible. Although some corporations can be created under federal law (mostly public and nonprofit organizations) each state makes and enforces its own body of corporate law. These laws may vary from state to state.

In 1945, a committee of ten from the American Business Association presented a draft of the Model State Business Compensation Act (MBCA). The MBCA sets standards for corporate practices regulating the creation and issuance of stocks. The influence of this act, although frequently amended, is widespread across the nation. This act does not become law until legally adopted by each state.

In 1984, the Committee on Corporate Law introduced a major revision of the MBCA. This revision called for the act to "be a convenient guide for revision of state business corporation statutes reflecting current views on social issues." This revision (RMBCA) also reorganized the language in which the original act was written, making it easier to comprehend.

In terms of corporate law, the MBCA and RMBCA have the most influence of any charter or legal ordinance relating to them. Not only do they define the nature of business, they also determine criteria which all companies follow.[6]

The Revised Model of Business Corporation Act (RMBCA) was drafted as a convenient guide for revising state corporation law. It is important to mention that RMBCA has never been adopted by any state in its entirety, yet it has had great influence on corporate laws in thirty-seven states. Because of this, individual state corporate laws should be consulted instead of the MBCA or RMBCA.[7]

The high standard of living enjoyed in this country is closely related to mass production and mass consumption. The availability of large quantities of goods at prices consumers can afford is an achievement of big business units. Although big business and corporations go hand in hand, it would be a serious error to assume that all corporations are large. There are many corporations that are as small or even smaller than the average sole proprietorship or partnership.

Corporations may be classified in several different ways, and each must meet certain criteria of classification. A corporation may be considered private or governmental, profit or nonprofit, stock or nonstock, domestic or foreign/international, closed or open, or industrial.

There are about three million established corporations in the United States, whose revenues are beyond the trillion-dollar mark. With great economic and political power these corporations have immense responsibilities. U.S. corporations today represent the ultimate in business performance. They also have achieved a remarkable status in improving social conditions. Along with government efforts, they have enabled our society to create an unprecedented economic well-being and standard of living. They have been responsible for many major economic, technological, and social achievements. These benefits are not limited to U.S. society; they have been extended to many other nations as well.

Despite these positive points, U.S. corporations and their executives are faced with a serious problem—the loss of public confidence. Corporate executives are definitely concerned about the generalized and diffused nature of diminished public confidence, since this lack of trust has been accompanied by extraordinary public criticism, undue government controls, and growing public expectations and demands for improved corporate performance.

Society now demands something more than the traditional large corporation. Issues of legal and ethical behavior, and the effects of technology, size, and complexity have become important in national public policy. Though the corporations share credit with government, education, and other professions for economic and social progress, they must also share the blame for many social problems including the unsatisfactory economic performance of the country.

These new expectations and criticisms reflect an enhanced image of large corporations that includes important social and political functions and responsibilities which arise from its basic economic activity. External pressures, social and political, are becoming a more decisive element in corporate functioning. In this atmosphere, the large U.S. corporation has become a center of public attention.

Traditionally, the performance of a corporation has been mainly determined by its financial gains, as seen by its net profits and return on investment, but to the political economist of the 1980s and 1990s, corporate performance means much more than its dollar earnings. These concerns include how corporations affect customers, employees, neighbors, and citizens as well as society's physical and social environment. The result is that today a corporation is judged by its overall performance—social, political, and technological impacts as well as economic and financial results.

Therfore, today's corporate performance involves marketplace achievements, net profits, financial reporting and control, public disclosures, legal and ethical behavior, quality of working life, employee citizenship rights, health, safety and the environment, technological innovation, political participation, social performance, and executive compensation.

When owners operate their own company, they are practicing ownership and management skills and there is little possibility for a distinction between governance and management. However, in large public companies, managing and governing roles are separated. The roles of the chief executive officer and the chairman of the board will be well defined in regard to who manages and who governs, as seen in figure 2.2.

Figure 2.2
Links Between Governance and Management

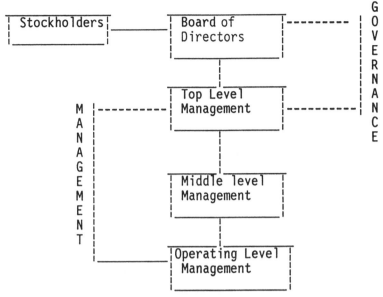

The establishment of a legal entity with a large number of shareholders in today's economy requires a separation between owners and managers. The underlying assumption of such separation is the appropriate allocation of corporate resources. Owners and managers might have a different interest in the existence of the corporation. Management focuses on how to run the entity efficiently and effectively through the traditional functions of planning, organizing, directing, and controlling. Management is also involved in the decision-making process concerning product design, procedures, financing, and product market. Ownership is mainly interested in the profitability or return on investment. The owners provide the necessary capital and consequently have the right to protect their property.

The issues of corporate performance in today's corporation involve how management should be accountable for the use of corporate power. Accountability of management, corporate boards of directors, and executives may be the answer to public concern about the use of corporate power.

RECENT BUSINESS LAW

Law is ultimately created by the ruling power of a particular area, region, or location. In order to substantiate why company law actually exists, we should ask what contributing factors caused its existence. The beginning of the century brought with it the formation of many businesses and hence, companies. Although the various companies had their own personal policies and operational strategies, there existed a necessity for some type of structured governance, or company law.

The roots of contemporary U.S. business law are based on a combination of U.S. civil law and English common law. Much of business law's development has been case-setting precedents which act as guidelines for the laws that pertain particularly to the field of business or "business law." "Business law" is a specialty or subdivision of civil and criminal law (an extension). Prior to the twentieth century there was not a concept called "business law" for the need for such specialty laws was not as pressing as today. With the number of companies constantly increasing, liability and power of ownership were the two issues that needed to be addressed. Thus, during the early part of the century, company law evolved to help limit liabilities and to distinguish ownership from actual management control.

During the 1960s and 1970s, U.S. government played the dominant role in exercising legal control over the various companies. The development of business law has gone through a rapid, reactionary process (based on court cases) as opposed to the precautionary development of other types of U.S. law (developed by legislature and government agencies). Since business law is classified as part of private law as well as public law, it covers a wide spectrum while remaining a specialty field in the law practice. Numerous attempts were made in the United States to produce a uniform body of laws relating to business transactions. Two major sets of laws, the Uniform Negotiable Instrument Law (1896) and the Uniform Sales Act (1906) were widely adopted by the states. Several other proposed uniform acts followed, although most were not widely adopted. In the 1940s, the need to integrate the partially adopted uniform acts became necessary and was realized in the creation of the Uniform Commercial Code. The Uniform Commercial Code (UCC) is a comprehensive commercial law (adopted by all of the states except Louisiana) that covers the law of sales as well as other specific areas of commercial law. The UCC deals with the formation and enforcement of sales contracts.[8] The UCC is basically the codification of common law and is also the framework for later business law to follow.[9] Some of the factors contributing to the evolution of company law were:

1. the interaction between ownership and management,
2. the interactions within other companies and competitors, and
3. the various environmental and societal factors (social issues, political situations, the economy, consumer behavior, etc.)

Beginning in the late 1960s, new federal regulatory agencies were formed to create law within a particular specialty field. Seven new agencies were created, some of which include the Consumer Product Safety Commission (CPSC), the Environmental Protection Agency (EPA), and the Occupational Safety and Health Agency (OSHA). These were created as precautionary law makers and to act as watchdogs over business practices. The first four years of the 1970s saw a doubling of the number of pages in the Federal Register, in which federal rules and regulations are noted. Most of this growth is caused by the impact of agency law developed as guidelines for general business policy.[10] A government agency is responsible for a limited area of regulation and consequently that agency develops an expertise from its continuous exposure to a particular area. An agency may be able to specify detailed rules of conduct in the development of sound policies that the courts, with limited resources and reactionary processes, are simply unable to meet. The expertise of the government agencies, in some cases, allow them to create policy/law before the problem arises, thus averting the crisis.

Therefore, today's "business law" is a unique mixture of precedent law from court cases (reactionary) and regulation law set by government agencies (precautionary and reactionary) which is continually being developed and adapted to regulate and protect society.

NOTES

1. Joseph Gross, *Company Promoters* (South Hackensack, N.J.: Rothman, 1972), p. 3.
2. Douglas North, "Corporation," *Encyclopedia Americana* (Danbury, Conn.: Grolier, 1980), pp. 12–13.
3. Alfred D. Chandler, Jr., and Herman Daems, *Managerial Hierarchies: Comparative Perspectives on the Rise of Modern Industrial Enterprise* (Cambridge: Harvard University Press, 1980), p. 11.
4. A. Aldo Charles, *College Law for Business* (Cincinnati: South-Western Publishing Company, 1963), p. 343.
5. North, "Corporation," pp. 5–6.
6. Richard A. Mann, Barry S. Roberts, and Len Young Smith, *Business Law and the Regulation of Business* (New York: West Publishing Co., 1987), pp. 766–69.
7. Ken Clarkson, Roger Miller, and Jentz Gaylord, *West: Business Law*, 3rd ed. (New York: West Publishing Company, 1986), pp. 643–44.
8. Louise E. Boone and David Kurtz, *Contemporary Business*, 5th ed. (Chicago: Dryden Press, 1987), p. 16.
9. R. I. Tricker, *Corporate Governance: Practices, Procedures and Powers in British Companies and Their Board of Directors* (England: Gower Publishing Company, 1984), p. 25.
10. Clarkson, Miller, and Jentz, *Business Law*, p. 749.

3

Forms of Business Organization

PUBLIC, PRIVATE, AND SUBSIDIARY COMPANIES

There is no legal distinction between private and public companies in the United States. Private companies can be of two types. One type is the small private company. Since this is an owner-managed company, there is for all practical purposes no distinction between the owners and the top-level managers. Whether there is one or a select few owners, they are in essence the board of directors for the whole business. The other type of private company is in most cases a family one in which the business is passed down from one generation to the next. This is where one finds more of a separation between the owners and the managers. In general, the shareholders for private companies are usually friends, relatives, or business associates of the promoters of the company.

Public companies are those that invite the public to subscribe for shares. If large amounts of money are needed, which private lenders will not or cannot make available, the public may be the only source of such money. This money may come from banks, insurance companies, or other institutional investors, including the U.S. government. This public financing is bound by federal and state regulations. The Securities and Exchange Commission (SEC), which is mainly under the Security Act of 1933, is in charge of these regulations. The SEC's main function is to ensure that investors are provided with the information necessary for future decisions. Therefore it requires publications and receives registration of prospectuses and periodic financial reports. The SEC also has the power to prescribe the methods to be followed in the preparation of the financial statements by specifying the form and content of those statements.

The SEC delegates some of its authority to other institutions in order to help monitor company operations. An example of this would be the Financial Accounting Standards Board (FASB). Since 1973 the FASB has been the designated organization for establishing standards of financial accounting and reporting. The basic philosophy of this act is the necessity of full disclosure in the offer of securities to the public. In public companies, the stockholders are perceived as investors with rights, but equal to those interests of the other stakeholders. In that the stakeholders' interests are fairly balanced, this gives the board of directors a great amount of power. This power is kept in check by independent auditors who report to the members. This system is supposed to adequately protect the interests of all.

Subsidiary companies are organizations that merge to form interconnected companies. In this situation, the parent company acts as the owner and consequently the manager. One could have a holding company which would incorporate the subsidiary companies. A holding board is appointed to oversee all of the subsidiary companies. The holding board will appoint a board of people to one or more of the subsidiary companies in order to make sure that they are run efficiently. The key here is to work as a group. Although a duality of governance exists, the right to managerial control still rests with the holding company.[1]

There are both advantages and disadvantages in taking a private company and going public. If all that one wants is capital, then the company should stay private. By going public, the company's credit position is improved because its securities acquire a market value based on actual purchases and sales of its stocks. Consequently, the company has a greater potential for growth. This creates a new and better image for the company. Relations with suppliers and dealers will also improve. Since the company has marketable stock, it can now compete in the job market for talented people because it can provide tax advantages to key employees. Right in line with the new company image goes the prestige that a major stockholder or officer will hold.

There are some disadvantages, however. The main disadvantage of going public is the fact that a company and the individuals involved in it have opened to the public the facts concerning many matters they formerly regarded as confidential.[2]

Information such as the company's business, the salaries it pays, the people who control its affairs and stocks, and the financial history are now available for public inspection. Also, if certain criteria are met, they will have to report to the SEC. The decision to go public also brings with it a variety of new laws to be abided by, such as those for shareholders and directors.

In "Going Private Is Unethical," Benjamin J. Stein refers to a strategic move by some companies to do just that. This type of strategy is known as insider buyouts or management buyouts. If the insiders in a company perceive a large difference between the going stock price and what they can get by breaking up the company, liquidating it, or redeploying the assets, they cook up an offer to buy back the company from the stockholders and "take it private."[3] (This will be explored further in section 4.) The returns to the insiders in such a deal have been forty to one in some cases, while the stockholders get a few percent on their money.

In conclusion, private, public, and subsidiary companies are each unique and it is important that we as managers or future managers be able to distinguish between them.

THE SIGNIFICANCE OF LARGE CORPORATIONS

Large corporations, which have been in the United States for over one hundred years, play very significant roles in the economy. Although they have gone through many changes, their main purpose is to earn profits. From the beginning, large corporations adopted the idea of dividing administrative structures so that power could be easily passed from owners, to managers, to employees. Later, it became more important to have this type of administrative structure due to the size of the corporations and the number of employees. By dividing the administrative structure, each division of the corporation can have its own manager and employees. This makes it easier for top officials of the corporation because they are concerned with the division managers, the production, and the efficiency of each division. They do not have to worry about each individual employee. The managers in turn deal closely with the employees. This reduces the burden on top officials since each division manager can evaluate employees' performance and decide whether to keep them. One of the most significant accomplishments of large corporations is the idea of division of administrative power, which in turn allows for a more efficient and profitable enterprise.

Dividing the corporation into different divisions also allows the corporation to cut costs. By having each division produce its own product the corporation is able to be more efficient and cut production, purchasing, and distribution costs. This is possible because each division handles its own aspects of production, and each knows exactly what it needs for production. This also helps the corporation adjust to customer needs since only one or two divisions would require changes, if necessary, not the whole corporation.

Another significant role that large corporations play in the United States is the continual improvement of the standard of living. Large corporations, through their size, power, and wealth, have molded the United States into an economically stable country. Large corporations employ a significant number of people, allowing the economy to constantly grow. If people are employed, they spend money, and if they spend money, the economy grows. Large corporations also improve productivity. By using their size capability they eliminate inefficient production techniques. These two factors alone have helped make this country economically stable and one of the most powerful countries in the world. Large corporations have used their size, power, and wealth to benefit all aspects of society, either directly or indirectly, domestically or internationally. They have given many other countries the helping hand they needed to get started.

Large corporations have also improved education and technology in the nation. By increasing the degree of competition among employees, corporations have raised the level of higher education. Each graduate needs to be better than his or her peers. This is good for the country because only the most qualified persons will be hired, which helps corporations improve their quality. Technology has improved tremendously due to competition among corporations. Each is trying to surpass the other, which ultimately helps society improve itself with better and more advanced products.

In summary, large corporations are significant in that they have provided us with administrative structure that provides the most efficient and effective way of operation a business can have. They employ a large number of people which helps keep the economy strong. They have also given economic stability and a higher standard of living, not to mention the help they have given countries that are in trouble. They have helped to improve the educational system and technological advancements through intense competition, giving further stability and confidence. And finally, large corporations are significant in that they control the greatest part of the industrial sector, and provide the United States with jobs, products, and economic security.

CORPORATE ACCOUNTABILITY AND REGULATION

Corporate accountability can be defined as the process of making corporate leaders responsible for their actions and goals. Corporations have become more accountable both morally and legally since their inception. The life of the corporation is no longer maintained behind closed doors. Corporations are accountable not only to the stockholders but also to the stakeholders.

From the British point of view, accountability functions in two types of context: the constitutional context and the proprietorial context. In the constitutional context elected representatives have a responsibility to be accountable to their electorate. According to the proprietorial context the responsibility to manage assets and obtain performance from such resources has been delegated by owners to managers or agents.

Accountability is exercised through a management stream for a subordinate company. In other companies, such as private or proprietorial companies, few problems arise because there is a close identification between owner, director, and manager. Accountability is fundamental for public companies.

In the United States, the Securities and Exchange Commission (SEC) perceives corporate governance as the method by which the corporation reaches decisions and takes action. The view of the SEC is that governance activities are mainly internal to the corporation through the election of stockholders to a board which oversees management. Overall, the SEC views accountability as the means by which those who manage and oversee the affairs of the company are held responsible for stewardship of corporate assets.

According to the SEC, shareholder interest lies primarily in the economic performance of companies, and because of this the SEC wants more information of board structure, composition, and functioning. The Companies Act (1980) states that a company must have regard for the interests of employees in general, as well as for shareholders, when making business decisions. Stakeholders' theories of accountability argue that the company is responsible to other constituencies, such as consumers, suppliers, creditors, local or other interests, and the general public.

Corporate accountability is used to help keep a company's head above water. A company needs to keep its head up by way of profits, because without profits a company will not survive. However, concentrating on short-term profit has been argued to be a major failing of U.S. and British company directors.

In 1970 the Institute of Chartered Accountants in England and Wales made several proposals on accountability. Among these proposals are:

1. narrowing the areas of difference and variety in accounting practices;
2. disclosure of accounting basis;
3. disclosure of departures from established definitive accounting standards; and
4. wider experience of major new proposals on accounting standards.[4]

As someone once remarked, "the exposure process stands in stark contrast to the total secrecy that had characterized the deliberations of the English Institute Council and Technical Committees."[5] Trying to establish standards has raised political problems in the accounting profession. There have been continuing calls for further disclosures, including proposals for greater disaggregation of published information by plant, product, and location. In the United States, the SEC lays down the requirements for accounting standards of public companies.

Corporations in the United States face regulation from both state and federal agencies; public and private companies are regulated by the state in which a particular company resides. Each state has its own set of regulations and expectations for a company. There also have been proposals for countrywide regulation, but nothing has materialized.

FORMS OF BUSINESS ORGANIZATION

There are three forms of business organization: sole proprietorship, partnership, and corporation.

Small or medium-sized businesses often operate as sole proprietorships.

Figure 3.1
Comparison of the Forms of Business Ownership

Number of business (14.5 million total)	1980	1985	Profits (in millions of dollars) 1985	
Proprietorship	70%	69.7%	($51)	24.8%
Partnerships	17%	10.3%	(-$7)	Loss
Corporation	13%	20%	($154)	75.2%
Total	100%	100%	Total ($205)	100%

These businesses are owned by one individual or a family and are operated by the owner or members of the immediate family. Professionals such as lawyers, doctors, management consultants, and CPAs when operating as individuals usually use the sole proprietorship form of business. Small services oriented to retail business also use this form of organization.

When two or more individuals jointly own a business it is called a partnership. It is similar to a sole proprietorship except there is more than one owner. These owners work together and share profits, losses, and liabilities. This form is commonly used by small businesses that wish to take advantage of the combined capital, managerial talent, and experience of two or more individuals. A partnership is most prevalent among professionals. For example, two CPAs (often with different areas of expertise) join together to provide clients with auditing and tax services or two doctors, each with a different speciality, operate a clinic jointly.

In the United States, the corporate form of business is the most dominant type of organization in terms of resources owned or controlled and revenue generated. *Fortune* magazine publishes an annual list of the largest five hundred companies (in terms of sales figures), all of which are corporations. Even though the corporate form of business is especially dominant among the largest companies, it is also used extensively by small companies that conduct business in a single location.

The form of business organization generally depends on the needs and objectives of the owners. These needs and objectives might change over time and, therefore, require a change in the form of the organization. A number of factors influence the type of organization. The *number of owners* influences the form of business organization. Most state laws require at least three individuals for incorporation. Three or more individuals from the same family are allowed to incorporate under many state laws. Therefore, the corporation may be family-owned or in the form of a partnership.

The *potential for raising capital* depends upon the financial position of the owner(s) and the availability of other sources of capital. The corporate form of business is the most advantageous for raising large quantities of capital because it enables the sale of capital stock to the public. In case more capital is needed for the future, the business entity can issue more shares to current or new stockholders as long as it does not exceed the authorized number of shares. The disadvantage of increasing the number of outstanding shares is that the earning per share will be smaller. In the three forms of organization, capital can be increased by having the existing owners contribute more capital or by borrowing from sources outside the business. The problem with borrowing capital is that it might cause a new business to start out with heavy debt and interest payment requirements that may strangle it. Borrowing agreements sometimes place restrictions on business operations, such as limiting the amount of dividends paid or requiring that certain cash balances be maintained.

Liability influences the type of organization. In a sole proprietorship, the owner is personally liable to creditors for all the debts incurred. In a partnership, each partner is individually liable to creditors for all or a portion of the debts incurred. Therefore, if a partnership becomes insolvent, the partners must contribute personal assets to settle the debts. This is a potential hazard in the partnership type of organization, while in a corporation the stockholders have limited liability. The corporation, which is a separate legal entity, is responsible for its own acts and obligations. It may acquire, own, and dispose of property. Similarly it may incur liabilities and enter into other types of contracts according to the provisions of its charter (also called articles of incorporation). Its creditors usually do not look beyond the assets of the corporation for satisfaction of their claims. Therefore, the financial loss that a stockholder may suffer is limited to the amount of investment. This limited liability was necessary for the growth of the corporate form of business organization.

Ownership transferability is an important factor. The stockholder (as will be discussed in the traditional model section) exercises control over the management of corporate affairs indirectly by electing a board of directors. It is the responsibility of the board of directors to meet periodically to determine corporate policies and to select officers to manage the corporation. Therefore, the owners of the corporation are not necessarily involved in the day-to-day management of the business. Accordingly, the ownership of the corporation may change with little or no disruption in its daily operation.

In noncorporate forms of organization, the ownership is directly involved in the conduct of the company and therefore has a great effect on the operation of the company. Consequently, when a sole proprietorship form of business grows or expands, it is difficult to transfer ownership. When the proprietor dies or decides to withdraw from the business, the business may have to be dissolved or sold. Similarly the partnership form of business experiences difficulties in transferring or increasing ownership. Most states have adopted the Uniform Partnership Act in which an existing partner cannot sell ownership interest and rights to a new partner; a new partner cannot be added by selling an interest; and heirs cannot inherit a deceased partner's ownership interest and partnership rights without unanimous approval from all existing partners. Usually when a partner retires, dies, or for some other reason wishes to withdraw from the company, one or more of the remaining partners may purchase the withdrawing partner's interest. Settlement for the purchase and sale is made between partners as individuals. Generally, in corporations ownership is transferred by selling existing stocks to anyone who wishes to purchase them. In a closely held or family-owned corporation, selling the stock might require the approval of the other stockholders.

Corporations are subject to additional *taxes*. Corporations must pay a charter fee to the state at the time of organization and annual taxes thereafter. If the corporation does business in states other than the one in which it is incorporated, it may also be required to pay annual taxes to that particular state. The earnings of a corporation may also be subject to state and federal income tax requirements. In addition, the remaining portion of the earnings that are distributed among the stockholders as dividends, are again taxed when they are added to the income of the individuals receiving them (this is called "double taxation"). Unlike corporations, sole proprietorships and partnerships do not pay income taxes for the organization as a separate entity. The sole proprietor pays taxes on all the business income. The partners pay income taxes on their shares of the partnership income. This income is usually added to their personal income (from other sources, such as salaries from other companies) and then pay taxes on the total. Since tax rates for individuals range as high as 34 percent (depending upon marital status and taxable income, sole proprietors and partners with large amounts of business income may find themselves paying very high personal income taxes to state and federal governments.

Sole proprietorships and partnerships are usually subject to the laws that affect individuals and to certain *government regulations* that relate to professional conduct. Partnerships are subject to the Uniform Partnership Act, while corporations are usually subject to more government regulation. Since it is a legal entity chartered by a state government, it is subject to certain state regulations. In addition corporations are more likely to be involved in interstate and international commerce, health and safety, transportation, and utilities, all of which are regulated by agencies of the federal government. Corporations that wish to trade their stocks in a public place through the stock exchange or the over-the-counter market are subject to operational and reporting regulations of the Securities and Exchange Commission (SEC) in addition to those of the stock exchange. The SEC's main function is to ensure

Figure 3.2
Characteristics of Business Organizations

Interms of Form of Business	# of Owners	Ability to Raise Capital	Owner's Liability	Transfer Ownership	Tax Position	Gov't. Regulation
Sole Proprietorship	One or Family	Weak	Liable	Difficult	Business income taxed as personal income	Low
Partner	Two or More	Fair	Liable	Difficult	Partner's share of bus-iness income taxed as personal income	More
Corporation	Three or More	Very good	Not Liable	Easy	Corporate income taxed as separate entity	Most

that investors are provided with information necessary for future decisions. It requires publications and receives registration of prospectuses and periodic financial reports. The SEC also has the power to prescribe the methods to be followed in the preparation of financial statements and the form and the content of these statements.

Figure 3.2 presents a summary of the characteristics of the three forms of business organizations.

NOTES

1. R. I. Tricker, *Corporate Governance: Practices, Procedures and Powers in British Companies and Their Board of Directors* (England: Gower Publishing Company, 1984), p. 16.

2. William S. Grayetal, *Manual for Corporations Officers* (Ronald Press Company, 1967), pp. 204–5.

3. Benjamin J. Stein, "Going Private Is Unethical," *Fortune* (November 11, 1985): 169.

4. Tricker, *Corporate Governance*, pp. 116–39.

5. Stephen A. Zeff, *Forging Accounting Principles in Five Countries—A History of and Analysis of Trends: Arthur Anderson Lectures.* Quoted in Tricker, p. 134.

PART TWO

Corporate Governance

4

Corporate Governance Models

In the following chapter, three models related to corporate governance will be discussed briefly. A supporting literature review will follow in future chapters. The models are: (1) the traditional model, (2) the European model, (3) the stakeholder approach.

THE TRADITIONAL MODEL

Most state laws in the United States under which corporations are established require that corporations be managed by a board of directors. The board is legally responsible for corporate actions and the impact and effect the corporation might have on society.[1]

According to Melvin A. Eisenberg, Rogene A. Buchholz, and others writing on the theory of corporate governance, stockholders own the property of the corporation and, therefore, have a legal right to control the corporation. Such control assures stockholders that their property is being used in their best interests.

In the United States, stockholders theoretically practice their legal right by voting at the annual stockholder meeting. The shareholders evaluate management's report on corporate performance and then elect their representatives (the board of directors). The function of the board is to elect the management and the officers of the corporation to run the business on a day-to-day basis. The board's responsibility is to meet periodically with management to decide on issues that need stockholder approval. The board also performs an overseer function to insure that the interests of the stockholders are looked after. Management, on the other side of the process, chooses the

Model 4.1
Traditional Theory

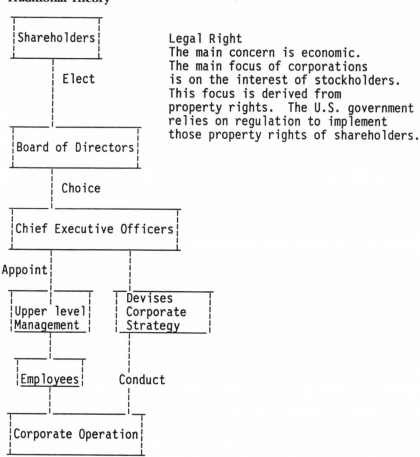

Legal Right
The main concern is economic.
The main focus of corporations
is on the interest of stockholders.
This focus is derived from
property rights. The U.S. government
relies on regulation to implement
those property rights of shareholders.

employees necessary to run the business and accomplish corporate goals and objectives.[2]

It is clear that in this form of organization the main theoretical emphasis is on the stockholders' interest. Management is concerned with more work and high pay while employees are concerned with high wages and other economic benefits. This theory is shown in model 4.1. In the traditional model of corporate governance ultimate control of the corporation rests in the hands of the stockholders. However, in real practice, most of the corporate powers are vested in the hands of management rather than the board of directors.

The separation between management and control was first discussed in the classic study of Adolf Berle and Gardiner Means in 1932.[3] Berle and Means classified companies based on the degree of management control versus owner control. They found that managers of the largest two hundred nonfinancial companies—*and not the stockholders*—had control over corporate resources. The study indicated that 44 percent by number and 58 percent by assets of these two hundred corporations were management-controlled.

The study also showed that none of the owners of these corporations had a stock ownership interest of 5 percent, the minimum needed to exert some influence. Their study confirmed that 65 percent of the corporations and 80 percent of their combined wealth were controlled either by management or a legal device, showing the degree to which ownership and control had become vested in two separate groups.[4]

Berle and Means were the first to direct attention to the corporate governance issue and how the separation of ownership from control constituted a fundamentally new economic structure. Subsequently, many authors and researchers have studied various attributions of corporate ownership.

In 1971, research replicating the Berle and Means study was done by Robert Larner using a 10 percent stockholder interest as a cut-off point. Larner reported that as of 1963, 85 percent of the top two hundred corporations were controlled by management.[5] In about thirty years the degree of management control had widened in the large corporations.

Berle and Means, Larner, Eisenberg, Williams, and others believe that even though the traditional corporate statutes require that the business affairs of corporations be managed by the board of directors, in practice this board rarely performs either as management or policy makers of the corporation. Buchholz believes that in reality ownership of most major U.S. corporations is widely dispersed throughout society. Such dispersion has left individual stockholders with small numbers of shares that are not large enough to make a difference in the voting process during the annual meeting of stockholders.

Holding small amounts of shares has led stockholders to think of themselves as investors rather than owners of the corporation. Therefore, when stockholders do not make enough return on their investments, they prefer to sell their stock rather than complain to management, because individually they have little power to effect change.

The corporation law of the State of Delaware states the position of directors as follows: "The business of every corporation organized under the provisions of this chapter shall be managed by a board of directors."[6] In spite of this requirement, there is substantial evidence that many large corporations have been managed and controlled by a chief executive and other top officers without adequate accountability to or monitoring by their boards of directors. In many cases, outside directors were poorly informed about corporate conditions which led to the collapse of a number of companies such as Penn Central, Bar Chris, Texas Gulf Sulphur, Anaconda, Lockheed, and others.[7]

In many studies conducted to determine public reactions to corporate governance and responsibility, the results were highly unfavorable. For instance, in 1968, Yankelovich, Skelly, and White conducted extensive research on public attitudes toward business. They reported that in national surveys

70 percent of the respondents thought that corporations try to achieve a fair balance between the public interest and profits. By 1976, the figure had dropped to only 15 percent of respondents. This indicates that business lost about 80 percent of its public support in eight years. This figure has not improved significantly since.[8] These results and others have served to increase public dissatisfaction and concern with corporate governance and accountability.

Many people call for reform of corporate governance in such a way that it will meet the new changes and requirements. The reform movement focuses mainly on the abuses of corporate power and on ways of dealing with such abuses. The present corporate system has failed to hold management and the board of directors responsible for the use of this corporate power.[9] Many proposals for reform have been made to reduce or control corporate power. Some of these have been implemented. For instance, the first steps have been taken to control environmental pollution, to adequately fund corporate pension plans, to control corporate political contributions, to control corporate foreign payments, and to implement affirmative action hiring practices.

The new reform proposals include: (1) improving the board of directors through more independent directors, audit, nominating and other committees with a majority of board and committee members from outside the corporation; (2) increasing management accountability through corporate chartering; and (3) increasing disclosure, public directorships, labor participation, and the like. Christopher D. Stone states that "we have to recognize that nothing we do at the board level is going to cure all or even most of the corporate problems people are concerned about."[10]

Lewis Solomon and others think that these proposals are too simple to deal with a very complex issue: "the problem of corporate reform is too complex and intractable to respond to so simple a solution as the reforms of corporate boards. Our efforts to review the board of directors are simply not realistic, new methods must be devised if we are to make corporate managements genuinely accountable."[11] A. A. Sommer states that "despite the proliferation of words concerning these matters, a great deal of confusion about these issues and the means of resolving them continue to exist."[12] Therefore, many people call for a new approach to the problem of corporate governance.

THE EUROPEAN MODEL

In Europe, the corporate governance issue is different. According to Joseph Monson, the main concern in the European corporate governance movement has been essentially ideological. "This ideological conflict is between the owners and workers and the issue of private ownership and public ownership. Thus there has been increasing pressure for employees to be put on boards

Model 4.2
European Model of Co-determination

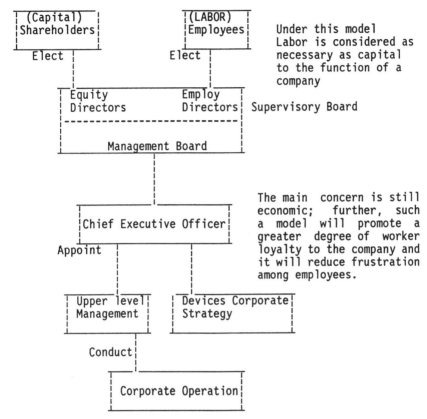

Under this model
Labor is considered as
necessary as capital
to the function of a
company

Supervisory Board

The main concern is still
economic; further, such
a model will promote a
greater degree of worker
loyalty to the company and
it will reduce frustration
among employees.

of directors and to play a larger and more dominant role in management."[13] Many European countries have established legislation providing for worker participation in the management of business firms. Through the use of co-determination schemes, these countries are promoting industrial democracy actively.

A brief discussion of the European co-determination model follows. However, the difference between the United States and Western Europe (represented by West Germany) will be discussed more thoroughly in a later chapter. Co-determination, similarly termed "worker's participation," is a European model for corporate boards of directors, which includes, by statute, representation of the work force. The idea of combining labor and capital, generated from post–World War II ideology, arises out of the concept of participatory decision making. Thus co-determination speaks to the involvement of labor in the decisions of the organization.[14] This is illustrated in model 4.2.

In theory, participatory decision making or participatory management can be viewed from the standpoint of protection of interests. In comparison with the United States, the interest of stockholders and creditors is protected by law and the government is responsible for the public interest. "However, the employees are connected with the fate of the organization in a special way. Their risk, although of a different nature than that of the stockholders, is in general larger."[15] Whereas investors are able to minimize their risk by diversifying their portfolio of investments, employees do not have the option of reducing their risk. For the most part, and practically speaking, they are employed by one corporation. It is not possible for them to work for several companies in an effort to minimize risk.

The realization of this concept led to demands by unions and workers in post–World War II European countries to increase their ability to minimize their own special risk by being included in the corporate decision-making process, vis-à-vis representation on the corporate board of directors. As defined by Robert Kuhne, co-determination describes a situation where employee participation takes the form of admitting one or more employee representatives as full members to the corporate decision-making board of an organization, together with the representatives of the owner. Kuhne further states that "the concept employee representatives applies to those members of the enterprise work force who are directly or indirectly elected or appointed by their colleagues, with or without direct recommendation of the trade unions who represent them."[16]

The European model of a board of directors typically consists of a supervisory board and a board of management. The supervisory board has the power to appoint and/or dismiss the lesser board of management.

In the European model of co-determination, employee representatives are usually concluded on supervisory boards, occupying between one-third and one-half of the seats. The task of the board of management is to oversee the day-to-day operations of the corporation.

While co-determination or worker control is acceptable in Europe, it is not acceptable in the United States and some think it is too radical for popular consideration.[17] Others think that the main reason for not considering the idea of co-determination seriously in the United States is that not only does management oppose it, but most U.S. labor unions are against it as well. They consider it to be a threat to their power and unnecessary because worker participation can be achieved through collective bargaining. James K. Brown reports that most unions in the United States are apathetic or indifferent to labor participation on the board of directors because co-determination is achieved through collective bargaining by the unions. Moreover if the unions are strong, labor influence can be extended beyond the factory walls to the whole community without a real need to adopt the co-determination model.[18]

THE SOCIAL CONTROL MODEL: THE STAKEHOLDER ALTERNATIVE

The level of criticism of corporate systems has increased tremendously in recent years. The performance of business and the power and privilege associated with large corporations have been called into question. Some have even questioned the corporate ability to deal with future problems.[19] Thus many people call for improvement in the social control of business or, in other words, an improvement in corporate governance. The government approach to dealing with the corporate governance problem was made through regulation.

Regulation can be defined as a societal response to actual and perceived problems in private industry. While regulation is an important device in handling the problems of a modern industrial economy, many regulations have placed heavy burdens on those subject to them. Societal control of private industries through regulation is now costing billions of dollars. The cost of compliance with regulations has forced a number of businesses to close their doors and has erected a formidable barrier to the entry of new firms.

At the same time, some of the regulations conflict with others, leaving businesses in the position of having to violate one or the other. In addition, the heavy cost burden imposed by filing of required forms, the hiring of employees to complete these forms, and the cost of changes in methods of operations required by some regulations has certainly added to inflation and a decline in productivity.

The existing policy of improving social control of businesses through regulation has failed to improve corporate performance. The growing feeling is that the government is not solving societal problems any better than private industries. And the cost of government regulations in most cases far exceeds the benefits to society and has created more serious problems than those solved. Therefore, it may not be appropriate to rely on increasing government involvement to improve corporate performance.

Most corporate reforms up to the present have suggested imposing external control on corporate behavior. Regulation has been the method of reform— traditional tools, political threats of one kind or another, jawboning, law suits, and antitrust. These reforms have proven to be very costly to corporations and society and have been only partially effective at best.[20] For example, the purpose of antitrust regulation was to re-establish market competition. The result was that faith in the market has decreased with the discovery of externalities and market breakdowns. The large corporations have become experts at protecting themselves from external control.[21] As a result society complains about the abuses of corporate power. Even stockholders are having difficulties exercising their legal rights (property rights). Stone thinks that society cannot continue to depend on external threats to the corporation but must reach directly into the decision-making structure and processes of the corporation to establish the kind of organization that will best respond to the legal and social pressures. Therefore, any new reform must rely on internal social control. Such reform will contribute to less government involvement, reduction of costs, improved productivity, and societal satisfaction. Social control mechanisms must be built into the internal structure of corporate governance.

Improving corporate governance internal control systems, therefore, is a substitute for increasing government regulation. Replacing external with internal controls where possible could improve the system and ultimately satisfy society. Social satisfaction will not occur unless society's expectations are met. Organizations are legitimate to the extent that their activities are congruent with the goals and the values of the social system within which they function.

This model gives more attention to the stakeholder notion. In addition to the stockholders, there are other groups to whom the corporation is responsible. The firm's objectives should be achieved by balancing the conflicting interests of the various constituencies in the firm, that is, the constituencies who have a stake in the performance of the corporation.[22] "While, as we shall see later, 'responsibilities and objectives' are not synonymous, they have been made one in a 'stakeholder theory' of objectives. This theory maintains that the objectives of the firm should be derived by *balancing* the conflicting claims of the various stakeholders in the firm: managers, workers, stockholders, suppliers, and vendors."[23] Therefore, the word *stakeholders* refers to those groups who have a direct interest in the survival of the organization and without their support the organization would ceast to exist. This includes shareholders, management, board of directors, employees, major suppliers, major creditors, major consumers, and the government. The concern for this approach, therefore, is not only economic, as the case in the traditional model; rather, the concern has expanded to fulfill the corporate responsibility to society as well.

In the social control model (see model 4.3), society's input to the corporation consists of physical and human resources. Society expects that corporations will meet its needs, values, and interests. It also expects the corporation to maintain control over its decision making so as to minimize the externalities (e.g., pollution) and assume greater accountability to correct social ills that inevitably occur. Violation of society's expectations by any firm will create a gap between business performance and societal expectations. S. P. Sethi states that "a continuously *widening* gap will cause business to lose its legitimacy and will threaten its survival."[24]

The author believes that improving corporate governance through stakeholder participation will narrow the gap between corporate performance and societal expectations. If this gap is narrowed, it means society's expectations

Model 4.3
Social Control Model

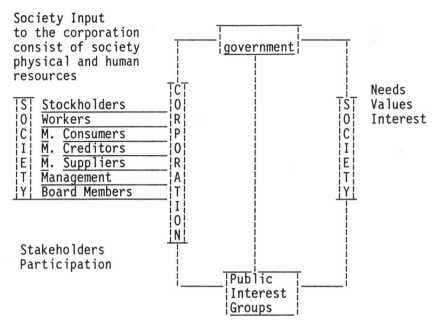

Society Input
to the corporation
consist of society
physical and human
resources

S	Stockholders
O	Workers
C	M. Consumers
I	M. Creditors
E	M. Suppliers
T	Management
Y	Board Members

C O R P O R A T I O N

government

Needs
Values
Interest

S
O
C
I
E
T
Y

Stakeholders
Participation

Public
Interest
Groups

Those groups interact with
both society and government.
When societal expectations are
not met, they will push for
more government involvement.

are being met to some extent; and, therefore, there would be no need to push for more government involvement. It is hoped that such improvement will result in reduction of government regulation. Increased reliance on internal controls will require the reconstruction of corporate governance. It is believed that this attempt might help determine who must be involved in the reconstruction of corporate governance. If the stakeholder notion proves necessary to improve corporate governance then corporate concern will shift from the traditional concept of the economic interest of stockholders to what is best in terms of society's interests. The corporate governance model can be presented as shown in model 4.4. The suggested model of corporate governance is a reform that may result in the discovery of ways of strengthening and protecting the various stakeholders' interests in the corporation, and of strengthening and enforcing public interest in corporate policy as expressed through democratic participation in a reconstruction of corporate governance.

Model 4.4
The Stakeholder Model

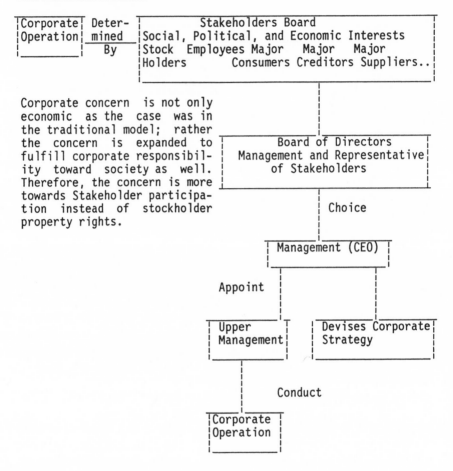

Corporate concern is not only economic as the case was in the traditional model; rather the concern is expanded to fulfill corporate responsibility toward society as well. Therefore, the concern is more towards Stakeholder participation instead of stockholder property rights.

NOTES

1. Harold Koontz, *The Board of Directors and Effective Management* (New York: McGraw-Hill, 1967), p. 1.

2. Rogene A. Buchholz, *Business Environment and Public Policy: Implications for Management and Strategy Formation* (Englewood Cliffs, N.J.: Prentice-Hall, 1986), p. 104.

3. Adolf A. Berle and Gardiner C. Means, *The Modern Corporation and Private Property* (New York: Macmillan, 1932).

4. Ibid., pp. 8–9, 93.

5. Robert J. Larner, *Management Control and the Large Corporation* (New York: Dunellen, 1971), pp. 9–24.

6. Delaware, *General Corporation Law of the State of Delaware, Revised on April 9, 1941, art. 1, chap. 65, sec. 9.*

7. J. Keith Louden, *The Effective Director in Action* (New York: Amacom, 1975), p. 3. See also Francis W. Steckmest, *Corporate Performance: The Key to Public Trust* (New York: McGraw Hill, 1982).

8. Harold M. Williams and Irving S. Shapiro, *Power and Accountability: The Changing Role of the Corporate Board of Directors*, 1979 Benjamin F. Fairless Memorial Lecture, Carnegie-Mellon University, p. 11.

9. Steckmest, *Corporate Performance*, p. 183.

10. Christopher D. Stone, *Where the Law Ends: The Social Control of Corporate Behavior* (New York: Harper and Row, 1975), p. 134.

11. Lewis Solomon, "Restructuring the Corporate Board of Directors: Fond Hope—Faint Promise?" *Michigan Law Review* (1978): 581–83.

12. A. A. Sommer, "Corporate Governance: Its Impact on the Profession," *Journal of Accountancy* 149 (July 1980): 52.

13. R. Joseph Monson, *Directions in United States and European Corporate Governance*, paper presented at the AACSB Conference on Business Environment/Public Policy, Summer 1979, p. 10.

14. Robert J. Kuhne, *Co-Determination in Business: Worker's Representatives in the Board Room* (New York: Praeger, 1980).

15. Ibid., p. 1.

16. Ibid., p. 3.

17. Thomas Jones, "Corporate Social Responsibility Revisited, Redefined," *California Management Review* (Spring 1980): 59.

18. Jeremy Bacon and James K. Brown, *The Board of Directors: Prospectives and Practices in Nine Countries* (New York: Conference Board, 1977).

19. Robert L. Heilbroner, *Business Civilization in Decline* (New York: Norton, 1976), pp. 101–24.

20. Murray L. Weidenbaum, *Business, Government and the Public* (Englewood Cliffs, N.J.: Prentice-Hall, 1977).

21. William M. Dugger, "Entrenched Corporate Power and Our Options for Dealing with It—A Pep Talk for Discouraged Reforms," *Association for Social Economics* (July 1980): 3.

22. Edwin M. Epstein and Dow Votaw, eds., *Rationality, Legitimacy, Responsibility: Search for New Directions in Business and Society* (Santa Monica, Calif.: Goodyear Publishing Co., 1978), p. 72.

23. Igor Ansoff, *Corporate Strategy: An Analytic Approach to Business Policy for Growth and Expansion* (New York: McGraw-Hill, 1965), pp. 33–35.

24. S. P. Sethi, "A Conceptual Framework for Environmental Analysis of Social Issues and Evaluation of Business Response Patterns," *Academy of Management Review* (January 1979): 65.

5

The Traditional Model

This chapter will examine the traditional theory of corporate governance and the main criticisms of it. It will also discuss in detail the various reform measures to improve corporate governance and explain why the issue is far from being resolved.

CORPORATE LAW REQUIREMENTS

The main function of corporate law is to regulate the rights and duties of various parties in the corporation and to limit the powers of the corporation vis-à-vis the external world. Most of the state laws in the United States under which corporations are established require that corporations be managed by a board of directors. The board is legally responsible for corporate actions and the impact and effect the corporation might have on society.[1]

According to Harold Koontz, the reason behind such a requirement is that the corporation is an artificial entity whose existence is established by a sovereign power through contract with a group of members (in business, the stockholders). This group of members, responsible for management, have historically been a plural executive called the board of directors.[2] Koontz maintains that anytime power or funds are entrusted by a group to individual managers or entrepreneurs, the logic is to establish a board to assure that the resources provided to the enterprise are well managed. Therefore, this board must be placed in a position of managing the corporation and assuring that the interest of those providing the funds are looked after.

This requirement simply calls for the board to undertake certain managerial functions itself and regularly pursue other activities to assure that the corporation is managed to achieve the goals and objectives set by the board.

Having a board of directors is not a new idea in the United States. It has been in existence ever since the inception of corporations. But in the last decade, boards have faced increasing challenges. "For good and sufficient reasons, boards have come under increasing scrutiny and even under fire. The point at issue is whether boards of directors as now constituted are obsolete, superfluous or little more than a necessary nuisance."[3]

The proper functions of the board of directors can be expressed in many different ways, but the ones discussed below are generally accepted by members of the legal, business, and academic communities.

The corporate affairs of a business are to be "managed by" or to be "managed under the direction of" the board of directors. This means that the board has ultimate company authority aside from matters requiring shareholder approval. "The board's primary function is to oversee and evaluate the performance of the management in running the company, and if that performance is not satisfactory, to do something about it."[4] Other functions of the board of directors include the following: (1) the approval and disapproval of the proposed major strategic business decisions; (2) the election and removal of the chief executive officer and other senior executives; (3) the recommendation of candidates for the board of directors; (4) the monitoring of the company's social and political impact; and (5) the establishment of performance and compensation of its top executives.[5]

Because the board of directors is legally responsible for the results achieved by the management of an enterprise and the board must delegate a major portion of these responsibilities to other people, it is extremely important that the board be well organized and efficient. Furthermore, it is necessary to spell out the reporting and controlling powers of the board as well as its relationship with the stockholders of the company. The next step in organizing an effective board is to prepare a position description of both the CEO and the chairman of the board. Even if one person fills both positions, a position description should be prepared because the chairman of the board is the board's agent and if he or she is also the CEO, he or she will be serving two different job positions.

Standards of performance should be established for the board of directors to guarantee that responsibility is satisfactorily performed. These standards should be agreed upon and put into writing before any action is taken. If board members are to act effectively, they must be aware of what is expected of them. Board members must serve capably as counselors to the CEO and other key members of management.

The chairman of the board is required to see that the work of the board is planned and performed on time and is acceptable. The chairman is also responsible for the organization of the committees of the board and for stockholder relations. Usually there are standard procedures developed to govern all board activities. The CEO, however, does not report to the chairman of the board but directly to the board of directors.

The frequency of board meetings contributes to a board's effectiveness. Meeting intervals vary from once a year to twelve times a year. The most effective interval is somewhere between six and twelve times a year.

Committees should be set up within a board of directors in order to explore in greater depth a specific area of a corporation's activities. It is important to realize that committees are part of the board structure and possess limited powers. This is important to realize because the committees may usurp the power of the board. The board cannot afford to let this happen because this would weaken the hierarchy of decision making.

It is good policy to include on the board both members outside the organization (outsiders) and members who engage on a daily basis with the activities of the organization (insiders). The size of the board ranges from somewhere between eleven and thirteen members for the most effectiveness.[6] At a board meeting insiders are no longer subordinate to the CEO but become in effect superiors of the CEO. This transition might cause conflict when a subordinate tries to challenge the CEO. Insiders make their greatest personal contribution as members of management and not as members of the board. It can be argued that outside members provide fresh viewpoints to the board of directors. Outsiders may also possess greater experience, expert knowledge, and judgments that might otherwise be missing from the company. It is apparent that the size of the board is not nearly as important as the quality of the members and the organization of the board.

The board must be properly informed, by management, of the activities of the corporation if it is to be truly effective. The board of directors as well as management must understand the financial and managerial statements of the corporation in order to recognize what is happening in the company. Goals and targets should be established by the board as well as by management in order to obtain the highest possibility of success for the corporation. The measurement of this rate of success enables the board to have a good understanding of how well final results compare to planned objectives. This in turn enables the board to control the organization by making suggestions and recommendations on how to improve in the future.

The majority of boards of directors in the United States today are ineffective. Many boards meet only three or four times a year for a few hours. This clearly is not enough time to effectively organize a corporation. Furthermore, the financial and managerial information of the corporation is often sent to board members hours before the meeting. This simply does not give them enough time to analyze and interpret the information.

THE DIFFERENCE BETWEEN THEORY AND PRACTICE

Critics of corporate governance allege that, even though the traditional corporate statutes require that the business affairs of corporations be managed by a board of directors, in practice the board rarely performs as either management or policy maker for the corporation. Rogene A. Buchholz (1986), Melvin A. Eisenberg (1976), Archie B. Carroll (1981), and others conclude that there is a gap between what theoretically has been set as the role and responsibility of the board of directors and what actually occurs in practice. According to Buchholz, theoretically the stockholders own the property of the corporation and thus should control the corporation. Therefore, the stockholders have certain legal rights to assure that this property is used in their best interests.[7]

Buchholz (1986) concludes that in theory ultimate control over the corporation's affairs rest in the hands of the stockholders, since they have the legal right to approve or disapprove major corporate policies. According to Eisenberg, shareholders elect the board and decide on major corporate issues. The board manages the corporation's business and formulates business policy. The executives are responsible for implementation of the policy established by the board and are, therefore, agents of the board. This theory assumes that the board manages the affairs of the business and formulates its policy. But Eisenberg thinks in reality the board does neither. He adds that in real practice most of the corporate powers are vested in the hands of the executives, rather than the board of directors.[8] In reality ownership of most of the major U.S. corporations is dispersed widely throughout society. Such dispersion has left the individual stockholder with a small amount of shares which really are not large enough to make a difference in the voting process during annual meetings of stockholders. Holding a small amount of shares has led stockholders to think of themselves as investors rather than owners of corporations. Therefore, when stockholders do not make enough return on their investments, they prefer to sell their stock instead of complain to management because individually they have little power to effect change.

In 1932, Berle and Means[9] conducted the first major empirical study about the separation of stock ownership and control in the largest two hundred nonfinancial corporations. The study found that managers of large corporations and not the shareholders have control over corporate resources. The research indicated that 44 percent by number and 58 percent by assets of those corporations were management-controlled. The study was based on an ownership stake of 5 percent, which was the minimum believed necessary to exercise some influence. The study confirmed that 65 percent of the corporations and 80 percent of their combined wealth were controlled by either management or a legal device. This showed the degree to which ownership and control had become separated.[10]

In 1971 a similar study was conducted by Robert Larner using 10 percent as the cut-off point. His study confirmed the earlier research done by Berle and Means. Larner reported that as of 1963, 85 percent of the top two hundred corporations were controlled by management.[11] Therefore, Buchholz's conclusion that management not only runs the corporation on a day-to-day basis but further exercises ultimate control over corporate resources is supported by research. Stockholders are not getting the information they need from management. Since management controls the corporation, they also control the proxy prospectus, and similar statements which are sent to the stockholder. Management control will influence stockholder votes to elect those directors who assure management reappointment and compatible working relationships.

Maitre J. Chambouline states that

the investor who puts into others' care the power to make his capital bear entrepreneurial fruit is not sufficiently informed. One need only attend annual stockholders meeting to realize this problem. Neither the reading of a balance sheet and profit and loss statement nor the examination of the Board's annual report can prepare one to evaluate a corporation justly. These statements are often either too specialized or too generalized.[12]

Francis W. Steckmest in *Corporate Performance: The Key to Public Trust* reports that chief executives and other top officers of many large corporations have dominant control over business affairs without sufficient accountability to or monitoring by their board of directors. He adds that there is clear evidence that some outside directors are poorly informed about corporate conditions. Such lack of coordination between management and the board of directors has resulted in the collapse of a number of companies including Penn Central Transportation Company, Texas Gulf Sulphur, Lockheed, Bar Chris, and Anaconda.[13]

Buchholz questions the board of directors' efficiency in protecting stockholders' rights and interests because the majority of directors of many companies are officers of the company (inside directors), and those outside members of the boards are "buddies" of management. Buchholz suggests that they are reluctant to disagree with chief executive policies. Steckmest agrees with Buchholz and thinks that the board members are subservient to the management. Therefore, it is unlikely they will oppose the chief executive's policies. Myles L. Mace asks: "How does an insider on the board serve as a discipline on himself? . . . How does an officer-director with aspirations of continued employment evaluate the president except in favorable terms?"[14] Christopher D. Stone voices a similar concern: "Why is there even a reason for insiders to serve on the board?"[15] Geneen has questioned the legality of the chief executive being on the board of directors, when the board's purpose is to represent the stockholder's interest.

Seventy-five percent of the companies that responded to the survey of Heidrick and Struggles (1980) have the chief executive as chairman of the board of directors, and this percentage increases with the size of the company.[16] Therefore, the chief executive officer (CEO) controls the flow of information to the board members. In many cases, board members are unaware of the real financial condition of their company. For example, in the Lockheed

Table 5.1
Distribution of Respondents: Personal Data (Management Position)

Level	Frequency	Percentage (%)
Lower Level Management	64	37.4
Middle Level Management	73	42.7
Top Level Management	34	19.9
Total	171	100.0

Corporation, the board of directors was unaware of the corporation's financial plight until it became publicly known.

Another good example is the case of Bar Chris. The problem, as J. Louden documents, lay in the misleading content and claims made in proxy statements. The board was negligent in signing without reading or even verifying the information in that statement. Louden raises the question of why the board simply accepted the word of management. "The board room is no place for euphoria or for dealing with vital matters in grand consul manner."[17] Buchholz argues that the nondemocratic way in which a large corporation is run and nonparticipation in major decision making by people who are most affected by it are some of the major factors which, together with the abuse of power by the limited few at the top, have resulted in the process of corporate governance getting closer attention from the educated masses of today. Those who regard the corporate form of organization as a public policy problem have thus questioned the legitimacy of this process and have advocated various types of reform measures.

THE STUDY

A recent study conducted by the author clarifies the issue of corporate governance from the management point of view. The study focuses on management perceptions alone. Then their opinions are compared with the models of the academic community.

A questionnaire was developed, and 400 questionnaires were distributed to managers in the large corporations. 171 completed questionnaires (or about 43 percent) were returned and constitute the sample of the study. The high rate of return for this kind of questionnaire-study is significant and gives more assurance about the validity of findings. (In the following pages the distribution of the respondents is based on various personal data presented in tables 5.1 and 5.2 for illustration purposes.)

Table 5.2
Distribution of Respondents: Personal Data (Sex Based on Position)

Position	Sex	Frequency	Percentage(%)
Lower Level Management	Male	52	81.25
	Female	12	17.75
Middle Level Management	Male	68	93.15
	Female	5	6.85
Top Level management	Male	34	100.00
	Female	0	0.00
Total		171	

Table 5.3
Frequency Distribution of Respondents

Question: "Stockholders who provide a certain percentage of the capital (such as 5%) should have an equal portion of influence on corporate policy."

Respondents Choice	L.L Mgt. Frequency		M.L.Mgt. Frequency		T.L.Mgt Frequency	
	Nos.	%	Nos.	%	Nos.	%
Total Agree	17	26.56	10	13.70	3	8.82
Indifferent	10	15.63	12	16.44	5	14.71
Total Disagree	37	57.81	51	69.86	26	76.47
Total	64	100.00	73	100.00	34	100.00

COMPARING MANAGEMENT PERCEPTION AND TRADITIONAL THEORY

Management perceptions depart from traditional theories of corporate governance. Stockholders are perceived to have little to say in corporate policy making, while boards of directors are seen as poor representatives. For example, the majority of the three levels of management disagreed that stockholders who provide a certain percentage of the capital should have an equal position of influence on corporate policy. Table 5.3 shows that a total of 26.5 percent of lower-level managers, 13.7 percent of middle-level managers, and only about 9 percent of top-level managers agreed that stockholders who provide a certain percentage of the capital should have an equal position of influence on corporate policy; on the other hand, a total of about 58 percent of lower-level managers, about 70 percent of middle-level managers, and more than 76 percent of top-level managers disagree with the statement.

The three levels of management agreed that stockholders should not form

Table 5.4

Frequency Distribution of Respondents

Question: "Stockholders who are many and distributed throughout society know little about how corporations should be managed and, therefore, they should not form corporate policy."

Respondents Choice	L.L Mgt. Frequency		M.L.Mgt. Frequency		T.L.Mgt Frequency	
	Nos.	%	Nos.	%	Nos.	%
Total Agree	41	63.98	60	82.19	25	73.53
Indifferent	6	9.38	6	8.22	4	11.37
Total Disagree	17	26.56	7	9.59	5	14.70
Total	64	100.00	73	100.00	34	100.00

corporate policy. However, they also believed that stockholders deserve adequate information. Table 5.4 shows that a total of about 64 percent of lower-level managers, 82.2 percent of middle-level managers, and 73.5 percent of top-level managers agreed that stockholders should not form corporate policy.

These results indicate clearly that management in general does not think that stockholders are necessary for corporate governance and should not influence corporate policy. This is a clear variation from the traditional theory of corporate governance which states that ultimate control of a corporation's affairs rests in the hands of the stockholders. These results also show a clear gap between theory and practice, between the academic community and state requirements and the real world or what is really in practice from the management point of view.

This concurs with the writings of many authors, such as Berle and Means (1932), Larner (1971), Eisenberg (1976), Sommer (1980), Geneen (1984), Nader and Green (1976), Aram (1987), Buchholz (1986), Weidenbaum (1985), and others. This agrees with the assessment, for example, that ownership of most U.S. corporations is dispersed widely throughout society. Such a dispersion has left individual stockholders with a small amount of shares which really are not large enough to make a difference in the rating process during the annual meeting of stockholders.

The conclusion, therefore, is that management does not want stockholders to influence corporate policy. Consequently, management is not only running the corporation on a day-to-day basis, but exercises ultimate control over the corporate resources. At the same time, managers agree that stockholders deserve adequate information. The study reveals that a total of 54.7 percent of lower-level managers, 67 percent of middle-level managers, and 57.6 percent of top-level managers disagreed with the statement that "stockholders demand more information than what is usually required by law through disclosure, and this information is costly to the corporation; therefore, management should not comply." While managers disagreed with stockholder participation in corporate policy, they agreed to provide stockholders with needed information.

Management seems to suggest that since stockholders use their voting rights to nominate board members, the board and not the stockholders should be involved. If the power to nominate and solicit proxies remains in the hands of management, as is now usually the case, management effectively controls the choice of the board members. This might also indicate that because management realizes that the stockholders are many and distributed throughout society, it is therefore difficult to get them to agree on who will represent them and the kind of influence they need.

NOTES

1. Harold Koontz, *The Board of Directors and Effective Management* (New York: McGraw-Hill, 1967), p. 1.

2. Ibid.

3. Francis W. Steckmest, *Corporate Performance: The Key to Public Trust* (New York: McGraw-Hill, 1982), p. 185.

4. Harold S. Geneen, "Why Directors Can't Protect the Shareholders," *Fortune* (September 17, 1984): 28.

5. Steckmest, *Corporate Performance*, p. 185.

6. Quoted in Melvin A. Eisenberg, *The Structure of the Corporation: A Legal Analysis* (Boston: Little Brown and Company, 1976), p. 142.

7. Rogene A. Buchholz, *Business Environment and Public Policy* (Englewood Cliffs, N.J.: Prentice-Hall, 1986), p. 239.

8. Melvin A. Eisenberg, *The Structure of the Corporation: A Legal Analysis* (Boston: Little, Brown and Company, 1976), pp. 3, 139–40.

9. Adolf A. Berle and Gardiner C. Means, *The Modern Corporation and Private Property* (New York: Macmillan, 1932).

10. Ibid., p. 93.

11. Robert J. Larner, *Management Control and the Large Corporation* (New York: Dunellen, 1971).

12. Maitre Jean Chambouline, *Directors and Board, Corporate Governance in the United States of America: Conclusion*, translated by Alexander Reed and Carolyn B. Kilbourne, Spring 1980, p. 28.

13. Steckmest, *Corporate Performance*, p. 183.

14. Myles L. Mace, "The President and the Board of Directors," *Harvard Business Review* (March–April 1972): 42.

15. Christopher D. Stone, *Where the Law Ends: The Social Control of Corporate Behavior* (New York: Harper and Row, 1975), p. 134.

16. Heidrick and Struggles, *The Changing Board: 1980 Update* (Atlanta, Ga.: Heidrick and Struggles, Inc., 1980).

17. J. Keith Louden, *The Effective Director in Action* (New York: Amacom, 1975), p. 127.

6

The Effectiveness of the Board of Directors

Since the board of directors can normally act only at meetings, the board has proven to be ineffective. The amount of time spent in meetings, as shown by studies, is very minimal and has proved to be insufficient to manage and direct a corporation's business affairs. Management claims that the amount of time spent does not enable the board of directors to rule efficiently. For instance, the Conference Board Study of 1967, which tested 454 manufacturing and mining corporations, concluded the following: (1) the boards of 45 percent of the responding corporations met six or less times per year; (2) 96 percent of these corporations met twelve or less times per year; (3) out of eighty-one public utility corporations, no boards met more than fifteen times per year; (4) out of forty banking corporations, 65 percent of the boards met between ten and seventeen times per year; 30 percent met thirteen times per year; and the remaining 5 percent met less than ten times per year. The Conference Board Study of 1972 (which tested 129 industries) showed that the boards of about 40 percent of the industries met ten times or more per year, while the boards of the remaining 60 percent met less than ten times per year.[1] A 1970 study of 474 industrial corporations by the management consulting firm of Heidrick and Struggles showed identical figures.[2] Koontz and others found that board meetings last only a few hours. Only a few boards spend thirty-six hours or more each year in meeting time, and about 50 percent of the board members spend eighteen hours or less. Based on such results, the board could not possibly manage the affairs of a large, publicly held corporation in an acceptable manner. Corporate presidents responded to Mace's interview as follows: "[the] board is handicapped in exercising the responsibility to measure management unless it has more than a casual amount of time to spend on the company's business... and I think the man who serves on several boards and has a full-time job some place just can't do it. He is not sufficiently knowledgeable; he is not sufficiently concerned, and he doesn't have the time to do it."[3]

M. Copeland and A. Towl,[4] Mace,[5] and Heidrick and Struggles report that the information given to the board of directors is controlled by the executives. "Another difficulty in measuring management is that the outside board member can respond only, or principally, to the material and data which are presented. It should be noted here that appraising the president's performance can be limited by what the president, who controls the sources of information, chooses to make available."[6]

Heidrick and Struggles showed that only 17.2 percent of the industrial corporations sent directors manufacturing data before the board meeting, and only 21.3 percent of the corporations sent marketing data. The same study showed that about 6 percent sent an agenda and 11 percent sent no information at all.[7] In many corporations the board was completely ignored by the executives.

In response to whether the board should have unrestricted information about the company's plans and operating data, 20 percent of the executives think that directors should not have unrestricted access to company information. One of the outside directors of Barnes Company said, "We outsiders on the Board got all our information on the threat of technological change through the president."[8] Others in management said, "we communicate with them [board of directors], but they are in no position to challenge what we propose to do."[9]

Relevant data is considered essential to meaningful decision making. From the facts and figures presented above, which show that boards lack data and the ability to evaluate data that is gathered, it is reasonable to conclude that boards are ineffective in making useful or meaningful decisions. It is evident that time spent by boards and the information flow to them have restricted board effectiveness and ability to manage business and make corporate policy. Time and the flow of information, however, do not show directly how board members are being subordinated to top executives.

What really restricts the board's ability and effectiveness is the composition of the board, that is, whether the board includes members who are economically and psychologically tied to or dependent on the chief executive officer or other executives in the corporation. Ten to twelve years ago, boards were designed primarily to support the decisions of management and the CEO. But since then boards have changed and their role has become more important. They now assume more responsibility for the direction of the corporation and are made up of independent, hard-working individuals. Because of this change, the board must be selected with great care and maintain a good balance between inside and outside directors.

Inside directors, known as functional, employee, management, or officer directors, are on the company payroll and are usually heads of divisions.

Since their primary affiliation is with the company and they are full-time directors, they are readily available for all board meetings. There are many advantages to having inside directors. They tend to have better technical backgrounds, more leadership ability, immediate availability for routine and emergency sessions, and a better understanding of the needs and disposition of the company. Management may find that it is better to have more insiders on the board during a crisis where management is facing the possibility of dismissal because insiders are generally more loyal to senior managers. Although their service is greatly needed insiders rarely receive any additional compensation for working on the board. Except for CEOs their directorship ceases after they leave the company.

Outside directors, referred to as honorary, independent, or professional directors, are made up of nonmanagement, nonemployee, and part-time individuals.[10] They are recruited from outside a corporation and form a highly diverse group. They mainly consist of bankers, attorneys, chairmen from other corporations, and retired businessmen. Having outside directors is extremely advantageous, for they provide independent assessment, have broader backgrounds, are more representative of stockholders and society, are stockholder-oriented, and give the best in checks and balances. The political role of outside directors is limited, however, because they are usually inadequately informed about the internal operations of the organization. Therefore, they must rely on senior management for information. Background information on outside directors is extremely important in order to know how to judge their potential behavior on the board. If it is known that the director is an outside director on another board or a chief executive in a critical organization, then it is fair to assume that he is knowledgeable and will be a great asset to the board.[11]

It is sometimes hard to distinguish between outside and inside directors. (An example of this difficulty would be distinguishing between private investors that are not employed and CEOs that continue after retirement.) The distinction can become blurred when an outside director is selected by one or two members of the senior management team. Such a director is most likely in the executive officers' "inner circle."[12] He therefore serves more as an inside director. In cases such as this, the purpose of the outside director is lost. He is no longer an independent outsider bringing in fresh ideas. Why would someone want to serve as an outside director? Pay is certainly not a motivating factor. Thomas S. Carrol of Lever Brothers Co. believes that "directors serve out of self-interest."[13] John Nash, president of the National Association of Corporate Directors in Washington says it is a great honor and good for the ego. As Stuart J. Northop, a former CEO at Huffy Corp. says, "a director has a wonderful situation. He's given very intense, excellent briefings on corporate problems and opportunities. Then he has the opportunity to give his input to management—but he doesn't have the pressure of implementing it and managing the operation."[14] Many believe serving on boards makes a good retirement career, while others make a living by serving on a number of boards. Hulett Clinton Merrit during his lifetime acquired 138 company directorates.[15] The ideal situation is for at least half of a board's directors be outside directors. The number of outside directors indicates the cohesiveness of a firm's management team. If there are too many insiders, the management team can become excessively cohesive. This sets up a very dangerous situation because the directors tend to derive their judgment only from colleagues. The scarcity of outside directors restricts outside influence and leads to close-minded decisions. On the other hand, the addition of many outsiders brings new information and ideas and allows the entire board to make sound decisions. Outside directors "provoke an independent and fresh review of long-term decisions, effectuate impartial, uncontaminated audits of managerial performance, and counterbalance the influence of top management."[16] Companies need strong, knowledgeable inside directors as well as independent outsiders in order to represent stockholders most effectively.[17]

Melvin A. Eisenberg thinks that a good number of seats on the board are occupied by executives themselves. The Conference Board Survey of 1973 showed that the boards of 29 percent of the 454 manufacturing corporations were occupied by 50 percent or more inside members.

Heidrick and Struggles, in their 1972 study, showed even higher percentages. Their study reported that 49.8 percent of the responding industries had 50 percent or more insider members. About 56 percent of the 1970 Fortune 500 corporations responded that 49.7 percent of the corporations had a majority of inside members.[18] Board members depend on chief executives for both retention and promotion. Mace remarks that it is unlikely that employee directors will disagree or depart from what has been determined by management before the meeting. Therefore it can be said that employee-directors (insider members) are highly dependent on the chief executive and most likely will not oppose him.

Furthermore, there is strong evidence that a good number of outside directors depend highly on the chief executive officer and therefore are less likely to disagree with his policy. Smith showed that 20 to 25 percent of the outside directors in large U.S. corporations are lawyers or investment bankers and perhaps the majority of them do business with the corporations on whose board they serve. They are thus unlikely to oppose the chief executive who usually controls corporate business and also those individuals with whom the corporation deals. These studies showed also that between 12 and 15 percent of outsiders are commercial bankers. They usually have a similar interest in keeping the corporation's business.[19]

The Conference Board Survey of 1973 showed that many of the remaining members of the board are either friends or colleagues of the chief executives, and therefore, are psychologically tied to them. Mace, in his 1971 interview with chief executives, showed ample support for the above conclusion. He quoted one chief executive as saying, "Here in Baltimore . . . individually and collectively their names are a credit to the boards they are on. They are friends of friends and new board vacancies are filled from their ranks and their rosters." Mace quoted others as saying, "Here in New York it is a system club. There are a group of companies that you can see and you know them as well as I do where the chief executive of company A has B and C and D on his board. They are chief executive officers of B and C and D and he is on their boards. They are all members of the Brook Club, the Links Club or the Union League Club. Everybody is washing everybody else's hands."[20]

The selection of board members is mostly done by the chief executive and not by the board. Many studies show that the power of selection of the outside members is in the hands of the top management. The chief executives will take into account the dependability of a new member before any selection takes place. Eisenberg thinks if top executives have the power to hire, then, logically, they have the power to fire. Mace believes that any unexpected challenge to the executives by an outside member would cause the latter to resign. Therefore the choosing of outside members by top executives assures the subservience of those members to top management. This implies that the member accepts that all power is possessed by the chief executive.

Mace quoted a president of a corporation as saying "in selecting new outside directors, I pick them very much like a trial lawyer goes about the selection of a jury." He quoted another president as saying, "Don't be surprised or disappointed if you find that most outside members are known to be non boat-rockers. What would you do if you were president? You control the company and you control the board. You want to perpetuate this control. You certainly don't want anyone on your board who even slightly might be a challenge or question to your tenure; so you pick personal friends with prestigious titles and names...you sure as hell are not going to ask Ralph Nader or Lewis Gilbert or...what's the name of that woman who is so unpleasant at stockholders' meetings?"[21]

These examples concur with Buchholz's and Steckmest's earlier remarks that the outside members of the board are "buddies" of management and subservient to management. It is clear that the chief executive controls the selection process just as he controls the flow of information to the board members and the stockholders. This indicates that the chief executive is the one who determines corporate activities. The state incorporation laws, as mentioned earlier, require that a company be managed under the direction of a board of directors. However, many large corporations have been managed and controlled by the chief executives and other top executives without sufficient accountability to their board of directors.

The board of directors of a corporation was primarily established to control and guard against the unrestrained self-interests of management. The board is supposed to protect the investments of stockholders by evaluating the performance of the managers and establishing a direction for the company's progress. Because the board represents the stockholders' interests, it must act as an overseer of the management. If management fails, it is the board's responsibility to replace the faulty managers. Although the board of directors supposedly protects stockholders' interests, stockholders feel that the job is being inadequately performed. Lately, life on the corporate board is becoming a tedious and unwanted task.

Because the stockholders have their money invested in specific corporations, they are concerned with how the business operates, and if the business makes a transaction that diminishes the value of their investment they, as investors, become very perturbed. In 1934 the government had to intervene and establish a Securities Exchange Act because there were many managers that were capable of making personal, rather than corporate, earnings. "The laws establish liabilities for presenting false information to the public in the sale of securities, and they define and outlaw practices of price manipulation and other deceptive devices."[22]

Although the government intervened, the board still inadequately continued controlling the corporations, for many boards were submissive and were misguided by false information distributed by management forcing corporations into financial disorder. A good example of management misrepresentation is Penn Central. "Penn Central directors said that they were handed expenditures lists to approve, and barely discussed in detail sketchy financial reports." When the managers at Penn Central forced the corporation into financial disorder, they blatantly showed that their board poorly evaluated their management.[23]

If the management of a company can misrepresent information to the board, there must be inadequacies present in the board's operations. People used to take positions on a board as an easy way to gain extra cash while also gaining prestige, but by taking this easy cash approach, they did not put their full effort into the matters of the board and problems arose. If a director did not have his own money invested in the corporation, why would he be overwhelmingly concerned for the efficient operation of the corporation? Most outside directors, for example, have rigorous jobs of their own, which barely allow them time to work on their own problems, let alone those of another company. It is also difficult for an outside director to take part in board discussions. If a director asks a question, he will be answered, but if he should persist in debating an answer he will usually be embarrassed by his lack of knowledge on that particular point of discussion. If the director keeps pushing for an answer he will become known as a trouble maker, and trouble makers do not last very long on boards.[24]

People who usually last on boards are those who can get along well with other people; they must be capable of working not only as individuals, but as part of a group. A person who keeps causing trouble and who goes against the majority just slows down the transactions of the board. Although the outside directors are nominated by the stockholders, the chief executive has the last word on the acceptance of the director. If the chief executive cannot work well with the potential director, that individual will not be hired.

Today, due to the inadequacies of yesterday's boards, having a seat on the board of directors is becoming a worrisome responsibility. Many directors feel that the legal risks and the time hassles are not worth it any more. The extent of the present problem started with Trans Union Corporation. The Trans Union Corporation held a meeting for two hours, and after the meeting the board agreed to a 690-million-dollar transaction with the Marmon group. The shareholders sued because the board acted too quickly and without sufficient information. "It's a signal that the pendulum has swung as far as it's going to in letting managements and boards do whatever they want without regard to the fundamental shareholders rights."[25] Many people are turning away the invitation to sit on a board, and companies are having problems finding replacements. Directors are afraid of liability judgments, for the cost of insurance has risen "tenfold in the last two years."[26] Because directors can be held liable for faulty business transactions, they will not join a board unless it has good insurance, which in turn is very expensive. Although the odds of a director's losing are low, many suits are settled out of court. The following quotation of a board of directors' meeting of a corporation is a good example of this issue.

> I serve on a board of the First Pennsylvania Bank and we just agreed to sell the bank to Marine Midland from Buffalo, New York, which I feel is a fantastic deal for our stockholders. There are now nine suits that have been instituted since the announcement of the merger, and all of these nine were instituted by well known so called ambulance chasers and unfortunately, they will probably get some sort of nuisance settlement which could range from $25,000 to hundreds of thousands of dollars, just to "go away," because it would cost the corporation more than that in legal fees to defend them.[27]

Because of this type of hassle, boards are becoming increasingly smaller with more outside directors. Besides the legal responsibilities deterring people from joining the board, there are also higher standards placed on the directors from shareholders. Directors today are expected to study issues more thoroughly now than before, for the directors are in fear of being sued for poor performance. Directors must then give up most of their time that they may need for running their own company. Before, if a person had his own business and a board position, he could get away with doing both adequately, for the board did not take much time. But the board today requires time and commitment. If a crisis surfaces, such as an unwanted takeover offer, board members can suddenly face weeks or months of constant meetings and telephone calls.

The resources of large corporations and much of society are thus controlled by a limited number of people. This is in contrast with a democratic system of control; in addition, this is a violation of state incorporation laws. Therefore great pressure has been brought recently to: (1) strengthen the board's role and accountability to the different interest groups; (2) assure consistency between theory and practice; and (3) emphasize internal corporate governance as a substitute to government involvement through regulation. Such regulation is considered to be costly to both society and corporations.

THE STUDY

According to traditional theory, boards of directors are not perceived as involved in or required for corporate policy making in general. The majority of the three levels of management agree that boards of directors should be responsible for all areas of corporate policy; however, they deny board participation in all aspects of corporate policy. While many boards have heretofore played a residual role in routine corporate policy making, intervening only in times of crisis, today this view has been challenged with increasing frequency by government and civil suits. The data in table 6.1 shows that the total of about 67 percent of lower-level managers, 51 percent of middle-level managers, and 56 percent of top-level managers agree that the board of directors should be responsible for all areas of corporate policy, while a total of about 17 percent of lower-level managers, 41 percent of middle-level managers, and 23.5 percent of top-level managers disagree.

The data in table 6.2 shows that a total of about 45 percent of lower-level managers, 31.5 percent of middle-level managers, and 47 percent of top-level managers agree that the board of directors should actively participate in all aspects of corporate policy. A total of about 41 percent of lower-level managers, 60 percent of middle-level managers, and 50 percent of top-level managers disagree.

The data presented in tables 6.1 and 6.2 reveals that while the three levels of management agree that boards should be responsible for corporate reviewing, top-level and middle-level managers disagree with board participation. This might raise the issue of why management accepts the board as responsible for corporate policy, yet does not accept their active participation. In general, managers are willing to comply with corporate law requiring board responsibility, but they are not ready to accept board interference. In addition, the law does not specify the kind of participation the board should have. According to traditional theory, the board of directors is supposed to represent the interests of the stockholders—the owners of the corporation.

The board's main role is to oversee and evaluate the performance of management in running the business, and if that performance is not satisfactory, the board should do something about it. The board's responsibility is to evaluate management performance, especially that of the chief executive, and to compensate or remove management as the board sees fit. That is what

Table 6.1

Frequency Distribution of Respondents

Question: "In recent years, corporate boards have been accountable for virtually all areas of corporate policy, therefore, they should be responsible for corporate policy."

	L.L Mgt. Frequency		M.L.Mgt. Frequency		T.L.Mgt Frequency	
Respondents Choice	Nos.	%	Nos.	%	Nos.	%
Total Agree	43	67.19	37	50.58	19	55.88
Indifferent	10	15.63	6	8.22	7	20.59
Total Disagree	11	17.18	30	41.10	8	23.53
Total	64	100.00	73	100.00	34	100.00

Table 6.2

Frequency Distribution of Respondents

Question"Boards of Directors should actively participate in all aspects of corporate policy."

	L.L Mgt. Frequency		M.L.Mgt. Frequency		T.L.Mgt Frequency	
Respondents Choice	Nos.	%	Nos.	%	Nos.	%
Total Agree	29	45.31	23	31.51	16	47.06
Indifferent	9	14.06	6	8.22	1	2.94
Total Disagree	26	40.63	44	60.27	17	50.00
Total	64	100.00	73	100.00	34	100.00

is supposed to happen but such evaluation usually does not take place according to management perception. According to the study, boards of directors are not perceived as involved in or required for corporate policy making in general. All levels of management disagree that the role of the board is to promote and compensate the CEO. Curiously, what earlier studies such as Mace's (1971) found was that, in the view of the board of directors themselves, this was the major, if not the exclusive, function of the board. The study reveals that a total of about 25 percent of lower-level managers, 18 percent of middle-level managers, and 23.5 percent of top-level managers agree that the board of director's role is to promote and compensate the CEO, while a total of about 54.7 percent of lower-level managers, 74 percent of middle-level managers, and 68 percent of top-level managers disagree. All levels of managers agree that the board should play an advisory role in corporate policy. The study shows that a total of about 69 percent of lower-level managers, 82 percent of middle-level managers, and 79.5 percent of top-level managers agree with the statement that "the Board of Directors plays an advisory role in corporate policy." These results suggest that managers see the board's role as an advisory one. While managers believe that the board should be responsible for all aspects of corporate governance, at the same time they deny the board's participation in all aspects of corporate policy as suggested by the theory. Rather, the current board role as management perceives it ranges from being merely advisory to negligible.

SUMMARY

The effectiveness of the board of directors is limited by several factors. In order to function effectively, the board should not be subject to time constraints, as is now the case. Board members are certainly hampered in their efforts to perform well by the amount of time allotted for the job. The complexity of the job demands more than an inconsequential amount of time divided among meetings spaced at lengthy intervals throughout the year. Another impediment to effectiveness is the quality and quantity of information available to directors. When management has the right to oversee and restrict pertinent data, the resulting gaps in the director's knowledge on a particular subject will affect any decision he must make. Perhaps the most significant element influencing board effectiveness is its composition. There are advantages associated with having inside directors as there are with having outside directors. For this reason, an ideal arrangement seems to be boards where both are represented in approximately equal numbers. The other perceived impediment to effectiveness is the selection process. It is important to keep in mind that the duty of a director as originally designed is to represent the interests of the shareholders. When management is involved with the selection of directors, this primary intent is thwarted. An appointee who feels a sense of obligation to management, rather than to the stockholders, will be reluctant to express criticism of management. Therefore, it is essential that those members selected to serve on a board are individuals who have the expertise, commitment, and objectivity to carry out the implied purpose of a role on the board of directors. This phenomenon is frequently not the case, although pressure is being brought to bring boards more in line with original expectations.

The study showed that the majority of lower, middle, and top management members believed that the board of directors should be responsible for all areas of corporate policy. This view is in opposition to the belief that participation by the board should be limited to routine matters or to crisis intervention.

When asked if the board of directors should actively participate in all aspects of corporate policy, 45 percent agreed they should, while 40 percent disagreed. However, middle-level managers had other views: only 31 percent agreed on participation, while 44 percent disagreed. All levels of management disagreed that the role of the board is to promote and compensate the CEO. All levels of managers agreed that the board should play an advisory role in corporate policy.

NOTES

1. Harold Koontz, *The Board of Directors and Effective Management* (New York: McGraw-Hill, 1967), p. 158.

2. Heidrick and Struggles, *Profile of the Board of Directors* (Atlanta, Ga.: Heidrick and Struggles, Inc., 1971).

3. Myles L. Mace, *Director: Myth and Reality* (Boston: Harvard College, 1971), p. 30.

4. M. Copeland and A. Towl, *The Board of Directors and Business Management* (Boston: Harvard University Press, 1947), p. 169.

5. Mace, *Director*, p. 30.

6. Heidrick and Struggles, *Profile*, p. 5.

7. Ibid., p. 6.

8. Mace, *Director*, p. 32.

9. Ibid., p. 43.

10. Stanley C. Vance, *Corporate Leadership* (New York: McGraw-Hill, 1983), pp. 45–46.

11. Johannes M. Pennings, *Interlocking Directorate* (San Francisco: Jossey-Bass Publishers, 1980), p. 78.

12. Ibid., p. 48.

13. James Braham, "An Inside Look at Outside Directors," *Industrial Week* (September 3, 1984): 39.

14. Ibid., p. 38.

15. Vance, *Corporate Leadership*, p. 47.

16. Pennings, *Interlocking Directorate*, p. 79.

17. Murray Weidenbaum, "The Best Defense Against the Raiders," *Business Week* (September 23, 1985): 21.

18. Ephraim P. Smith, "Interlocking Directors Among the Fortune 500," *Anti-Trust Law and Economics Review* (Summer 1970): 47, 49, 56.

19. Ibid., pp. 48–49; and table 2.

20. Mace, *Director*, p. 99.

21. Ibid., pp. 79–81, 99.

22. John D. Aram, *Managing Business and Public Policy: Concepts, Issues, and Cases* (Marshfield, Mass.: Pitman Publishing, 1987), p. 323.

23. Ibid., p. 324.

24. Harold S. Geneen, "Why Directors Can't Protect the Shareholders," *Fortune* (September 17, 1984): 28.

25. William B. Alaberson and William J. Powell, Jr., "A Landmark Ruling That Puts Board Members in Peril," *Business Week* (March 18, 1985): 56.

26. Laurie Baum, "The Job Nobody Wants," *Business Week* (September 8, 1986): 56.

27. Questionnaire reply from Herbert Lotman, Equity Meat Corp., Philadelphia, Pennsylvania, November 1986.

7

Board Liability

INTRODUCTION

This chapter will discuss the issues surrounding the board of directors' liability to shareholders. Membership on a board of directors was once considered a prestigious position. Recent trends have shown many board member candidates have not felt this way; they have been turning down the invitation to become board members. This chapter will not only discuss the reasons why this has occurred, but also ways this trend can be reversed.

This fact may seem ironic considering the possible benefits of becoming a board member. Most board members are paid a base salary of no less than $21,000 dollars per year for an average of 112 hours of work.[1] Some board members belong to as many as twelve different boards of directors at one time and are still presidents of other corporations on top of that; as a consequence, the possible yearly income is astounding.[2] In the past board members have had quite lucrative positions; they were well paid and not expected to do much in the way of making real decisions. The main function of many board members is that of figure head. Gerald Ford, for example, received a salary of $92,000 per year at the mining company Amax Inc., an industry in which he had no previous experience.[3]

THE PROBLEM

Why are candidates turning down such opportunities? The main reason is liability. Although many executives may cite other reasons for the sudden decline in the acceptance of board positions, all stem from the increase in the lawsuits against the board of directors. The problem that many boards of directors face today is the fact that they are liable to shareholders if the company should fail. If the board fails to act in the best interest of its shareholders the outcome may be a lawsuit. Even if board members only appear negligent, they may find themselves pulled into court by nervous shareholders.

There are a number of goals which a board of directors is expected to meet. One is to separate itself from the management of the company. This separation insures that the board is not unduly influenced by top management so that both will work in the best interest of the company's shareholders. The board is also expected to insure proper management of the corporation's resources, including human resources. According to Harold Geneen, a former chairman of ITT, "the board's responsibility is to sit in judgment of the management, especially on the performance of the chief executive officer, and to reward, punish or replace the management as the board sees fit."[4] A director's duty is not to earn a quick return on investment; it is to insure the best possible results for the shareholders which elected him or her to represent their interests. This puts directors in a touchy situation; every move that the board makes must be taken carefully.

NEW TRENDS

There are at present three main trends in the board's reformation process. First, many corporations are seeking outside directors with no previous affiliation with the corporation. Second, many corporations are hiring more outside directors than inside directors. Third, corporations are seeking board members who have various skills.

An example is an auditing committee. This committee would make sure that the company's accounting books are accurate. These trends, if continued, will have many positive advantages for the corporation which uses them. One would be a reduction in poor decisions, which in turn would reduce the risk of a board being sued by its shareholders. The use of outside directors has proven valuable in providing shareholders with a nonbiased board of directors. Using a larger number of outside directors stops the common practice whereby inside directors overrule objections of the outside members by using the powerful majority vote. The use of outside directors with various skills can often improve the decision-making process of the board.

An example of this would be if a former president of a steel-producing company were to serve on the board of an automobile manufacturer. The former steel president could provide useful information on how steel prices react to present and future economic conditions. This information is very valuable to auto manufacturers because they use steel to such a large degree. There are also disadvantages associated with these emerging trends. One is the fact that outside board members are becoming harder and harder to find and even harder to hire. Another disadvantage is the opposition of top-level managers to the hiring of outside managers. Top-level managers tend to view these trends as a threat to their strength and power in the corporation as the main policy makers.

Another problem is that the hiring of outside directors does not always insure that these outsiders are "true" outside directors. Frequently so-called "outside" directors have some connection with the company that is not easily seen by the shareholders. They may be the friends or business partners of management, which may possibly result in biased decisions. Many directors are also chosen because of their famous names instead of their qualifications. In the case of Allegheny International Inc., the outside directors included such prestigious people as H. J. Heinz, Alexander Haig, and Richard Cyert, president of Carnegie Mellon University. All of these men were well known by the public, yet none of them were well educated in Allegheny's industry and all lacked necessary knowledge to make proper judgments while sitting on the board. As a result, the shareholders filed a lawsuit against the board for negligence and conflict of interest.[5]

Proposals for restructuring boards of directors includes special interest directors and employee directors. Special interest directors provide expertise in specialized areas, such as serving as trouble shooters in a corporation. An example would be the hiring of an accountant to help with difficulties in the finance department. Using employees on the board can also be a valuable asset for management. Employees can help provide information to the board in such areas as production proposals and possible employee reactions to new policies. The Chrysler Corporation has had a member of the employees' union on the board for a number of years to help in the decision-making process. This has proved to be a profitable venture for both employees and the corporation itself. Although these proposals for restructuring the board of directors are in the process of being developed, the liability issue is still at stake.

BOARD LIABILITY

The issue of the board of directors' liability to the corporation's shareholders has seemed to surface overnight. Although common sense tells us the liability issue has only gradually grown, it is only now being publicized. Why do corporate directors have such a difficult time with liability to the shareholders? This question could be answered simply with three words: *mergers, takeovers,* and *buyouts.* All three processes deal with the change in the ownership of a corporation, which makes stockholders nervous. As high tech and powerful buying ability has increased in today's successful corporation, it is up to the directors to make sound judgments on mergers, takeovers, and buyouts. If these judgments are not responsible in the eyes of the shareholders, the board fears that they will be sued by the shareholders. "Angered shareholders that are dissatisfied with the dealing of the board, stand poised to sue corporate officers and directors for management malpractice."[6] These lawsuits are very expensive to defend; consequently, cases are settled out of court. Even if a corporation believes that it might win the case, they will usually elect to settle because it is cheaper and they will not suffer public disgrace.[7]

Another example is that of Allegheny International Inc. Allegheny had been having financial difficulties for several years and yet nothing was done to remedy the situation. The stockholders were finally able to take action after the board was asked to address the problems itself and did not do so. "We gave the board the opportunity to take action itself and, by not doing so, that triggered the right of the shareholder to sue the board in the name of the company."[8] The shareholders soon brought Allegheny International to court on a number of counts.

The suit was against the chairman and the CEO of Allegheny International, Robert J. Buckley, for recovery of certain corporate funds. This situation might have been avoided if the CEO had not been so influential in the determination of board members. The board members he chose were people with popular names, yet with little expertise in this particular industry. One such board member was Alexander Haig, former secretary of state. Haig was a very popular man, yet he could be easily manipulated because of his lack of experience. The blind ignorance of board members often leads to poor, one-sided board decisions. If a board is truly objective in its analysis of the CEO and the company (which is precisely its function), such problems probably will not arise. If they do, they will be stopped before significant damage is done to the company. The board in this case was protecting the CEO and itself, not the shareholders they were supposed to protect.

Due to the increase in the number of lawsuits against board members, many corporations have been attaining insurance for their board members. Lawsuits have become so prominent recently that insurance companies are demanding higher premium rates. These higher premium rates are affecting the makeup of the board itself. The average increase is 362 percent over the past five years.[9] Many corporations, because of this, are asking outside members to resign. In contrast, inside directors are already protected by the company's insurance. In the case of the Zonic Corporation, top management was facing a tenfold increase in insurance premiums for coverage of four outside directors. Knowing that they could not afford to pay this price, Gerald Zobrist, the president of the company, was forced to fire all of the outside board members—one was his own father, Joseph Zobrist.[10]

The problem of the board's liability to the shareholders has become so acute that many major corporations are trying to pass new laws. These laws will protect many directors from this burden of liability. Although these corporations would like to have such bylaws, most stockholders will not agree to them because this gives the board of directors the right to do virtually anything without punishment. Corporations such as Pillsbury, General Motors,

Bank of America, and General Mills are among those asking shareholders to accept such bylaws to protect the directors.

These new bylaws are being viewed as "corporacy" at its worst. Top management is not trying to protect the board from liability suits. The following statement exemplifies the attitudes that many shareholders have toward the new bylaws: "At a time when managers and directors of corporate America most need to be held accountable for their actions, they are trying to insulate themselves instead."[11]

The problem of board room liability has become so critical that many companies are now forced to hire professional recruiters to search for qualified and intelligent board members. These professional recruiters are not enjoying success for a number of reasons. Not only is the process of hiring professional recruiters expensive but it is also time-consuming and often unsuccessful. Approximately five years ago, four of every five executives approached by recruiters accepted board positions. Today only two of five executives accept these positions.[12] This too has had a major impact on the makeup of the board of directors.

The boards of today are becoming smaller and smaller and members are increasingly inside directors, because it is so difficult to find top-flight executives to accept these board positions. The directors of today are expected to know more than the directors of the past. The responsibilities thrust upon board members are greater than in the past. Directors are now expected to sacrifice more time and energy than ever before. The extra time and effort needed to be a director is yet another reason why the decline in the acceptance of outside directors to the board continues to grow. Directors are less willing to put effort into an outside company if it may take away from effectiveness in their own companies.[13]

Due to the fear that shareholders will realize the potential for liability suits against board members, there has been a halt and even a turn-about in the process of attaining outside directors. This turn-about is quite a change from the trend of the past. In the 1960s the prevailing trend was to use as many outside directors as possible to insure a strong board. Today the fear of liability has overridden the trend toward outside boards and it may have a severe effect on the competence of present-day boards. Inside directors have more to lose by speaking their mind than do outside directors. Today, boards are composed of a good number of inside directors. Although outside directors are preferred, board room liability is having a major impact on the modern corporation, actually changing the way many directors view the once prestigious position.

A landmark ruling by the Delaware Supreme Court has virtually opened the door to board member liability. The Trans Union Corporation, which leased railroad tank cars and water and waste equipment, gave approval to the Pritzker family's Marmon Group Inc. take-over bid. It took the Trans Union board approximately two hours to accept Marmon Group's bid of $690 million. The Trans Union board was immediately fighting a shareholders' suit that would result in every board member being personally responsible for the fair value of Trans Union. The shareholders of Trans Union charged the board for selling the corporation at an unfair price. The stockholders also charged the board for acting too quickly and hastily in accepting the offer. The Delaware Supreme Court ruled that the ten directors of Trans Union were fully responsible for paying the difference between the Pritzker family's bid and the fair value of Trans Union. This ruling opened the door for board room liability to the shareholders. "It's a signal that the pendulum has swung as far as it's going to in letting managements and boards do whatever they want without regard to fundamental shareholder risks."[14]

It was estimated that the Trans Union Corporation may have been worth as much as $200 million more than what the Pritzker family paid. Also it was estimated that Trans Union had a $20-million insurance policy taken out to protect its directors. Although Trans Union had insurance, the board could still face $180 million in liability damages.

Since this Trans Union case there have been many similar cases. For example, the ten directors of Continental Illinois National Bank and Trust Co. have been forced to step down. This public display of accountability was exacted by the Federal Deposit Insurance Corporation as the price of government buyout. The Chase Manhattan Bank and Bank America Corporation are also pursuing a suit against its former managers. They claim that these managers were negligent, resulting in millions of dollars of losses.

Eight of ten directors on the board of Armada Corporation, a steel company located in Michigan, left their jobs. These eight board members resigned because Armada's liability insurance premium had increased drastically. This drastic increase in premium forced Armada to discontinue its liability insurance.[15] These brief examples of board room liability demonstrate why outside directors are turning down board room positions. If shareholders never accept bylaws, which keep directors from being liable, there will be no such thing as outside directors.

Corporate directors must perform in a careful and intelligent manner, in the best interest of the shareholder. If the board does not perform in the best interest of the shareholder, then it must face the consequences. Today, board members cannot attend a half hour of eating doughnuts, meeting, and voting yes or no on a major issue before playing golf. Board members now must be business analysts and forecasters. Major corporations, such as IBM, are determined to get the most intelligent and worldly directors for future success.

POSSIBLE SOLUTIONS

Now that some relevant board room liability cases have been detailed, it is pertinent to determine some resolutions to board room liability. The following solutions to board room liability appeared in *Fortune* magazine (1987): (1) Stock options for board members should be installed in every corporation. With stock options, board members can relate to the same concerns that shareholders have. (2) Board members should be paid the prevailing wages for their duties. Also boards should be kept small. (3) The board should include as many outside directors as possible. To be an inside director, one must own a substantial amount of company stock. (4) It would be beneficial to a corporation and its stakeholders to have an accounting firm randomly present with the board. (5) A chairman without a full-time position should be involved in the board. (6) Institutional investors must be concerned about the quality of directors. (7) Too many directors are often overly concerned with making a quick buck. This is often done at the long-term expense of the corporation. (8) The board's concern for high short-term earnings is probably the main issue of board room liability. Board members should have more concern for the long-term health of the corporation.

Its future is what the corporation of the present relies on for existence. Another possible solution to the problem of board room liability is the possible re-education of potential board members as to their proper functions. Board members are in the position to oversee the management of the corporation's assets by the management of the corporation. They must also establish and approve the corporation's mission, objectives, and strategies.

The board must also review management's actions in light of the corporation's performance relative to the goals of the corporation. Finally, the board is expected to hire and fire the principal operating officers of the company based on their performance. Simply, the board is there to direct the affairs of the corporation, not to manage it.

The ability to stay on the board and out of trouble is a goal that all directors hope to attain. The following are six tips for accomplishing those goals: (1) Be open and state your own opinions on specific topics. (2) Ask questions and know all the relevant material about a particular topic at hand. (3) Become a business analyst, not a business spectator. (4) Try to attend and participate in every meeting. (5) Make certain you are insured in case of a liability suit. (6) You must not be apprehensive about telling the CEO what you are thinking. Your thoughts may be greatly appreciated by the CEO or the corporation as a whole.

In the opinion of many, if board members do not use their expertise and knowledge in the best interest of the corporation and shareholders, then they are guilty of malpractice—just like negligent doctors. From a business viewpoint, the patient is the corporation, the doctor is the board, and the shareholders are the family that sues the board for malpractice.

NOTES

1. Laurie Baum, "The Job Nobody Wants." *Business Week* (September 8, 1986): 56.

2. Laurie Baum, "Professional Directors: So Many Boards So Little Time." *Business Week* (September 8, 1986): 59.

3. Ibid., p. 59.

4. D. J. Dunn, "Directors Aren't Doing Their Job," *Fortune* (March 16, 1987): 119.

5. "No More Rubber Stamps in the Board Room," *Business Week* (December 1, 1986): 117.

6. Tony Mauro, "Liability in the Board Room," *Nation's Business* (May 1986): 46.

7. Christopher Farrell, "If Directors Are Doing Their Jobs, They Don't Need Insurance," *Business Week* (September 8, 1986): 61.

8. Ben Powell, "Is It Safe to Go Back into the Board Room?" *Newsweek* (March 18, 1985): 54.

9. Mauro, "Liability," p. 117.

10. Ibid.

11. Baum, "The Job Nobody Wants," p. 56.

12. William B. Alaberson and William J. Powell, Jr., "A Landmark Ruling That Puts Board Members in Peril," *Business Week* (March 18, 1987): 56.

13. Mauro, "Liability," p. 117.

14. Alaberson and Powell, "Landmark Ruling," p. 56.

15. Dunn, "Directors," p. 119.

8

Reform of Corporate Governance

Corporate critics suggest that the existing system of corporate governance has failed to hold management and the board of directors accountable for the use of corporate power. Critics recommend reforming the internal structure of corporations thereby opening up the decision-making process to a wider set of influences. Their concern is whether decisions made in large corporations are sufficiently representative of society as a whole to ensure protection of the public interest as well as the interest of the corporation.

The U.S. Senate has held numerous hearings in Congress on the concentration of corporate power and the ownership of large corporations. For instance, Senator Edward M. Kennedy (Dem., Mass.) worked to secure the adoption of legislation that would limit conglomerate acquisitions. Such actions were considered necessary to protect the consumer from adverse effects created by large, powerful corporate entities. Senator Howard M. Metzenbaum (Dem., Ohio) also headed many hearings to find out "what, if anything, the American people should be doing to make corporations more accountable to their stockholders and to the public."[1]

During the late 1960s and early 1970s a series of financial debacles were discovered; some of these were considered outright fraud and many were complicated by questionable accounting practices. These actions reduced the confidence of the public in regulators and legislators alike. The leadership of U.S. business in general was called into serious question. The result was a call for reform of corporate governance; and the issue became what can and must be done to increase the effectiveness of corporate governance and improve the present system. The reforms suggested by different sources are summarized in this chapter.

DISCLOSURE

Disclosure was first brought to light by the special prosecutor involved in the Watergate scandal. A large number of U.S. corporations were engaged in questionable practices, both at home and abroad, some of which were illegal. The SEC first encouraged corporations to voluntarily disclose these questionable practices in 1977. The SEC mandated such disclosure after their investigation showed that over five hundred U.S. corporations had disclosed practices that were considered to be illegal or questionable. "As a consequence of the SEC investigations . . . over five hundred U.S. corporations have disclosed . . . illegal or questionable . . . conduct at home or abroad."[2] This investigation showed that the amounts considered to be improper payments were immaterial by traditional economic standards.

In July 1978, the SEC expanded the disclosure requirement—principally in the proxy statement. Such expansion was designed less to provide vital information to investors than to prod corporations in the direction of corporate governance reform. Rogene A. Buchholz thinks that the motivation behind increased disclosure is to increase corporate responsibility to the interests of the stockholders and society as a whole.[3] Now the SEC requires additional information to be disclosed: (1) the relationship between directors and candidates for election to the board or to the corporation; (2) the various committees' duties and membership; (3) the procedures for submission of shareholders' proposals; (4) the procedures for the shareholders' suggestions to the nominating committee, if there is one; and (5) the election of and votes against directors.

Reform in this area will provide stockholders with more information about how corporations are trying to help them in their future investment decisions. The shareholders have the opportunity to vote against the individual directors. Harold Williams, the former head of the SEC, advised corporations to provide their shareholders with the necessary information to make the corporate accountability process work in its present form or there will be more radical reforms and more government regulations.[4]

The SEC is not the only establishment to demand increased disclosure. In the last decade, the Financial Accounting Standards Board (FASB) has continued efforts toward self-regulation and establishment of uniform standards of disclosure. For instance, inflation accounting has been debated and proposed in various forms over the years. In 1979, the FASB issued Statement No. 33, "Financial Reporting and Changing Prices," which mandates inflation-accounting disclosure in annual reports to shareholders of large public companies. It requires only public companies having $1 billion of assets or $125 million of inventories and gross properties (before accumulated depreciation) at the beginning of the year to present supplemental information. The FASB, however, encouraged all enterprises to make this disclosure.

The principal supplemental disclosures required by Statement No. 33 are:

(1) current year income from continuing operations and information about both the historical cost/constant dollar basis and the current cost basis; (2) a five-year summary of selected financial data; and (3) certain narrative explanations of inflation-adjusted information. In March 1976, the SEC issued Accounting Series Release No. 190. The SEC adopted rules requiring certain public companies to disclose replacement cost data in Form 10K. The FASB current cost basis of Statement 33 created a second standard that addresses accounting for specific price change. The SEC then issued ASR 271 waiving the requirement to report replacement cost information and accepted FASB 37. The SEC and the FASB were concerned with providing additional information to aid users in understanding the effects of inflation on the financial statements of the company.

Irving Shapiro recommends that the board of directors use disclosure as a means of building the public's and the shareholders' confidence. He adds that the corporate board should implement policies that can help restore trust and respect.[5]

FEDERAL CHARTERING

Governance of all U.S. corporations, with few exceptions, is based on a charter issued under the provisions of state law. These state laws deal with management of the internal affairs of the corporation (e.g., stockholders' rights, the meeting of the stockholders and directors, the duties and liabilities of directors, managers, and financial structure).

Francis W. Steckmest believes that management is not accountable to state governments because state charters are too permissive.[6] Other critics believe that states compete by lowering their charter requirements in order to gain more charter revenues. For example, the State of Delaware has more than 110,000 corporations under charter; at least 40 percent of these corporations are listed on the New York Stock Exchange.[7] Ralph Nader found that 134 of the largest 1000 companies reincorporated in Delaware between 1967 and 1974; and 448 of the largest 1000, 251 of the largest 500, and 52 of the largest 100 corporations were incorporated in Delaware in 1974.[8] Therefore, the call for federal chartering as a method of corporate reform was increased. Federal chartering would provide uniform standards for internal governance and regulatory law to control the external conduct of large corporations. Some people think that federal chartering would be a radical change in the present system of corporate governance.[9] However, others think it has been in the system for some time.

William Dugger explains how national banks have operated under federal charter since the Civil War. He argues that nonfinancial corporations also used this practice. He adds that three presidents of the United States have suggested such chartering to Congress (Teddy Roosevelt, Taft, and Wilson).[10] Senator Joseph O'Mahoney, a populist from Wyoming, also supported the idea in his closing statement to the Temporary National Economic Committee (TNEC) in 1941: "It is idle to think that huge collective institutions which carry on our modern business can continue to operate without more definite responsibility toward all the people of the nation than they have now. To do this it will be necessary in my judgment to have a national charter system...."[11]

The idea of federal chartering has been in the public arena for quite some time. The call for corporations to obtain their charter from the federal government rather than from the state is a new reform to current practice. Ralph Nader in 1976 proposed comprehensive federal chartering including a law that would demand all industrial, retail, and transportation corporations, which sold over $250 million in goods and services, or which employed more than ten thousand employees in the United States in any one of the last three years, to obtain their charter from the federal government.[12]

The major advantages of federal chartering are: (1) Competition between states in charter laxity would be eliminated. States like Delaware would no longer be able to compete with other states merely by lowering their charter requirements. (2) State incorporation according to Nader makes no sense because boundaries are not relevant for corporate commerce. Therefore, federal chartering would provide a regulatory law and uniform standards for corporate governance to control the external conduct of large corporations. (3) Certain provisions for the composition and behavior of corporations could be imposed by the federal government. In the Nader proposal, provisions deal with the following areas:

Internal governance of the corporation. Such a provision would require companies under federal charter to establish a nine-member board of directors with specific duties. In addition to approving corporate policies, each director would be assigned a specific area of responsibility such as employee welfare, shareholder rights, environmental protection, consumer protection, or community relations. Such a provision would not only restrict management's behavior but management would also be subject to harsh penalties should they violate laws related to corporate operations.

Dealing with the public. Under this provision corporations would have to publish in detail a corporate register, listing all social and economic data. This information would include any pollution caused by the company, the steps taken to overcome this pollution, how much toxic material is used in each plant location, and statistical information about the number of employees, analyzed by race, sex, and income. This provision would also require companies to disclose information about their largest one hundred security holders, the thirty highest-paid executives, and financial reporting by product line, lobbying activities, joint ventures investments, annual tax returns, and the like.

Employee citizenship rights. To protect the employees this provision would involve a "bill of rights" which would prohibit companies from firing, penalizing, and intimidating employees in violation of their constitutional rights. This provision would also prohibit companies from firing employees for blowing the whistle.

Industrial structure. This final provision bases power on an arbitrary share of the market, and would prohibit mergers in concentrated industries.[13]

Representative Benjamin S. Rosenthal (Dem., N.J.) introduced the Corporate Democracy Act of 1980 in the House of Representatives. The bill would impose some federal requirements on large corporations and calls for all public policy committees to respond to public complaints against the corporation. This committee would recommend policies to the board on socially important issues. The bill also calls for a supervisory committee to deal with internal governance matters. A. A. Sommer thinks that such legislation will not move in Congress swiftly.[14]

According to Steckmest, many attorneys and professors of law and business have joined corporate leaders in rejecting not only federal chartering, but also any other federal legislation that affects the internal structure of the corporation. Some of their claims are the following: (1) "There has been no failure of state laws. Those laws provide the basis for the existence of a corporation and establish standards for its internal management." (2) "A single set of standards prescribed for a large number of corporations proposes a simplistic answer to a situation that involves a wide variety of circumstances and calls for flexible response. Disclosure is particularly well suited for that purpose." (3) "Federal chartering or another version of federal regulation of the internal governance of the corporation is an inappropriate way to curb errant corporate conduct. Specific legislation for identified problems is preferred to a single omnibus bill that would regulate governance and such problems as antitrust, pollution, equal opportunity, and occupational health."[15]

Others think it would be difficult to convince fifty state governments to agree on a common action. Some states are gaining good revenue from the existing corporate chartering process. "One local resident makes money telling people how to start a Delaware corporation for less than $100."[16] Some people defend their choice of chartering in the State of Delaware. They claim that they registered with Delaware not because its laws are loose and authorities are looking the other way but because the code of Delaware is a modern one. In addition, members of the legal profession together with the corporations trust the stability and wisdom of Delaware courts. Many corporations consider Delaware home and prefer to have their affairs chartered in that jurisdiction rather than anywhere else. "Nothing in the record suggests that stockholders and the public are therefore badly served."[17]

Steckmest claims that even though many federal chartering proposals have been introduced, there is little chance that federal chartering will be adopted in the near future. However, the possibility of some kind of federal chartering remains a threat.

IMPROVEMENT OF THE BOARD OF DIRECTORS

Many people believe that the board of directors is a major factor in the issue of corporate governance. Steckmest states that "the corporate community was forcefully reminded that effective performance of corporate boards is an indispensable factor in the governance process."[18] Some critics of the board report that even though the board is important it still does not manage the corporation's affairs.

"Under the system of directors which has developed in this country among large, listed companies, directors are unable to manage corporations in any narrow interpretations of the word. . . . Directors do not and cannot direct corporations in the sense of operating them."[19]

Those critics and others report that major policies are formulated by executives and not boards of directors. Steckmest believes that management is not accountable to the board members because those members (directors) are too subservient to management and the chief executives.[20] For these reasons and others, pressure to reform the board of directors has greatly increased in recent years.

Harold M. Williams, who supports the reform of the board of directors, maintains that voluntary corporate initiatives are by far preferable to further government intervention. He calls for boards to be truly independent of management. He believes that management is naturally interested in compatible and comfortable board members who will not be detrimental to their plans and policies. He calls on large corporations to improve board composition and accountability in order to assure the public that they are capable of self-discipline.[21]

Suggested reforms are in two main areas. The first one deals with the composition of the board. More outside directors should serve on the board because the current composition of the board does not allow board members to be independent. Therefore, the suggested reforms insist on a majority of outsiders as members, which could be achieved either by expanding the current board or by dropping some of the inside members.

The American Law Institute (ALI) has described the objectives of the business corporation as "corporate profit and shareholders gain." It recommends that large corporations have a majority of outside members on the boards; and it separates the functions of the board and of management.[22] These efforts will make the board more independent from management and assure that the board can perform its required function of reviewing management's actions to determine if they are in the stockholders' interests. The major focus of these reforms is on the board of directors. The increasing problem with corporate governance has reminded the business community that the board is an indispensable factor in the governance process.

Some critics have gone further and suggested that the board should have only one member from management and that he or she must not be allowed to be the chairperson. Harold Williams, former SEC chairman, presents the ideal board as one consisting entirely of outside directors except for the chief executive officer; and he adds that the chief executive officer should not be the chairman of the board.[23]

According to Eisenberg, these suggestions would be effective if two conditions were clarified. The first deals with the definition of independence. The definition must be rigorous. Any person who is an executive of the firm or who has a professional relationship or material business dealing with the firm and/or any close relatives of such persons should be treated as *not* independent. The second condition is that any person considered to be independent should be independent in fact as well as form and should have effective power to select and remove top executives and chief executive officers.

These two conditions can be met only when independent directors control the de facto power to select and dismiss members of the board who ultimately have the power to select and dismiss the executive directors. Currently, this power is vested in the hands of chief executives. They can select or dismiss any member of the board. Individual directors cannot oppose the chief executive because of domination of the board members or at least the majority of the board. Unless the majority of the board members are from outside the corporation the board will continue to be subservient to the chief executive officer.

The recommended outside directors are to protect the interests of the shareholders and the expectations of society on an unbiased basis. Therefore, these individuals must not currently be members of the firm's management and have no business relations with the firm they serve or its board. For example, the firm's legal counsel, bankers, major suppliers, or retired officers are not to be considered outsiders. Instead, executives of other unrelated businesses, college professors, professional directors, and the like, are considered to be independent outsiders.

The second area deals with the functions of the board. Christopher D. Stone thinks that formal job descriptions exist for just about everybody except directors. There is almost no authoritative guide to a director's function.[24] Some of the board's responsibilities that have been defined by state corporation laws are: "adoption of by-laws, calling shareholders for special meetings, declaration of dividends, election and removal of officers, proposing amendments of incorporation, and prior review of such matters as mergers requiring shareholder approval."[25]

Some critics have assumed that the board of directors of many large corporations have not performed some or all of their functions adequately and therefore society's expectations have not yet been met. Thus the suggested reform is meant to improve the performance and the accountability of the board through the board committees.

The Roundtable study suggests that the board has four major functions:

(1) provision for management and board succession, (2) consideration of decisions and actions with a potential for major economic impact, (3) consideration of major social impacts, and (4) establishment of policies and procedures to assure law compliance."[26]

The American Law Institute has recommended that the board be required to select, evaluate, remove, and replace the principal senior executives and to monitor not only the selection and evaluation of other senior executives but also the conduct of the corporation's business. It must determine whether the company's resources are managed within the new legal definition of the corporation. The board is also required to review and approve the major corporate plans, policies, commitments of corporate resources, and all other major corporate plans.[27] However, the head of the Business Roundtable's corporate responsibility task force and the chairman of Champion International, Andrew Sigler, expresses his total opposition to ALI's stance as a "ludicrous imposition of an unworkable method by a bunch of people who don't know anything about anything."[28] The three main objections raised by Business Roundtable are: (1) the structure of the board, (2) the ease of shareholders to bring derivative actions and the difficulty for the corporation to dismiss them, and (3) the director's liability. The ALI's words *rational basis* open the doors to further litigation. The ALI has also defined the composition, power, and function of certain board committees.

The *audit committee* is one of the most important committees, composed entirely of outside directors to monitor the firm's accounting procedures and to ensure the accuracy of all information presented in the annual report. According to Ralph Lewis,[29] audit committees are very important and serve various purposes such as the following: (1) review of the major accounting decisions, problems, and disclosure of information; (2) monitoring the internal control system and providing necessary investigation into the weak areas of operation discovered by the audit; (3) prevention of company violations of the code of conduct and appropriate procedures for disclosure; (4) supervision of the scope, timing, and costs of independent auditors; and (5) scrutiny of the letter to management from auditors with regard to the internal control systems and management responses.

The purpose of having entirely independent auditors is that they will be out of management control and will therefore comply with the rules and laws more freely and responsibly. Audit committees have been acknowledged to play a necessary role in the effectiveness of corporate control by various groups such as government officials within the SEC, certified public accountants, and legislators.[30] These committees are not new in the system. They were first proposed by the SEC in the 1930s. The SEC proposed the outsider audit committee to the board of the McKesson and Robbins Company. The SEC discovered that 22 percent of the company's reported assets were fictitious.[31] Then in 1967 the American Institute of Certified Public Accountants (AICPA) announced in favor of audit committees.[32]

The SEC statement in 1972 included: the "commission...endorses the establishment of all publicly-held companies of audit committees composed of outside directors."[33] In 1973, the New York Stock Exchange strongly recommended that all listed companies form an audit committee consisting of three to five outside directors. The SEC issued another release that required all registered corporations to disclose in their proxy statement information about the composition or nonexistence of an audit committee. The adoption of the Foreign Corrupt Practices Act (FCPA) came in 1977. This act included two provisions on accounting matters that were originally in the Senate version of the FCPA but were eliminated in committee: (1) the corporation should maintain accurate books and records; and (2) internal control should be mandated to meet specific objectives.

The SEC made it clear that it is unlawful for the corporation to make false entries on the books or on the corporate reports or to deceive auditors in the review of corporate financial statements. While these have been eliminated from the FCPA, the SEC came back in April 1979 to propose this missing part again. The SEC proposed rules that would require all reporting companies to: (1) indicate annually whether internal controls were in compliance with the act; and (2) have independent auditors state their opinions on the company's internal controls.

However, because of the large number of opposing companies, the SEC withdrew this proposal at least for the time being. The conclusion is that the audit committee is necessary and important and that it is difficult to imagine an effective corporate control system lacking such a committee. "The SEC may well take the position that the only appropriate control over certain activities is the establishment of an audit committee of the board of directors."[34]

The *nominating committee* takes away the executive officer's power to nominate a new member to the board. This committee consists of a majority of outsiders who organize the selection of a person to fill a board position. Thus, it prevents the chief officer from nominating friends, colleagues, or relatives. Such a committee would be required to have a majority of its members from outside the corporation so that it would be more difficult for the executive officers to control the new board members. According to a SEC study conducted in 1980, 29 percent of the 1200 companies surveyed had such nominating committees.[35]

Nominating committees and auditing committees have been required by the SEC. The SEC demands the disclosure of information on: (1) relationships between directors and candidates for election to the board; (2) information about duties and membership of the various committees; (3) the procedure of submission of shareholder proposals; (4) the procedures if there is a nominating committee; and (5) a disclosure of whether the shareholders have an opportunity to vote against particular directors.

In addition, the SEC demands a disclosure of any director's economic or personal relationships with the firm. Disclosure of this information is important to the investing public and it also increases corporate responsibility. The interests of shareholders are best served by a board of directors which is able to exercise independent judgment, ask probing questions of management, and bring to the company a broader perspective than that of management.[36] The SEC also requires information to be disclosed on board composition and function. The corporate proxy statement must indicate: (1) employment relationship to the corporation in the last five years; (2) ties to any of the company's executive officers; (3) economic relationships; (4) any association with the corporation's law firm during the last two years; and (5) any association with an investment banking firm providing services to the corporation.

Through these and other requirements, the SEC is seeking to direct reporting corporations toward the acceptance of new and better structures of corporate governance and consequently strengthen opportunities for stockholders' participation in director nomination. This required information in annual proxy statements will provide the public the opportunity to view the overall nature of board function and composition.

Compensation committees would evaluate and compensate top executives. This committee must have all its members from outside the corporation in order to act freely and independently from management. *Public policy committees* would receive complaints against the corporation and recommend to the board policies on socially important issues. *Supervisory committees* would be concerned mainly with internal governance matters.

Some people think that in order to improve management's perception of public values, corporations must have a public director on the board. They think that the arm of the public must penetrate deeply inside the corporation to extract information and to ensure performance. The advocates of this reform suggest that the number of public directors in the company vary depending on the size of the company. The larger the company, the higher the percentage of public directors. The prime responsibility of these directors would be the implementation of public policy within the corporation and verification of performance. The public director, as suggested by its advocates, would have an office in the company headquarters and have access to all company files. He would attend all the board meetings and report, through at least two press conferences a year, the company's handling of social issues. Also, he would report directly to the Occupational Safety and Health Administration (OSHA) the Equal Employment Opportunity Commission (EEOC), and other federal agencies.

The board of directors should include a public director who would be nominated by a federal commission and approved by the board of the company involved. Public directors, according to Stone, would spend at least half of their time on the business of the company. They would be paid on the same basis as the highest-grade civil servants, would have a full-time staff, and would be responsible for seeking out potential social and legal problem areas in the corporation.

The suggested public director is not a new position. In 1940, William O. Douglas proposed a similar idea. He stated that "salaried, professional experts would bring a new responsibility and authority to directorates and a new safety to stockholders."[37] Such directors, according to Townsend, would be chosen by legislative committees of Congress on an ad hoc basis. (This means that they would be employees of the federal government.) Then they would be sent to a specific corporation by lottery. They would keep senior executives informed of all new developments in public policy, behaving as ambassadors from government agencies such as OSHA and EEOC.

This reform could result in improved cooperation between government and the corporation. Public directors could form a bridge connecting public expectations and corporate interests. It seems likely that the pressure for reform of corporate governance will be directed at having more outside directors, auditing and nominating committees dominated by independent outsider members, and adoption of codes of conduct. Unless corporations, mainly large ones, start to respond to these pressures, there is little hope for any improvement in business-government and public-business relations. However, this does not mean that the implementation of these reforms will be easy or inexpensive for the corporation. The opposite is clearly true. The suggested reform proposals to improve corporate governance are considered to be simplistic solutions to very complex, intractable problems. Professor Lewis D. Soloman in 1978 reported that: "The problem of corporate reform is too complex and intractable for a response so simple to be a solution to the reform of the corporate boards. Our efforts to review the board of directors are simply anachronistic. New methods must be devised if we are to make corporate management genuinely accountable."[38]

SOCIAL AUDIT

A social audit is an attempt to identify, measure, evaluate, report, and monitor the effects a corporation is having on society that are not covered in traditional financial reports. Unfortunately, none of these tasks is easy.

In identification of effects, should a corporation measure the total impact or only specific problems? Also, should it measure in multiple or single ways? Once it is measured, what does it mean? Moreover, in reporting the question arises about whether information should go to the public or be only used for internal purposes. And, if it does go to the public, since no common measures of reporting exist, it is very difficult to compare performances of different firms. Finally, in order to effectively monitor, a corporation needs more than a one-time social audit.

Six types of social audits are commonly used by corporations:

The inventory approach. This is simply a listing and brief description of social programs a corporation has developed to help solve social problems. The information may appear on a page or two of the annual report, or in special booklets describing the company's social activities. Unfortunately, it is not very useful to management or external constituencies in evaluating, because of the difficulty in comparing different costs and results with performance evaluation; it is also impossible to compare different companies.

The program management approach. This approach focuses on specific social problems, but is a more systematic effort to identify costs and evaluate achievements. However, this approach seems to be of most use in the management of social programs and not very useful for external reporting.

This approach is also of little value in the selection of priorities and relatively little information is provided about the impact of a program on a particular social problem of concern to the community or society in general.

The process audit. This approach focuses on specific social programs, but it provides more information about those programs. The process audit consists of four steps: (1) an assessment of the circumstances under which each social program being audited came into being; (2) an explanation of the goals of the program—a statement of what the program is intended to accomplish; (3) the rationale behind the activity, specifying how the goals are to be attained; (4) what is actually being done as opposed to what the rationale says ought to be done. This also has the disadvantage of a deficiency in external reporting.

The cost or outlay approach. This approach focuses on the costs or other outlays associated with a given social program. There is also some attempt to determine whether the amounts involved are appropriate. However, problems with this approach make its usefulness limited. Efforts to allocate the costs of various functions between social programs and day-to-day business operations could be difficult.

The cost-benefit approach. This approach attempts to measure the total social impact of a corporation, not just those activities that are voluntarily undertaken. This approach tries to tally up aggregate social costs and benefits of all corporate activities as they affect society. Efforts to allocate such costs, however, is very difficult—especially in the areas of discrimination, work-related injuries and illness, and environmental damages.

The social indicator. All of the previously mentioned approaches are not sufficient. This approach is the only one that would be beneficial. First, one needs to perform an external audit of community well-being through the use of social indicators. The second step is to measure internal corporate activities that are related to these community indicators. The major advantage of this approach is the measurement of corporate activities in relation to community needs and the impact that this can have on the planning process. Therefore, using this approach will help to meet the purpose of social audit. For instance, management decisions will be objectively broadened about social priorities.

With this information, accountability can be more formally realized and solved without direct government interference. (Buchholz 1986).

In spite of the pressure for reform of corporate governance the problems are far from being solved. Sommer in 1980 noted that "the most discussed issues in corporate circles, if not in society at large, are those of corporate governance and corporate accountability.... Despite the proliferation of words concerning these matters, a great deal of confusion about the issues and the means of resolving them continues to exist."[39]

A CASE STUDY: THE AMERICAN LAW INSTITUTE (ALI)

The corporation has been described as seductive because of its appealing characteristics. The seductive qualities of the corporation include the ability to raise capital from small investors who have no interest in daily management of the corporation, limited liability for these investors, and the perpetual life of the corporation. Perhaps the most interesting characteristic of the corporation is the separation of ownership from control, meaning that the corporation is owned by stockholders and run by management. Stockholders elect the board of directors to serve in their best interests.

The board of directors is responsible for the corporation's actions and the results of those actions. The term *corporate governance* refers to the mode of structure and the power that determines the rights and responsibilities of the various groups involved in the running of an organization. It involves the legitimacy expectation of the business, the method of operating, and the overall accountability of management for the board of directors. The growing concern over corporate governance is due to popular opinion that management does not always act in the best interest of the stockholder, and by commission or omission the board of directors allows this activity. Corporate governance is sometimes in need of repair.[40]

The American Law Institute's Corporate Governance Project

The American Law Institute (ALI) in Philadelphia has assumed the task of restating the law as it applies to corporate governance. The ALI Corporate Governance Project was authorized in May 1978, as a three-year project to restore trust in corporations. Begun in 1980, the project continues today with no targeted completion date.

The ALI researches and drafts proposals on issues of importance, in this case corporate governance. The ALI offers "precise, authoritative distillations of principles of existing law"[41] that have had a definitive influence on the outcomes of many legal cases. For this reason the ALI Corporate Governance Project has attracted vast attention from the business community.

The project was initially titled *Corporate Governance and Structure-Restatement and Recommendations*. The title upset the corporate community in that it implied the project was merely a restatement of what the law read, when in fact the project was calling for changes in the law. The name of the project was changed and stands today as *Principles of Corporate Governance: Analysis and Recommendations*.[42]

Michael Greenwald states that the project is very controversial, and for this reason is moving very slowly. The ALI is currently working on the seventh draft of the project, with portions of each draft rewritten time and time again. There are yet areas, such as takeovers, that have not been addressed in the project, and may not be addressed due to their extremely controversial nature.[43]

The theme of the project remains that management cannot be trusted to act in the stockholder's best interest; therefore, corrective measures must be adopted. The ALI Corporate Governance Project seeks to increase the responsibility and potential liability of directors, as well as requiring directors to become more involved in the formulation and execution of corporate policies. The project would like to make shareholder suits easier to pursue and harder for the corporation to defend. A critic of the project, Walter B. Wriston, retired chairman of Citibank, contends that the ALI Corporate Governance Project "would create a legal environment in which risk would be discouraged and American business would be put at a further disadvantage in the global marketplace."[44]

The project's tentative first draft, presented in 1982, received substantial criticism. The opinion of this draft was that incompetence on management's part can only be restricted by increased supervision and involvement of the board of directors of the corporation. Extended duties of independent directors and precise liability standards for nonperformance of those duties was implied as the means to the end of increased director involvement.

This draft divided corporations into a three-tier system by total assets and number of shareholders, establishing an inflexible board and committee structure for large corporations. The draft asserted that first-tier corporations of $100 million in assets and two thousand stockholders were to maintain a board of directors, the majority of directors being independent or free of significant relationships with management. An audit committee was required, composed solely of directors such as these. A nominating committee was also to be established, having control over the selection of directors. This committee, as well as a compensation committee, could have an officer or employee of the corporation as a member.

The project recommended that second-tier corporations be defined as smaller, publicly held entities with $3 million in total assets and five hundred stockholders. These corporations should maintain, according to the project, at least three independent directors on their board. Likewise, an audit committee was recommended in second-tier organizations.

In addition to the structure of the corporation, the ALI project addresses such issues as duty of care and the business judgment rule, duty of loyalty, and transactions in control. These sections of the project deal with increased liability and negligence of directors, legitimate corporate transactions, and director responsibilities in transactions involving control (i.e., hostile takeovers).

Six drafts later, the original concepts of the project remain unchanged. The latest draft calls for a distinct board committee structure and duties for large corporations. The audit committee continues as a requirement of the corporation. Responsibilities of directors remain in expanded form. Director liability has been restated, but is less protective than the existing law.

Criticism of the ALI's Corporate Governance Project

In the years following the first ALI proposals, criticism has flowed from the corporate community in an attempt to influence the content of future proposals. Of all the critics of the project, among whom are the New York Stock Exchange, the American Society of Corporate Secretaries, and the American Bar Association, the Business Roundtable is perhaps the project's most vocal critic.

The Business Roundtable is a business membership association whose function is to follow public policy issues where these issues could be implemented with business impact. The Roundtable is composed of chief executive officers from two hundred major U.S. corporations, 95 percent of which are Fortune 500 companies. The CEOs serve on standing committees, following issues such as taxation, ethics, and antitrust.[45]

The Business Roundtable's May 1984, comments on the project first attacked the inadequate time the ALI permitted its members to review the data prior to a vote. The Business Roundtable felt that the ALI's philosophy of increased liability of directors, reliance on independent directors, and complex web of regulations ran contrary to existing law and practice. Further, the Roundtable asserted that the ALI had no foundation for the proclamation that the existing corporate governance system needed to be changed. In the Roundtable's words, "the little empirical data currently existing indicates that some of the drafts' proposals would have a detrimental impact on United States corporations."[46] Finally, the Business Roundtable felt that ALI had not consulted significant interest groups, such as experienced business managers, economists, and business school faculties, with regard to the project.

Comparison of Corporate Governance Models with ALI Proposals

The traditional model of corporate governance, the prevalent model in the United States, holds that shareholders' property rights are paramount. The shareholders, or owners of the corporation, elect the board of directors to act as an intermediary between the owners and management of the corporation. The board appoints the management and officers to run the corporation on a regular basis. Management exercises its authority over the firm's employees in daily operations to attain corporate objectives.

The co-determination model, or European model, of corporate governance exists in many European countries. This system maintains that both capital and labor should be represented in the process of corporate governance. Employee representatives and owner representatives together comprise the board of directors. One practical version of this model promotes a two-tier board structure, with a supervisory board and a management board. The supervisory board performs the oversight functions while the management board is involved with daily operations of the corporation. The supervisory board has ultimate authority in that it can select and dismiss members of the management board.

The stakeholder model of corporate governance asserts that all constituencies with a stake in the performance of the corporation, not just employees and owners, should be represented in the governance process of the corporation. Interests of the stakeholder will be taken into account when employees, customers, environmentalists, bankers, and other parties are represented on the board of directors of the corporation.

The ALI proposes an independent board of directors whose function is monitoring rather than the typical managing role of today. The board would focus on audit function under the ALI proposals, reviewing management, operations, staffing, and execution to assess the competency of the CEO and senior staff of the organization. In actuality, the monitoring board would be a new level of top management. In addition to the monitoring board, the ALI recommends an audit committee, a nominating committee, and a compensation committee. These models are illustrated in table 8.1.

Conclusion

It is evident that the American Law Institute's Corporate Governance Project has evoked strong opposition from members of the business community, and the debate is certain to continue for years to come. It is felt that the proposed changes, while not entirely unfounded, should be more of a matter of choice on the part of the corporation rather than mandate by law. The argument continues that the increased participation and liability of directors undoubtedly turns directorship into a full-time job. While quality directors and more responsible boards are the focus of the project, the requirements of directorship will make it impossible to attract quality directors to the corporation. Testimonies of executives such as Harold S. Geneen[47] substantiate the claims that reform is necessary in the area of corporate governance. Compromise between the business community and the ALI should result in

Table 8.1
Comparison of Corporate Governance Models

TRADITIONAL MODEL	CO-DETERMINATION (EUROPEAN) MODEL	STAKEHOLDER MODEL	ALI PROPOSALS
Stockholders (Owners)	Capital and labor	Social, Political & Economic Interests	Independent Monitoring Board of Directors
Board of Directors	Supervisory Board	Stakeholder Participation on Board of Directors	Audit Committee
Officers & Managers	Management Board	Management	Nominating Committee
Employees	Management	Employees	Compensation Committee
	Employees		Management
			Employees

a structure of corporate governance that will be beneficial to both the modern corporation and the shareholder.

NOTES

1. Rogene A. Buchholz, *Business Environment and Public Policy: Implications for Management and Strategy Formulation* (Englewood Cliffs, N.J.: Prentice-Hall, 1986), p. 112; Francis W. Steckmest, *Corporate Performance: The Key to Public Trust* (New York: McGraw-Hill, 1982), p. 168.

2. A. A. Sommer, "Corporate Governance: Its Impact on the Profession," *Journal of Accountancy* (July 1980): 112.

3. Buchholz, *Business Environment*, p. 112.

4. "Business Must Tell Holders More or Face Tougher U.S. Controls, SEC Chief Warns," *Wall Street Journal* (September 30, 1977); Buchholz, *Business Environment*, p. 113.

5. Irving S. Shapiro, "Corporate Governance," in Irving Shapiro and Harold Williams, *Power and Accountability: The Changing Role of the Corporate Board of Directors* (Pittsburgh, Pa.: Carnegie Mellon University Press, 1979).

6. Steckmest, *Corporate Performance*, p. 171.

7. Shapiro and Williams, *Power and Accountability*, p. 42.

8. Ralph Nader, Mark Green, and Joel Seligman, *Taming the Giant Corporation* (New York: W. W. Norton and Company, 1976), p. 57; Ralph Nader and Mark Green, eds., *Corporate Power in America* (New York: Grossman Publishers, 1973).

9. Buchholz, *Business Environment*, p. 113.

10. William M. Dugger, "Entrenched Corporate Power and Our Options for Dealing with It—A Pep Talk for Discouraged Reforms" *Association for Social Economics* (July 1980): 9.

11. Nader, Green, and Seligman, *Taming the Giant Corporation*, p. 57.

12. Nader and Green, *Corporate Power*, p. 79.

13. Nader, Green, and Seligman, *Taming the Giant Corporation*, pp. 233–36.

14. Sommer, "Corporate Governance," p. 58.

15. Steckmest, *Corporate Performance*, p. 174.

16. Shapiro, "Corporate Governance," p. 42.

17. Ibid.

18. Steckmest, *Corporate Performance*, p. 175.

19. John C. Baker, *Directors and Their Functions: A Preliminary Study* (Boston: Harvard University Press, 1945), p. 12; Robert A. Gordon, *Business Leadership in the Large Corporation* (Washington, D.C.: Brookings Institute, 1945).

20. Steckmest, *Corporate Performance*, p. 168.

21. Shapiro and Williams, *Power and Accountability*, p. 42.

22. American Law Institute, "Principles of Corporate Governance and Structure: Restatement and Recommendations" (1982).

23. "Management Should Fill Only One Seat on a Firm's Board, SEC Chairman Urges," *Wall Street Journal* (January 19, 1978): 3.

24. Christopher D. Stone, *Where the Law Ends: The Social Control of Corporate Behavior* (New York: Harper and Row, 1975), p. 141.

25. "The Role and Composition of the Board of Directors of the Large Publicly Owned Corporations" (New York: Business Roundtable, 1978), p. 8.

26. Ibid., p. 15.

27. Kenneth R. Andrews, "Rigid Rules Will Not Make a Good Board," *Harvard Business Review* (November–December 1982): 34–35.

28. Tamar Lewin, "The Corporate Reform Furor," *New York Times* (June 10, 1982): D-1.

29. Ralph F. Lewis, "What Should Audit Committees Do?" *Harvard Business Review* (May–June 1978): 22, 26, 172, 174.

30. John D. Aram, *Managing Business and Public Policy: Concepts, Issues, and Cases* (Marshfield, Mass.: Pitman Publishing, 1987), p. 28.

31. Securities and Exchange Commission, Accounting Series Release No. 19, "In the Matter of McKesson and Robbins, Inc." (December 5, 1940).

32. "AICPA Executive Committee Statement on Audit Committees of Boards of Directors," *Journal of Accountancy* (September 1967): 10.

33. Securities and Exchange Commission, Accounting Series, No. 123 (March 23, 1971).

34. Hurd Baruch, "The Foreign Corrupt Practices Act of 1977," *Harvard Business Review* (January–February 1979): 38.

35. "Corporate Governance Faulted in a Study by SEC Staff," *Wall Street Journal* (January 28, 1980): 10.

36. "Shareholders Communications: Shareholders' Participation in the Corporate Governance Generally, Final Rules" (Securities and Exchange Commission Release No. 34-15384), *Federal Securities Law Reporter*, para. 81, 766 (December 6, 1978): 58, 523.

37. William O. Douglas, *Democracy and Finance* (New Haven, Conn.: Yale University Press, 1940), p. 121.

38. Lewis Soloman, "Restructuring the Corporate Board of Directors: Fond Hope—Faint Promise?" *Michigan Law Review* (1978): 581–83.

39. Sommer, "Corporate Governance," p. 52.

40. George A. Birrell, et al., *The American Law Institute and Corporate Governance: An Analysis and Critique*, January 1987, p. vii.

41. George A. Birrell, "Legal Scholars vs. Business," *Across the Board* (July–August 1987): 7.

42. Mike Greenwald, American Law Institute, telephone interview, March 23, 1988.

43. Ibid.

44. Birrell, "Legal Scholars," p. 7.

45. Rob Martinez, Business Roundtable, telephone interview, March 30, 1988.

46. *Comments of the Business Roundtable Concerning the American Law Institute's Corporate Governance Project*, New York, May 4, 1984, p. 5.

47. Harold S. Geneen, "Why Directors Can't Protect the Shareholders," *Fortune* (September 17, 1984): 28.

9

The European Model

This chapter will review the major ideological differences on corporate governance in Western Europe and the United States. This discussion will include comparisons of modern labor union ideologies, institutional effects of labor unions on management policies, management-labor relations, and a suggestion as to why this model cannot be applied in the United States, at least for the time being.

DIFFERENCES BETWEEN U.S. AND WESTERN EUROPEAN IDEOLOGIES

Major changes in corporate governance occurred during the 1970s in both the United States and Western Europe. However, the two areas used different approaches based on ideological beliefs and the definitions of the existing problem. For example, the foremost concern in the United States is to make the corporation more accountable to stockholders. This can be clearly seen in the emphasis on property rights for stockholders. A second concern is corporate social performance. A third is unethical business practices.

In Western Europe, the dispute is over who should control the property in the business corporation. The concept of private property has divided Europe into two different ideologies, the left and the right.

The United States does not experience such ideological conflict because it began as an open frontier society with continual westward movement. This effectively drew off the problems of surplus population. Also, there is a materialistic approach to problems in the United States. "While populism has been a strong strain, particularly in the midwest, in American thought, it too still regards the solving of problems in a pragmatic way. Thus the approach to the corporation has not yet been an ideological one."[1] Western Europe is different because modern industrial development stemmed from the feudalistic society and the existence of a class structure. For example, in Britain, a person's accent automatically betrays his or her class origin. This gave rise to much concern about organizing property and resulted not only in strong ideological differences but in pitting capitalism against socialism in most countries in Europe.

The United States approaches corporate governance problems through various forms of government regulations. Such an approach is based on the idea that any problem can be regulated and solved. If the government of the United States at any level is persuaded that the competitive market has failed beyond redemption, its most common response is to regulate rather than supersede the private market by government ownership. In recent years, however, business and society have started to complain about the increasing cost of regulation and the reduction in productivity and efficiency.

European countries deal with corporate governance problems in a number of ways.

Nationalism. Most European countries have nationalized a substantial sector of their economy. Austria, for example, now has about 50 percent of its industry nationalized and, of the fifty largest industrial corporations in Europe, nineteen are controlled or owned by the state. These figures continue to increase year after year along with the spread of ownership and control of the largest companies by the state. The role of the state is to maintain a balance between private property and nationalization. The effect of this on the economy has been severe.

Influencing change on corporate governance. The states of Western Europe are practicing industrial democracy concepts as a type of control over the boards of the companies. The basic idea of industrial democracy is the extension of political democracy to economic life. In this concept, labor is considered as important as capital to the functioning of the company.[2]

For example, West Germany has been traditionally considered a capitalist country. However, in recent years, many laws have been issued that require boards to have worker participation. This model has become the point of departure for industrial democracy in other West European nations. Similar models were adopted in Denmark, Norway, Austria, and Sweden. In these countries, a law has been passed requiring firms to have directors elected by unions or employees.[3]

If such changes continue, these will have a strong impact on labor-capital relations, not only in West Germany but throughout the West, as industrialists experience unrest, labor complaints, and threats of nationalization. It has been reported that businessmen in Germany still do not approve of co-determination (worker participation), fearing this might lead to socialism.

COMPARISON OF MODERN LABOR IDEOLOGIES

While West German union ideology accepts strong economic and social roles for unions as social change agents in German life, unions in the United States emphasize the economic role benefiting their ideological identification as "business unions," with pragmatic goals benefiting their members. Unions in the United States place greater emphasis on collective bargaining (the private contract between corporations and unions), while West German unions emphasize co-determination of working conditions and legislative recourse (the public domain).

Unions in the United States have emphasized greater involvement in the political sphere since World War II. This shift to the legislative recourse has de-emphasized the one-time exclusive reliance on collective bargaining to meet union goals and objectives. West German collective bargaining, in comparison, involves broad-based industrywide agreements between employer trade associations and unions. Finally, both U.S. and West German unions follow the practice of not formally identifying with any political party, thus allowing greater freedom to choose candidates who are sympathetic to trade union objectives.

COMPARATIVE INSTITUTIONAL EFFECTS OF LABOR UNIONS ON MANAGEMENT POLICIES

Management policies involve senior executives and the board of directors in the formulation and implementation of the mission, strategy, and plans of the corporation. To compare the institutional effects of labor unions on management policies, a review of those mechanisms used by employers and unions to formally interact with management is in order.

The United States

Modern labor-management relations in the United States are based on two major pieces of federal legislation: the National Labor Relations Act (1935) and the Labor Management Relations Act (1947).

The National Labor Relations Act made collective bargaining compulsory if a majority of employees in a bargaining unit agreed to it. A Federal National Labor Relations Board was created to keep employers from preventing employees from choosing union representation, and to create and administer the rule making under which collective bargaining was to take place. Agreements were not required to be concluded. Unions could order their workers to stop working (strike). However, once an agreement was reached and accepted by the National Labor Relations Board, it had to be placed in a formal written contract.[4]

The Labor Management Relations Act added to the National Labor Relations Act, which had specified employer unfair labor practices, a list of union practices that were banned. However, collective bargaining essentially remained unchanged.[5] Collective bargaining rather than compulsory arbitration or legal enactment has always been favored by U.S. trade unions. Collective bargaining is an implied readiness to enter into a written collective agreement with employers governing all terms and conditions of employment.

This collective agreement is broad in its scope. Many concerns that are included in collective bargaining agreements involve "wages, hours, and other terms and conditions of employment." Other usual areas covered include vacations, technological change, severance pay, grievance procedures, arbitration, seniority, fringe benefits, management rights, bans on strikes and lockouts, union security, antidiscrimination provisions, and employee allowances.

There are national agreements in apparel, steel, automobile, and telephone industries, but bargaining by employer associations, common in Europe, is rarely practiced in the United States. From the start, U.S. employers have preferred to do their own bargaining rather than entrust it to professional negotiators.

West Germany

Major national labor-management legislation in West Germany includes the Collective Agreements Act, the Co-determination Act (1951), and the Works Constitution Act (1976). The Collective Agreements Act is the cornerstone of collective bargaining that enabled legislation in West Germany. It recognizes the autonomy of unions and employers, but strictly regulates the procedures of bargaining. The act also provides guidelines for recognizing the legitimacy of strikes and lockouts.

Collective bargaining has developed as a two-tier structure. Normally, industrywide agreements between unions and employer associations are implemented on a regional or national level. However, there has been increasing use of firm-level agreements, primarily with profitable corporations by local unions. The usual wage agreements, one year in duration, cover wage rates and categories. "General agreements" include occupational classification, wage groupings, and principles of job evaluation. A third major category is "general frame agreements," and includes basic conditions of work, such as working time and days of annual leave. A final category, "specific agreements," relates to such matters as conciliation or arbitration procedures, protection for workers against technological unemployment, and the rights of shop stewards.

Recent trends in collective bargaining have shown a general widening of subject matter, including the German "collective agreements." Although labor relations still hold a prominent place in the setting of norms for labor-management relations, the importance of collective bargaining has tended to increase.

The Co-determination Act of 1951 was the first step in the development of worker representation and industrial democracy. This act provided for "parity co-determination" in the management of firms in the steel and coal industries. Parity co-determination means that there is effective equal representation on the supervisory (director) board and a labor director on the managing (operations) board.[6]

The Works Constitution Act of 1976 dealt with labor-management relations at the shop-floor and plant level. Worker councils were established to represent workers' interests.

The Co-determination Act of 1976, which covers all enterprises with more than two thousand employees, provides for "near parity co-determination" for labor. Near parity co-determination means that, while labor is formally equally represented on supervisory (director) boards, in case of tie votes the chairman, always a representative of shareholders, can cast the deciding vote. Also, employees in managerial positions are entitled to elect, within the allotted labor seats, a special representative to the board.

Co-determination is viewed differently by unions and employers. Unions believe that only "parity" representation can guarantee true industrial democracy, where social and labor policy will be equally as important to management as traditional marketing and production concerns. Co-determination also takes care of plant-level worker problems which industry-level collective agreements do not cover. Employer trade associations believe that co-determination is incompatible with the concept of collective bargaining, private ownership rights, and managerial efficiency.[7]

MANAGEMENT-LABOR RELATIONS

Labor unions in the United States have traditionally stayed out of the management of the firm. The ideology behind "business unionism" was predicated on the adversary relationship that exists between labor and management. Each has its place and responsibility clearly defined in the socioeconomic structure of a capitalist democracy. Management is there to satisfy shareholders; unions are there to get all they can for workers in terms of wages and working conditions.

Due to its legal responsibilities to stockholders, management in the United States contends that it has the duty to oppose union attempts to share in managerial decisions, because the union represents interests not necessarily compatible with those of the owners. Management argues that they alone are responsible for business policy. And although they may be willing to share their authority, management cannot escape full responsibility. It is therefore unreasonable to expect management to relinquish authority and yet retain the responsibility for actions not of their choosing.

Management is necessarily separate from the workers at the compliance level. There is neither time nor moral justification for mutual participation or "industrial democracy" at this level in the management function.[8] Most members of management feel that there should be some boundaries limiting the degree of union penetration into the area of corporate policy. Some of the reasons behind such feelings are: (1) management fears that worker penetration will threaten the very organization of business by destroying unified final authority; (2) union penetration prevents management from the discharge of its responsibilities; (3) union penetration endangers the efficiency of industrial organization; (4) management objects to the lack of union responsibility; (5) management feels that union leadership is inadequate; and (6) management is fearful of the ultimate result of union penetration.[9] West German unions, however, have a socialist ideology which is built around the concept of "industrial democracy." Management planning under the concept of "industrial democracy" involves management *and* labor planning policies and strategies for the enterprise.

The present status of labor's institutional effect on management planning in the United States is virtually nil. Unlike West Germany, where legislation provides that enterprises with two thousand or more employees must have employee representation on half the seats on supervisory boards, the United States has no such legislation. Both business management and labor unions are strongly opposed to the concept of co-determination. There are also antitrust and state corporate law considerations that could impinge upon labor representation on corporate boards of directors.

Presently, the steel and coal industries in West Germany are under parity co-determination. Labor and management have a 50 percent share on the boards of directors of firms as well as a one-to-one ratio of votes in these industries. Thus West German labor "co-determines" the planning of the future corporate strategies and policies in these industries. In firms with two thousand or more employees, parity co-determination has not yet been reached since the chairman of the board, normally elected by the shareholders, has a double vote in case of a tie. Nevertheless, West German labor still has a significant institutional presence and effect on policies and decision making in the average West German enterprise.

FINAL REMARKS

The last five years have witnessed a change in the way U.S. and West German businesses have recognized labor's institutional presence and impact regarding corporate planning and decision making. In the United States an agreement was reached in 1979 whereby U.A.W. President Douglas A. Fraser would be nominated, on a managerial-backed slate, to the twenty-member board of directors of the financially ailing Chrysler Corporation. Chrysler Chairman Lee A. Iacocca nominated Fraser to the board on May 13, 1980, in return for wage and benefit concessions made in the fall of 1979 and for the union's cooperation in lobbying Washington for the company's government loan guarantee plan.

In October 1981, Pan American World Airways agreed to recommend that its shareholders elect a director proposed by four unions who sit on the Pan Am Labor Council. This union request was granted in return for the union taking a 10 percent pay cut through 1982. Corporations such as Pan Am, Chrysler, General Motors, Uniroyal, United Airlines, and the New York Daily News are opening their financial records to direct union inspection or neutral verification procedures. Confidential information regarding production costs, competition, and long-range investment decisions are now being divulged. If this trend continues, it could lead to direct union influence on future decision making and planning regarding investments, plant closures, and plant locations.

In West Germany the co-determination movement has come up against stiffened employer opposition. In June 1977, the president of the top employers' organization, The Confederation of German Employer's Association (BDA) brought a lawsuit challenging the 1976 co-determination legislation, claiming it was unconstitutional in that it infringed on basic, legally guaranteed ownership rights. This effort failed but the bitter feelings it engendered have remained.

In 1981 a law was proposed in the Bundestag that would allow large steel and coal firms to shift control of their works to a separate subsidiary, thus allowing the parent firms to have less than half of their sales in steel and coal production. These parent firms will then be able to operate under the 1976 co-determination law which gives shareholders the voting edge over labor on supervisory boards. The steel and coal subsidiaries will still be under "parity co-determination," however. Under a compromise bill, the present "parity co-determination" in the steel and coal industries would remain unaffected for six years after passage of the law.

The shift from faster-growth Western economies that existed in the 1960s and early 1970s to the slower growth, "shake-out" economies of the late 1970s to the present has resulted in a noticeable change in labor-management relations. Closer cooperation between labor and management has resulted during recent years in the United States while in West Germany a schism has developed and management is reasserting its power of exclusive decision making. Since this employer movement has grown, West German labor unions are taking a tougher stance with management in collective bargaining negotiations, moving toward a more traditional U.S. labor-management adversarial relationship.

The U.S. trend is rather modest. A few large financially distressed firms in industries seriously affected by international competition or regulatory reform, have acquiesced to union demands, usually in return for wage and benefit concessions, for a labor representative on the board of directors, and independent (or union) audits of financial records. The majority of large U.S. corporate managements and the AFL-CIO are still strongly opposed to this embryonic movement. The AFL-CIO opposes board-level representation because it might tend to "diffuse" union power and because it would blur traditional distinctions between workers and management.[10]

There are still significant problems that could arise to challenge this movement toward labor directors and the sharing of confidential financial information.

1. Management essentially has to agree to the election of a labor representative to the board.

2. State corporation laws in the United States do not provide for "special interest directors" to represent the interests of only one group of shareholders or employees on a corporate board.

3. Violations of Section 8 of the Clayton Act, dealing with interlocking directorates, and the Security and Exchange Commission's antitrust rules dealing with disclosure of confidential information, could arise "as union officers occupy seats on the boards of competing companies."[11] Both private shareholders' derivative suits claiming conflict of interest and government antitrust suits challenging the legality of such representation, would eventually result. For example, a U.A.W. attempt to place a labor representative on American Motors Corporation's board of directors in 1981 was blocked by a Justice Department advisory opinion.

4. Employers fear the effect of co-determination on the collective bargaining system.

It is therefore doubtful that labor representation on U.S. boards of directors will continue to grow. A shift in recent depressed economic conditions could result in either management or labor backing off from their recent cooperative stance and returning to a traditional adversarial relationship. Certainly having one labor representative director on corporate boards will have a minimal impact on corporate policies and decision making. "Co-determination" West German style is based on an ideology alien to both U.S. management and labor.

THE STUDY

Management is not ready to accept the European model of co-determination but might accept employee participation at a lower managerial level. All levels of management strongly disagree with the desirability of a board composed of an equal number of representatives from stockholders and workers. The higher level of management, the stronger the disagreement. The data in table 9.1 indicates that a total of about 67.2 percent of lower-level managers, 79.5 percent of middle-level managers, and 82.3 percent of top-level managers disagree that workers should be equally represented with stockholders on the corporate board. However, the same study shows that management might

Table 9.1
Frequency Distribution of Respondents

Question: "Some people have suggested that workers are equally represented with stockholders on corporate boards."

Respondents Choice	L.L Mgt. Frequency		M.L.Mgt. Frequency		T.L.Mgt Frequency	
	Nos.	%	Nos.	%	Nos.	%
Total Agree	3	4.69	5	6.85	4	11.77
Indifferent	18	28.12	10	13.70	2	5.88
Total Disagree	43	67.19	58	79.45	28	82.35
Total	64	100.00	73	100.00	34	100.00

Table 9.2
Frequency Distribution of Respondents

Question: "It is wise for operation division management to include some employees in their policy decisions."

Respondents Choice	L.L Mgt. Frequency		M.L.Mgt. Frequency		T.L.Mgt Frequency	
	Nos.	%	Nos.	%	Nos.	%
Total Agree	47	73.44	60	82.19	26	76.47
Indifferent	6	9.38	6	8.22	2	5.88
Total Disagree	11	17.18	7	9.59	6	17.65
Total	64	100.00	73	100.00	34	100.00

be ready to accept some form of worker participation. This conclusion is supported by management's high agreement on employee participation with operating division management.

The data in table 9.2 indicates that a total of about 73.4 percent of lower-level managers, 82 percent of middle-level managers, and 76.5 percent of top-level managers agree that operating management should include some employees in their policy decisions.

The study also shows that management at these levels gives a moderately high stake but low influence to the employees in general. For example, on a scale from one to five where one is low and five is very high, management gave white-collar employees a stake score of 3.47, 3.33, and 3.56 from lower to top level management, respectively, while they gave an influence score of

1.94, 2.12, and 2.21, respectively. The study reveals that the three levels of management gave blue-collar employees a moderate stake of 3.38, 3.22, and 3.44 from lower to top level, respectively, in the corporation, while management thinks that blue-collar workers have low influence on corporate policy (1.67, 1.77, and 1.62, from lower to top, respectively).

INTERNATIONAL BUSINESS MANAGEMENT

The preceding discussion indicates that the concept of co-determination is alien to U.S. business. Other forms of participation which have been adopted in North America, however, seem to have their roots in economic necessity rather than in higher-order ideals of beliefs, commitments, or managerial pursuits. In fact, preference for some type of participative model flows from the nature of work and structuring or organization. In contrast, the co-determination concept in Western Europe stems from the belief in the distribution of power and organizational social responsibility. This belief found its roots in the historical and economic development of European societies. For example, co-determination in Germany can be traced back to 1834 when consultative work councils were first introduced, and 1881 when they were first instituted.

What are the implications of the findings reported here to multinational corporations (MNCs)? The first implication is concerned with the recruiting and selection of international managers. U.S.-based MNCs may find it difficult to compete in the international market without acquiring and developing international managers. These managers, aside from having all the qualities that make good managers of domestic corporations, are also mobile, receptive, and at ease in cultures other than their own. Emphasis should be placed on selection rather than on training alone. Belief in worker participation does not come intuitively; rather, it develops over a long period of time. This implies a need for a responsible policy in recruiting international managers, a policy sensitive to other cultures. Failure of MNCs' operation is attributable to a lack of understanding and conflicts in decision making.

MNCs can realize success in international markets only if the orientation and values of its managers abroad are consistent with the society's values. Familiarity and sensitivity to host countries are prerequisite for present and future success in operations.

The second implication is related to human resource planning in the international arena. People with appropriate skills and knowledge are a scarce commodity. For many years MNCs tended to rely on expatriate managers for overseas assignments. Unfortunately, experience indicates that this policy is often costly and inappropriate. A long-term perspective of recruiting and developing indigenous personnel to assume managerial responsibility is an imperative task and should not be left to chance. Furthermore, developing international managers gives MNCs a competitive edge and strengthens their market position.

CONCLUSION

Management in U.S. corporations is not ready to accept the European idea of worker participation. For some the idea is too radical, for others the opposition of management and labor unions makes it impractical since it interferes with their power. Management also fears that labor participation will hinder the smooth functioning of business, decrease efficiency, and cause undue interference in corporate policies. They think that worker participation can be achieved best through collective bargaining.

Recently effective worker participation in corporate governance has proven attractive to many corporations. Combining an equity stake and board membership has been a means of establishing lower pay scales in highly competitive industries. It has begun to emerge as a condition of government assistance for corporations in financial distress. Finally, employee buyouts of failing firms and subsidiaries have created many firms with "employee-capitalists" at the helm. For example, in 1982, the British government sold its largest freight handler, National Freight Consortium, to its 12,000 employees. By August 1983, a share of this company was valued at about $5.10, which is an increase of 3.4 times more than the price in 1982. Sales and profits were increased because of the boost in employee motivation. These expedients have posed the possibility, even the desirability, of co-determination. But, they have not yet established the "right" to participation in the eyes of current managers.

NOTES

1. R. Joseph Monson, "Directions in the United States and European Corporate Governance," paper presented at AACSB Conference on Business Environment and Public Policy, Summer 1979, pp. 1–2.

2. "The State in the Market: Public Sector Enterprise," *Economist* (December 30, 1978): 39–40.

3. James Furlong, *Labor in the Board Room: The Peaceful Revolution* (New Jersey: Dow Jones, 1977), pp. 1–3.

4. Ibid.

5. John T. Dunlop and Walter Gulenson, *Labor in the Twentieth Century* (New York: Academic Press, 1978), p. 41.

6. Ibid., pp. 175–76.

7. Furlong, *Labor*, pp. 64–76.

8. H. A. Clegg, *A New Approach to Industrial Democracy* (New York: Blackwell and Mott, 1963).

9. Neil W. Chamberlain, *The Union Challenge to Management Control* (New York: Archer Books, 1969), pp. 129–36.

10. Robert J. Kuhne, *Co-determination in Business: Worker's Representatives in the Board Room* (New York: Praeger Publishers, 1980), p. 93.

11. Ibid.

10

The Stakeholder's Model

Earlier arguments presented in this book have concerned the nondemocratic way in which a large corporation is run and nonparticipation in major decision making by people who are most affected by its activities. In addition, the abuse of power by the limited few at the top corporate level has led many people to question the legitimacy of this process and to call for various types of reforms. This chapter, in an attempt to deal with the issue of corporate governance, uses the relatively new concept of stakeholder. It will review this concept and its importance in corporate policy, and compare management perception of stakeholder representation at the board level.

THE CONCEPT

Stakeholders has been defined in this book as those groups with a direct interest in the survival of the corporation; without their support the corporation might cease to exist. This concept refers to the obligation that a corporation might have to constituent groups in society other than stockholders.

According to the definitions of numerous writers, the stakeholder theory of corporate governance includes many groups. These range from individuals operating inside the corporation, to those operating outside the corporation: stockholders, board of directors, management, employees, major consumers, major creditors, major suppliers, unions, government (state and federal), communities, and trade associations. The interest of these stakeholders vary. For example, principal stockholders' interests range from security appreciation to dividends, while unions are interested in comparable wages, employment stability, and opportunity for advancement. Government, on the other hand, looks for support in its programs and adherence to laws and regulations. Therefore, it is essential that the stakeholder theory identify the main set of actors in the environment of a corporation to whom it is responsible, and whom it interacts with. Consequently, the objectives and goals that management sets should be arranged with these stakeholders in mind. The corporation should balance the conflicting interests of the external environment (such as community, unions, and consumers) with those of the internal environment (such as management and stockholders).

THE EVOLUTION OF STAKEHOLDER THEORY

The first appearance of the word *stakeholder* was in 1963 in an internal memorandum at the Stanford Research Institute (SRI) with the purpose of generalizing the notion of stockholders as the only group to whom management need be responsive. The SRI suggested that the firm's executives must understand stakeholder needs and concerns because the lack of such understanding might threaten the firm's survival.[1]

Eric Rhenman applied the concept to industrial democracy in Sweden.[2] Even though his approach was similar to that of SRI, it was more exclusive. For instance, instead of defining the stakeholder concept as any group whose support is necessary to the survival of the company, he defined it as "any group who places demands on the company and on whom the company has claims." He added that the application of such a concept might lead to the industrial democracy notion. By the 1970s the concept began to emerge with innumerable definitions with its variances as "strategy, policy planning, and corporate social responsibility." For instance, Bernard Taylor emphasized the concept of stakeholder, assuming that businesses in the 1970s would pay attention to other groups besides stockholders (1971).

In *Strategic Planning and Policy*, William R. King and David I. Cleland suggested a way of analyzing "clientele groups," "claimants," or "stakeholders."[3] W. Rothschild, in *Putting it all Together* (1976), applied the stakeholder concept to the planning process established at General Electric. Hussey and Langham, in *Corporation Planning: The Human Factor* (1978), used the stakeholder concept in a model to analyze the role management plays in the corporate planning process.

In *Corporate Strategy*, Igor Ansoff maintains that the objectives and responsibilities of the corporation are not "synonymous"; however, in the definition of a stakeholder they are made to be so. The stakeholder theory states that "the objectives of the firm should be reached by balancing the conflicting claims of the various stakeholders in the firm: managers, workers, stockholders, suppliers, and vendors."[4] Ansoff believes objectives should be separated into economic and social matters with the latter being a secondary objective.

Russell Ackoff emphasizes stakeholder concepts that fall within an organizational system. Ackoff believes that stakeholders interacting with the organization system will solve a number of societal problems. Ackoff rephrases Ansoff's argument and defines a method for stakeholder analysis of organizational systems—an open systems view. The main argument stems from societal problems that can be resolved by the redesign of fundamental institutions with the support and interaction of the stakeholders in the system—in short, focusing or analyzing the whole system or "synthesis." Ackoff argues that system design can only be accomplished by stakeholder participation, and thereby argues for the inclusion of stakeholder groups in solving systemwide problems. He stresses stakeholder participation as an important part of the system and the one that can contribute most to solve such problems.[5]

Corporate social responsibility advocates during the 1960s and 1970s placed the satisfaction of society as a whole rather than owner satisfaction as an important goal. This implies the importance of other constituencies in addition to stockholders. A. B. Carroll maintains that social responsibility includes the economic, legal, ethical, and discretionary expectations placed by society on organizations at a given point in time.[6]

Rogene A. Buchholz contends that the concept of social responsibility is based on the grounds that corporations have helped cause many social problems. Therefore, corporations have the responsibility to devote some of their resources (financial, capital, human) to the solution of social problems.[7] K. Davis states that "it is the obligation of decision makers to take actions that protect and improve the welfare of the society as well as their own interest."[8]

Others like Sethi (1971–1981), Preston (1978–1982), Votaw (1974), Post (1981), Steckmest (1982), Anshen (1980), and Frederick (1978) all suggest real changes in organizations within the social context in order to guide corporate responsibility toward the public, the consumer, and the community. They argue that any institution is allowed to exist only because it performs useful functions in society. Thus, if business wants to survive it must respond to change in society and do what society demands.

W. Dill has applied the stakeholder concept to strategic management. He argues that "we have been reluctant, though to admit the idea that some of these outside stakeholders might seek and earn active roles with management to make decisions."[9]

The Business Roundtable study specified four crucial roles for the board of directors which include the following: provisions for management and board supervention; giving attention to decisions that have the potential for economic impact as well as social impact; and establishing policies and procedures that will assume compliance with the law. It also approved the trend toward the reconstruction of the board to include a majority of outside directors. The Roundtable study believed directors should exhibit a variety of experience and background. It maintained that political models (stakeholders) are totally undesirable and irrelevant because the primary goal of an organization is to supply goods and services and it is already subject to the discipline of competition and a myriad of legal, social, and political restraints: "effective operation in this environment requires an internal organization which is cohesive, not divided, and which is fast moving, responsive, and flexible, rather than bound by excessive bureaucratic regulation or formalities, either internal or external."[10]

R. Edward Freeman in his review of the stakeholder notion has assembled the various uses of the concept to develop a strategic management approach. Freeman calls for a global definition of the stakeholder. He defines the concept as "a stakeholder in an organization as (by definition) any group or individual who can affect or who is affected by the achievement of the organization's objectives."[11]

MANAGEMENT AND STAKEHOLDERS

The present stakeholder theory focuses on the responsibilities of management within the organization. Management is to recognize stakeholder relationships in a manner that achieves the purpose of the organization. Management is responsible for setting the goals and objectives of the organization with respect to all stakeholders. They should not favor one group over another. Management must set its objectives using input from the internal and external environments. Therefore, for the corporation to be viewed solely as an economic enterprise would not be feasible. It would virtually eliminate those stakeholder interests that are not profit-oriented.

Viewing the corporation as a multipurpose organization omits the narrow road of economics, and broadens management's scope toward other interests. "Stakeholder interests range through a pendulum of economic, social, and political welfare. In responding to these concerns, the corporation becomes a multipurpose institution producing economic and social betterment, and to the extent the corporation strengthens rather than weakens the political system (perhaps one could also say political betterment)."[12] The corporation's decision-making and management process should carefully weigh the impact of decisions and balance the interests of various constituents. A happy medium is achieved through compromises and tradeoffs. All views must be accounted for, but it is impossible to assure that all will be satisfied. Rather than seeking to maximize profits, the multipurpose institution seeks to balance the interest of various stakeholders so that everyone is equally satisfied. Rather than relying solely on an economic calculus in making decisions, the multipurpose institution relies on compromise and negotiation to reach a conclusion.

THE PUBLIC AND STAKEHOLDERS

The public attitude toward government, big business, and major economic institutions has mainly been one of distrust and disapproval. Maximizing immediate shareholder value appears to be the basic purpose of a business enterprise today! By focusing on short-term economic goals, publicly held businesses will see their competitive position decay, their resiliency in difficult times undermined, and their standing in society compromised. But society's attitude toward business is not a new one; it has taken a turn for the worst. These changes began in the 1960s and 1970s, and continue today to some extent. The social movements of those decades started the ball rolling for civil rights, equal rights, and consumer legislation. These movements resulted in changing public expectations of public enterprises; society now feels that "executives should manage corporations in ways that:

1. Assure quality products at reasonable prices manufactured, distributed, and disposed of under publicly acceptable conditions;

2. Help to provide a cleaner environment and lessen risks to human health and safety;

3. Improve the quality of working life by employee participation in workplace decisions, job satisfaction, and advances in on-the-job rights and entitlements;

4. Are open and ethical, and provide greater public accountability for corporate performance, including aspects that heretofore were of little public interest.[13]

The basic business system in this country has worked well. It has been, by and large, efficient. It has produced the world's highest standard of living for its citizens. We must be very sure that in an environment of expenditures—with some willing to manipulate corporate structure for quick profits—we do not end up compromising the basic strength of this unique system. A corporation's success over time is almost totally dependent on its ability to attract and retain good people as employees—in terms of talents, integrity, and willingness to sacrifice at times for the good of the company. But for a corporation to expect this kind of commitment and dedication from its employees, it must reciprocate. It must evidence a greater breadth of purpose than short-term maximization of per share stock prices. It must also be more aware of social concerns and be willing to adapt new methods to address these new concerns. Community interests range from contribution to community development through taxes, participation in charitable activities, and the employment of local people. By focusing on these and many other issues, the corporation will show society it cares and society will respond in a positive fashion.

Social factors shaping the external environment influence the development and resolution of corporate performance. Some of these factors also conflict with traditional corporate economic and political concerns. As a result, many public issues confronting the nation and corporations today focus on deciding between growth and environmental protection, between inflation and unemployment budget constraints.

As society's most visible economic institutions, corporations are held at least partially responsible for national and international economic problems. Stubborn economic realities such as business cycles, high interest rates, an increasingly global economy, and periodic resource shortages demand innovative responses from managers. The classical economic model can be traced back to the eighteenth century, when businesses were owned largely by entrepreneurs. Competition was vigorous and short-run profits were the overriding concern. Of course, the key to attaining short-run profits was to provide society with needed goods and services. According to Adam Smith, the father of the classical economic model, an "invisible hand" promoted the public welfare. Smith believed that the efforts of competing entrepreneurs had a natural tendency to promote the public interest when each tried to maximize short-run profits. In other words, the public interest was best served by individuals pursuing their own interests.

This model has survived into modern times. The well-known economist Milton Friedman has no doubts about the role of business in society. According to Friedman, "few trends could so thoroughly undermine the very foundations of our free society as the acceptance by corporate officials of social responsibility other than to make as much money for their stockholders as possible."[14] Thus, according to the classical economic model of the corporation, short-run profitability and social responsibility are one and the same thing.

ETHICS AND STAKEHOLDERS

The stakeholder framework described thus far raises a number of ethical issues. If we view business as a network of stakeholder relationships, then we can clearly trace a line between business and ethics. Ethics is concerned with how various individuals or organizations interact on important matters. It deals with the distribution of benefits and burdens, rights and duties, and provides more fundamental reasons for the decisions that managers make. The stakeholder model offers a different way of looking at business; it shows us that many business decisions concern a number of parties, each of which is harmed or benefited to some degree.

An ethical issue at the heart of every organization is the determination of precisely what a business sees as the nature of the stake of each stakeholder. If the organization decides that a particular group has no real stake, then it may choose to ignore that group's claims. In a sense, the firm can choose its stakeholder—those groups it wants to serve. This choice is known as enterprise strategy, and involves setting the rules for the management of all stakeholders.[15] The organization which chooses to serve only stakeholders will answer in a different way than the firm which chooses to serve both stockholders and the community. For example, government might be called in to fill the gap between society and business, which could result in additional governmental regulations. Ultimately the organization will have to oblige and conform to the rules. However, by recognizing the various stakeholder groups present, the organization can eliminate the excess cost of regulations and benefit from a higher rating by society, perhaps in the form of profits.

Organizations are like political systems that must organize power among groups that differ. Like social leaders, managers can be susceptible to biases and assume possessive attitudes toward corporate decisions. Exclusive governing in the corporation, either by design or by neglect, bypasses interests of people with a stake in corporate success. These neglected issues may later surface as moral dilemmas for managers.

This point is exemplified in the current debate on the ethics of corporate takeovers. Managers of target companies express anguish over their conflicting obligations to shareholders, on the one hand, and to employees and community citizens on the other. As much as shareholders benefit from a takeover, employees and communities dependent on the firm are at risk under new management. Managers and their sympathizers claim multiple loyalties and decry their difficult ethical dilemma.

Yet if obligations to employees and communities are present at the time of the hostile bid, certainly they were also present prior to the takeover attempt. The source of the manager's dilemma lies in the poor definition of these obligations and weak methods of accounting for them. Similarly, corporate leaders may at any time define the corporation possessively and weaken, rather than strengthen, its checks-and-balances feature.

To avoid ethical pitfalls, questions must be focused on the issue: How are the firm's obligations determined, and how can they be expressed? Are explicit decisions made to balance the interest of some groups, such as employees, with the interest of other groups, such as shareholders? Do constituencies need to sacrifice short-run interests in order to strengthen the corporation and achieve long-term benefits sought by all? Are sacrifices equitable? By failing to answer these questions, managers risk creating zero-sum tradeoffs between interests when a crisis arrives. Corporate leaders need to recognize mutuality of interest between the entity and its constituents and have the skills to manage an inclusive process.

Writing a code of ethics is an important step toward building an ethical corporation; but to be effective, it has to be backed by support structures throughout the organization to ensure adequate communication, oversight, enforcement, and review. The structure of decision making at high levels represents a melting pot of roles and relationships conducive to particular interests and values. There are two significant questions a manager must ask: Does the unique configuration in this organization cast a sufficiently wide net to capture the variety of interests that ultimately bear on the corporation's success? And does the structure of roles and relationships ensure that personal oversights, distortion, and biases will be minimized so that personal interest cannot override corporate interest and corporate interest does not override those of the stakeholders?

THE IMPORTANCE OF THE STAKEHOLDER APPROACH

It has been demonstrated earlier in this book that the stockholders who own the corporation and have legal rights to control it do not really own and control the business as an individual owns or controls his or her personal property. This is because most of the large corporations have thousands of stockholders distributed throughout society, many of whom own only a small number of shares, not enough to make a difference in the voting outcome at an annual meeting.

This has led many stockholders to think of themselves as investors rather than as owners of the corporation. When they do not get enough return, they sell their stocks. In addition, the present corporate governance system has failed to hold management and boards of directors accountable for the use of their corporate power. Managers of corporations, therefore, have come under fire. Their ability to manage corporate affairs and satisfy stockholders is being called into question.

Management is not accountable to the board of directors because members of the boards are too subservient to management. Management has grown in power and the boards of directors, theoretically representing the owners, are increasingly remote and ill-informed about the operation they are supposed to direct. The results of these problems in the corporate system have led critics to conclude that the best way to make management fully accountable for the use of corporate power is to impose external control on government systems.

One way to do this is to reform the system. Reform has proved costly to both business and society. The relationship between business and government has never been easy or simple. However, difficulties in recent years have increased as each has grown in power and complexity. Many regulations have placed heavy burdens on those subject to them. The cost of compliance with regulations has forced some firms to close their doors and has restricted the entry of new firms. The expansion of government activities and regulations resulted mainly from distrust of business practices and conduct. Few people think that business can be counted on to do what is right unless pressured to do so. Therefore, the need for regulation is mainly blamed on business, not on the public or government. If business could have secured public trust, then government involvement, created by public pressures, might not have occurred. Government bureaucratic systems have also contributed to inefficient regulation.

However, if the public had not pressured government, then the public would have had to bear the cost of the problem (i.e., be injured, be killed, sacrifice a healthy environment, be discriminated against in employment. Thus society is paying both ways; and society definitely prefers to have government involvement since the market mechanism may not work efficiently.

Social dissatisfaction has widened the gap between society's expectations and business performance; therefore, business's legitimacy and its survival are questionable. Not only has corporate performance been called into question, but the power and privilege associated with large corporations are also questioned.

Improvement in the internal social control of the corporation means that major business decisions are more socially responsible. If business can make a proper response that effectively meets societal expectations, government regulation may be avoided altogether. Therefore, the stakeholder approach is a substitute for increasing government regulation. Replacing external controls with internal controls where possible could improve the system and ultimately satisfy society. This concept, therefore, applies the obligations corporations might have to groups in society other than stockholders, beyond the obligations prescribed by law or union contract. These groups represent society's physical and human resources to the corporation. It is expected by society that corporations will meet the needs, values, and interests of society. It is also expected that the corporation will maintain control over its internal decision making to minimize externalities (e.g., pollution) and assume greater accountability for social ills that inevitably occur.

Violation of society's expectations by any firm will create a gap between business performance and societal expectation. "An institution is allowed to exist only because it performs a useful function in society, and business's charter can be amended or revoked at any time if it fails to live up to society's expectations. Thus, if business wants to continue in existence, it must respond to changes in society and do what society demands. If society wants business to respond to social values, it must do so or be threatened with extinction."[16]

In order to narrow the gap between corporations and society, major corporate decision making must be shared with those groups with economic and social stakes in the corporation. Since corporate decisions on corporate policy made by management affect many others within the corporate system as well as society, finding out who must be considered in such decisions will reflect real industrial democracy. It means decisions are not necessarily made by the few. Stakeholder participation will assure the interest of the various groups involved and, ultimately, the interests of society as a whole.

It is the author's hope that this attempt will help determine who must be involved in the reconstruction of corporate governance. If the stakeholder notion proves to be necessary to improve corporate governance, then corporate concern will shift from the traditional concept of economic interest of the stockholders to what is best for society as a whole. This concept provides a new way of thinking about corporate governance and how corporate policy should be directed.

Ansoff states that "stakeholder behavior is taken as given, or as a strategy."[17] We formulate strategy against a static environment, which can be forecasted in the long run. The stakeholder concept is a gathering mechanism that can more accurately predict environmental opportunities and threats.

According to many advocates of the stakeholder concept, this is an accurate way to predict environmental problems such as conflicts with various stakeholders. By predicting possible results from actions taken by a corporation, conflicts can be avoided by setting objectives for a company using the knowledge of the total environment.

IMPLEMENTATION

The stakeholder concept of corporate governance implies that management of the organization should take all relevant participants into account when making decisions. The main argument supporting this premise is that management should consider the external forces. However, this is not an easy job. It is often the temptation of management to overlook smaller, weaker stakeholders as a means of cutting cost, pacifying such stakeholders only when necessary. Examples of this type stakeholder include consumers, suppliers, and community leaders. The powerful stakeholders such as stockholders, the board of directors, the government, and unions, have leverage or bargaining power that can be imposed on management.

An obvious solution to this swinging pendulum between management and major and minor stakeholders is to establish a collision. (This is similar to the two-tiered board in West Germany.) Affiliation of stakeholders with the most influence should be represented—major suppliers, major consumers, major leaders/creditors, government agencies, community leaders, employees or union representatives, and stockholders. The "collision" would be composed of individuals within each group, equally represented, with all interests being equally weighted. Specific responsibilities of the stakeholder board should be established.

According to Stanley Kaplan, a former professor at the University of Chicago Law School, "we are just trying to tell directors what their responsibilities really are in this economic climate. With so many Chapter 11 bankruptcies and so many suits charging mismanagement, directors are entitled to a better clarification of their duties. The law as it stands now is very confusing."[18] Therefore, each company is advised to develop its own expectation of the board. In general, board roles and responsibilities can be summarized as follows:

1. Determine the status of the chief executive officers of the corporation.

2. Determine the compensation of the CEOs.

3. Approve financial decisions of material importance to stockholders, such as dividends, issuing stocks, or major strategic investments.

4. Audit corporate performance to assure that management is doing what it says it is doing.

5. Oversee the management of the company's assets.

6. Participate in the making of corporate strategy.

7. Participate in all policy decisions—operational or organizational.

In order to implement this form of structure, the organization needs to identify the internal and external stakeholders. It must have an accurate picture of the corporate environment. Then it needs to develop a list of the various groups who have a stake in the company. It should pay more attention to those groups with a direct interest in the survival of the company, such as stockholders, employees or unions, major consumers, major creditors/lenders, major suppliers, and government agencies. Once the group is identified a committee from the existing board (outsider) should be established. This committee should review the chart with information provided by the management. It then should classify stakeholders, using categories of stake, role, interconnection, and multidimensions. Many stakeholders have more than one role, and usually belong to more than one stakeholder group. Stakeholders also have interconnections (stakeholders may band together to fight certain issues). Stakeholders are also "multidimensions," when categorizing them by degree of commitment, interest, and power. Based on these classifications the board committee will establish the process of stakeholder relationships. This is a visual picture of who the stakeholders are and the strategies used currently for managing relationships and interactions of stakeholders.

Managers need know stakeholders in order to solve the problems of various groups. Since these groups represent the corporation's physical resources, their participation at the board level will improve corporate performance and satisfy society's needs and expectations (see figure 10.1 and model 10.1 for the stages that need to be followed in implementing the suggested stakeholder approach).

Once the stakeholder board is established, the next concern will be how to improve the moral and ethics of the corporation. An internal mechanism for self-control which includes a business code of ethics and a corporate social audit should be established. Institutionalizing ethics means getting ethical issues into corporate policy making at the board and the top management levels through development of a formal code, thereby integrating ethics into all daily decision making and work practices for all employees in the institution.

THE STUDY

According to the author's study, management is not ready to accept the stakeholder approach to corporate governance, which is designed to include various internal and external parties with an interest in the corporation.

All levels of management strongly disagree about whether major buyers and suppliers, community leaders, and major creditors should be represented

Figure 10.1
Suggested Stakeholder Implementation

     1. <u>Identification Stage:</u> To identify the internal and external stakeholders after careful appraisal of the corporate environment.

     2. <u>Development Stage:</u> To prepare a list of the various groups who have stake in the company.

     3. <u>Formation Stage:</u> The current board form a committee called the stakeholder committee (all outsiders).

     4. <u>Reviewing Stage:</u> The stakeholder committee reviews the list of the stakeholders, provided by management.

     5. <u>Classifying Stage:</u> The committee classifies the stakeholders into levels of stake, either based on their economic stake or in their interest to participate and be active in corporate policy.

     6. <u>Processing Stage:</u> The committee will establish a process of stakeholder relationship.

     7. <u>Strategy Stage:</u> Develop the strategies that need to be taken with regard to different stakeholder groups or classifications.

Model 10.1
Stakeholder Implementation

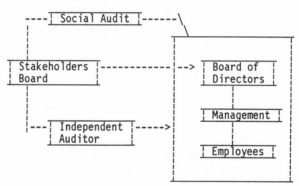

on the board. The higher the level of management, the higher the disagreement. The data in table 10.1 relates to the issue of whether "major buyers or suppliers should be represented on the board of directors" and reveals that the three levels of management highly disagree. A total of 77.4 percent of lower-level managers, 83.6 percent of middle-level managers, and 94 percent of top-level managers disagree. The higher the management level, the higher the disagreement tends to be on this issue. The data in table 10.2

Table 10.1

Frequency Distribution of Respondents

Question: "Major buyers or suppliers should be represented on the board of directors."

Respondents Choice	L.L Mgt. Frequency		M.L.Mgt. Frequency		T.L.Mgt Frequency	
	Nos.	%	Nos.	%	Nos.	%
Total Agree	4	6.24	7	9.59	1	2.94
Indifferent	10	15.62	5	6.85	1	2.94
Total Disagree	50	77.44	61	83.56	32	94.12
Total	64	100.00	73	100.00	34	100.00

Table 10.2

Frequency Distribution of Respondents

Question: "Community leaders, with no business expertise, but with an active interest in the corporation, should be represented on the board of directors."

Respondents Choice	L.L Mgt. Frequency		M.L.Mgt. Frequency		T.L.Mgt Frequency	
	Nos.	%	Nos.	%	Nos.	%
Total Agree	9	14.06	19	26.03	6	17.65
Indifferent	17	26.56	12	16.44	5	14.70
Total Disagree	38	59.38	42	57.53	23	67.65
Total	64	100.00	73	100.00	34	100.00

relating to the issue of whether "community leaders, with no business expertise but with an active interest in the corporation, should be represented on the board of directors" indicates that the majority of management respondents disagree. The data shows that a total of about 59.4 percent of lower-level managers, 57.5 percent of middle-level managers, and 67.6 percent of top-level managers disagree. In comparison, a total of about 14 percent of lower-level managers, 26 percent of middle-level managers, and 17.6 percent of top-level managers agree.

The data in table 10.3 relates to the issue of whether "major creditors who support the corporation, such as banks, insurance companies, etc., should be represented on the board of directors" and reveals that the majority of management disagrees. The data shows that a total of about 51.5 percent of lower-level managers, 52 percent of middle-level managers, and 55.9 percent of top-level managers disagree with major creditors' participation on corporate boards. In comparison, a total of about 30 percent of lower-level managers, 29 percent of middle-level managers, and 32.4 percent of top-level managers agree.

Table 10.3
Frequency Distribution of Respondents

Question: "Major creditors who support the corporation, such as banks, insurance companies, etc., should be represented on the Board of Directors."

Respondents Choice	L.L Mgt. Frequency		M.L.Mgt. Frequency		T.L.Mgt Frequency	
	Nos.	%	Nos.	%	Nos.	%
Total Agree	19	29.68	21	28.76	11	32.35
Indifferent	12	18.75	14	19.18	4	11.77
Total Disagree	33	51.57	38	52.06	19	55.88
Total	64	100.00	73	100.00	34	100.00

Table 10.4
Frequency Distribution of Respondents

Question: "Decision could be improved by wider participation of all levels of management."

Respondents Choice	L.L Mgt. Frequency		M.L.Mgt. Frequency		T.L.Mgt Frequency	
	Nos.	%	Nos.	%	Nos.	%
Total Agree	47	73.44	63	86.30	21	61.77
Indifferent	10	15.63	2	2.74	4	11.77
Total Disagree	7	10.93	8	10.96	9	26.46
Total	64	100.00	73	100.00	34	100.00

Management, surprisingly, disagrees with stockholder participation in corporate policy. The majority of managers who responded do not think that stockholders are necessary for corporate governance.

Management thinks that though both insider and outsider directors are important to the corporation, outsiders must not be the majority. Lower-level and middle-level management highly agree that decisions could be improved by wider participation by all levels of management. The top-level management also agrees, but significantly less enthusiastically. For example, the date in table 10.4 shows that a total of 73.4 percent of lower-level managers, 86.3 percent of middle-level managers, and 62 percent of top-level managers agree to wider participation of all levels of management.

The study shows that management might be ready to accept some form of employee participation, but only at the operation level of management. Management, therefore, is not ready to accept the stakeholder alternative, as proposed, which is designed to include various internal and external parties with an interest in the corporation. Management opposition to the stakeholder approach is consistent with the Business Roundtable's strong opposition to the political models.

The Business Roundtable study felt strongly that the political models (stockholders) are totally undesirable and irrelevant because the primary goal of an organization is to supply goods and services, and it is already subject to the discipline of competition and a myriad of legal, social, and political constraints—"effective operation in this environment requires an internal organization which is cohesive, not divided, and which is fast-moving, responsive, and flexible, rather than bound by excessive bureaucratic regulations of formalities, either internal or external."[19]

Management might think that stockholder participation is a shift that is more political and social than economic. It is clear that most, if not all decision making, involves politics. Therefore, widening participation in a more responsible way by including the stockholder is a continuation of past managerial practices. Management needs to recognize the importance of the stockholder in the process of corporate governance. Improving relations with these groups might save the corporation much trouble.

Since many regulations have placed heavy burdens on corporations, restricting their activities in many ways, corporate reform must rely on internal control. Such a strategy will contribute to less government involvement, reduced cost, increased productivity, and social satisfaction.

CONCLUDING REMARKS

Issues of corporate governance and involvement of social factors in corporate activities are recent phenomena. These are a direct consequence of the turmoil and debates of the late 1960s and early 1970s. The debate is still shaping up on the campuses of business management schools and new ideas are emerging from this debate.

The stakeholder concept of corporate management is new to American society. Americans are very conservative in many aspects. Their corporate business concept is almost two centuries old and is based on traditional stockholders, board of directors, and management theory. For many the problem of corporate governance does not exist at all; others recognize that there is something wrong in corporate functioning but are not sure it needs to be repaired. Most corporate executives, however, concede that change is inevitable; but human nature makes it difficult to accept new changes.

Most of the debate on these issues has so far taken place in academic circles, while corporation personnel have only recently entered into the picture. With a continuing dialogue between various parties, things are slowly taking shape. Though people now have a better understanding of corporate governance issues, it is still unclear for the majority of people. The stakeholder approach to this problem, as already mentioned, is relatively new. Few graduates of business schools now in corporate management have had any academic exposure to this view of corporate governance. It is, therefore, imperative that academicians and the media educate the public about all aspects of the governance issue and its possible solutions.

NOTES

1. R. Edward Freeman, *Strategic Management: A Stakeholders Approach* (Boston: Pitman Publishing, 1984), p. 31.

2. Eric Rhenman, *Industrial Democracy and Industrial Management* (London: Tavistock Publications, 1968), quoted in Freeman, *Strategic Management*, p. 41.

3. William R. King and David I. Cleland, *Strategic Planning and Policy* (New York: Van Nostrand Reinhold, 1978).

4. Quoted in Freeman, *Strategic Management*, p. 37.

5. Ibid., p. 41.

6. Archie B. Carroll, *Business and Society: Managing Corporate Social Performance* (Boston: Little, Brown and Company, 1981), pp. 34–35.

7. Rogene A. Buchholz, *Business Environment and Public Policy: Implications for Management and Strategy Formulation* (Englewood Cliffs, N.J.: Prentice-Hall, 1986), p. 415.

8. Quoted in Freeman, *Strategic Management*, p. 37.

9. W. Dill, "Public Participation in Corporation Planning: Strategic Management in a Kibitzer's World," *Long Range Planning* (1975): 57–63.

10. "The Role and Composition of the Board of Directors of the Large Publicly Owned Corporation." (New York: The Business Roundtable, 1978): 25.

11. Freeman, *Strategic Management*, p. 46.

12. Buchholz, *Business Environment*, p. 459.

13. Francis W. Steckmest, *Corporate Performance: The Key to Public Trust* (New York: McGraw-Hill, 1982), pp. 221–22.

14. Milton Friedman, *Capitalism and Freedom* (Chicago: University of Chicago Press, 1962), p. 133.

15. R. Edward Freeman and Daniel Gilbert, Jr., "Managing Stakeholder Relationships." Quoted in S. P. Sethi and C. M. Falbe, *Business and Society: Dimensions of Conflict and Cooperation* (Lexington, Mass.: Lexington Books, 1987), p. 397.

16. S. P. Sethi, "A Conceptual Framework for Environmental Analysis of Social Issues and Evaluation of Business Response Patterns" *Academy of Management Review* (January 1979): 65.

17. Igor Ansoff, "Managing Strategic Surprise to Weak Signals," *California Management Review* 18 no. 2 (1975): 21–23.

18. "The Role and Composition of the Board of Directors," p. 25.

PART THREE

The Implications of
Corporate Governance

11

Corporate Social Responsibility

INTRODUCTION

In recent years there has been a change in how businesspeople view the issue of corporate social responsibility. There has been a concerted effort to define the issue and ways to control the problems it causes. This chapter will address the topic of corporate social responsibility. First, we will give a brief summary of how the issue has been defined and why it is an issue. Then we will discuss some different views on social responsibility. Finally, we will discuss the future of corporate social responsibility.

DEFINITION

A working definition of the term *corporate social responsibility* is difficult to formulate. One reason for this is that in order for the definition to be of use to corporations and acceptable to the public, it would have to include all those issues for which society feels corporations should be held responsible. However, for two reasons, a definition of this type would be difficult, if not impossible, to translate into a policy that corporations could follow. First, every individual in society would have a different concept of what the corportion's primary responsibilities are to society. Second, these concepts would be forever undergoing change as new problems arose, thus making a definition quickly obsolete.

According to S. Prakash Sethi, "social responsibility ... has been used in so many different contexts that it has lost all meaning. Devoid of an internal structure and content it has come to mean all things to all people."[1] With these problems in mind, the definition needs to be exact so that guidelines may be set, yet flexible enough to change with society's concerns in the future.

The older view of the relationship between business and society prior to the 1960s was based on the tenet that economic growth was the source of all social and economic progress. In other words, the basic mission of business was to produce goods and services at a profit.

Today's view maintains that this singleminded pursuit of profit causes detrimental effects in society. The best solution to these problems is to impress upon business the idea that it has a responsibility to society to work for social and economic betterment. This new view does not invalidate the old view; it only adds to it.

The idea of social responsibility then, is that decision makers have a moral obligation to society to protect and improve the welfare of the community. Along with being socially responsible, corporations today also strive for traditional economic goals.

The definition of corporate social responsibility and its implementation is highly relevant to today's corporations and society as a whole. This is especially true as corporations grow larger and profits become smaller, causing some corporations to cut corners and to think less about their responsibilities to the public.

ISSUES OF CORPORATE SOCIAL RESPONSIBILITY

Most leading businesspeople and economists agree that corporate social responsibility is the corporation's obligation to interact with society and to gain insight and judgment on public policy. While the concept of corporate social responsibility may have been conceived as early as the 1930s, it was not actually implemented until the mid–1960s to early 1970s. At this time society's values were changing and there was a need for a response from a corporate world. Business executives responded by implementing specific programs to educate people on social issues. Schools of business and management offered new courses that oriented students to the new social responsibilities of businesses.

Corporations now have an obligation to society to help solve social problems, some of which they helped create. An example of this is the high content of pollution emitted from industrial factories. Business must devote its human, financial, and capital resources to finding solutions to these problems.

ARGUMENT FOR CORPORATE SOCIAL RESPONSIBILITY

There are several valid arguments in favor of corporate social responsibility. One argument is that public expectations of business have changed, and business has no choice but to adapt to these changes. It must respond to the demands of society to stay in existence. Another argument is that profit maximization should be seen over a longer time period than in the past. It is the long-term self-interest of business that produces changes in environmental conditions. Further, business will develop a more positive public image by being socially responsible. It may also be able to avoid government regulation. Some authorities feel that business has vast resources that would be useful in solving social problems. Finally, there is a moral argument that business is obligated to help society due to the many problems that are a direct result of business operations.

ARGUMENT AGAINST CORPORATE SOCIAL RESPONSIBILITY

Critics feel that social responsibility has been addressed in so many contexts that it has lost all meaning. Some corporations create operational problems in trying to be too specific about their social responsibilities. The rights of corporate managers are questioned in determining public policies for their organizations. When managers assume this right, they completely ignore any preestablished guidelines for public policy, which are for all society in general. Another argument against corporate social responsibility is that the sole responsibility of the corporation is to its shareholders. Managers must abide by the rules for profit maximization. In addition, corporate social responsibility is fundamentally a moral concept. Therefore it is difficult if not impossible for organizations to respond to it. Finally, it is felt that the doctrine itself undermines the principles on which the free enterprise system is based.

Several key issues concerning corporate social responsibility are as yet unresolved, the first being the operational definition of responsibility. Is it possible to effectively allocate resources? With which problems should the corporation concern itself? Corporate social responsibility provides no clear guidelines for managerial behavior and does not even consider the competitive environment with which all business is faced. Lastly, corporate social responsibility is a moral issue, and to define "moral" would be impossible because people's individual views are so drastically different.

DIFFERENT VIEWS

According to Milton Friedman, the social responsibility of business is to increase profits. Businesses do not have responsibilities, only people can have responsibilities. First we have to determine precisely what is meant by the "social responsibility" of business and to whom it applies. A corporate executive has a direct responsibility to his employers. "That responsibility is to conduct the business in accordance with their desires, which generally will be to make as much money as possible while conforming to the basic rules of the society, both those embodied in law and those embodied in ethical customs."[2] Thus, the corporate executive's primary responsibility is to the individuals who own the corporation. What if an executive were to refrain from increasing prices to prevent inflation, make expenditures beyond the best interest of the corporation to present pollution, or hire unemployed workers who were poverty stricken instead of better-qualified ones? In each case, the corporate executive would be spending someone else's money to benefit the general public. The stockholders would not be getting their returns, consumer prices would go up, and the employees' wages would decrease. The executive would have to spend money the same way stockholders, customers, and employees would have spent their own money. If the executive were to spend the money as they saw fit, it would be equivalent to implementing a tax, thus leading to "taxation without representation." What if an executive were to spend this money for "social responsibilities"? Would the customer and employees accept his choice? No, they would leave the company and support an organization less scrupulous about social responsibilities.

Friedman believes that there are four basic obligations that an organization has to society:

1. A corporation must obey the law.

2. A corporation must provide goods and services.

3. A corporation must employ resources efficiently.

4. A corporation must pay resource owners fairly in accordance with the market.[3]

These four factors are designed to function in a competitive market system. A corporation is designed to raise the standard of living, and cannot meet the needs and wants of everyone.

Thomas M. Jones asks if we should adopt corporate social responsibility, and if so, how to implement it. His definition of corporate social responsibility resembles that of Buchholz's. Jones defines corporate social responsibility as "the notion that corporations have an obligation to constituent groups in society other than stockholders and beyond that prescribed by law or union contracts."[4] It is very important when discussing corporate responsibility that we do not begin to expect more of corporations than we do of other social and political institutions. Corporations will go through the process of social policy to be fair, but there are no promises of the results. An analogy with the law can be applied to the process. "The law cannot guarantee that an innocent person will be found innocent, but promises a fair trial."[5] Corporate responsibility ought not be seen as a set of outcomes, but as a process. If the corporation makes an effort to implement the process, then the results cannot be criticized. As previously stated, it is very difficult to judge the outcome of a social process since the whole concept of social responsibility is so vague.

By defining corporate social responsibility in terms of a process, Jones suggests that corporations are obligated to view the impact of their decisions on the social environment before the decisions are levied so that the consequences of the choice can be kept to a minimum or eliminated altogether. It becomes the responsibility of the corporation and its management to dwell on the social aspects when they formulate their course of action. Many aspects are currently the concern of top officials, due to imposed government regulations; however, still other aspects need to be kept within the minds of the executives on a voluntary basis.

Jones contends that in the process of fulfilling corporate social responsibility, organizations must beware of two potential problems. "First, there is a danger that alterations to the decision-making process will become ends in themselves."[6] For example, corporations may satisfy their obligations by placing women on their boards, but also may disregard any input they offer, thus defeating the purpose. "Second, process changes will not necessarily result in changed corporate behavior."[7] It is often difficult to incorporate alterations into actual transformed actions. The intentions of the corporation may be valid but they are not a guarantee for correct behavior. As long as management is aware of these hurdles, Jones claims that they will not pose any obstacle to proper corporate social responsibility.

Christopher D. Stone opposes Friedman's argument. Stone asks, "Why shouldn't corporations be socially responsible?" Friedman argued that corporate executives make a promise to stockholders to maximize profit. Even if this is so, Stone believes that an ordinary person would not "interpret it to mean maximize in every way you can possibly get away with, even if that means polluting the environment, ignoring or breaking the law."[8] Stone also suggests that most people would agree that such a promise would need to be broken in some cases.

What is the role of the corporation? Are corporate executives solely responsible to stockholders? If we consider parents to be responsible for their child, are they not responsible for taking care of the house and earning a living? Parents cannot give every moment of their attention to a child. Corporate executives are in the same situation: they cannot give all their attention to stockholders. Friedman suggests that if stockholders do not agree with how a corporation is spending their money, then the stockholders can simply sell their stock. But what about the employees of the corporation and the consumers? They cannot simply make a phone call to remove themselves from the influence of the corporation. In conclusion, Stone believes that the forces of the market and the law ought to be used to keep corporations within desirable bounds. "It may be better to trust them than to have corporate managers implementing their own vague and various notions of what is best for the rest of us."[9]

Rogene A. Buchholz states that "the pursuit of economic growth and profits does not necessarily lead to social progress. In many cases it has led instead to a deteriorating physical environment, discrimination against certain groups in society, poverty for others, urban decay, and other social ills."[10] An example of such disregard for social responsibility may be taken from America's Industrial Revolution. Workers were underpaid and forced to work in terrible conditions for long hours with little thought given to the environment. Although such blatant disregard for responsibility is not existent in today's corporations, there are other issues at stake for which society holds corporations accountable. Therefore, the study and implementation of corporate social responsibility is important so that the errors of the past do not become problems of the future.

Since the issue of corporate social responsibility is not new, studies have been conducted to survey executive viewpoints as to how they, as individuals, and their corporation view this issue. In 1975, Sandra Holmes of the University of Texas distributed questionnaires to top executives of large U.S. corporations concerning their attitude and their corporation's attitude toward corporate social responsibility. The results showed that 60 percent of the executives expected businesses to be socially responsible. They also predicted an 8 percent increase in adherents of this view by 1980 (table 11.1).

In the winter of 1981–1982 Richard T. De George published an article entitled "Can Corporations Have Moral Responsibility?" He described two extreme philosophies of corporate social responsibility: the organizational view and the moralistic view. In the organizational view, a corporation is a legal entity established for certain limited purposes such as profit, production, the provision of services, and similar restricted ends. It is organized to fulfill these specific tasks.[11] This means that a person who works for an organization should work toward the goals of the corporation, regardless of his or her personal moral values.

In the moralistic view individuals do not cease to be moral persons simply because they are employed by corporations; nor are corporations or other organizations or legal entities, such as nations, immune from moral evaluation and criticism.[12] This view holds the corporation responsible as well as the people involved. These views are extreme opposites. We feel that a middle of the road approach would be more appropriate. Although these two approaches differ in thought they both lack legal procedures and rules to support their philosophies. De George suggests five different ways of internally assigning responsibility for corporate actions. These actions are as follows:

1. the person assumes all of the responsibility assigned to the corporation from without.
2. partial responsibility to all members of the corporation who have direct involvement with the decision.
3. the corporation is held fully responsible.
4. full corporate responsibility with individual responsibility also.
5. responsibility for corporate actions only to the corporation, not to individual members.[13]

Table 11.1
Social Responsibility Survey

Executives' Opinions and Firms' Philosophies about the Social
Responsibilities of Business: 1970, 1975, 1980

	Percentage of executives who selected statement to describe their opinion	Percentage of executives who selected statement to describe their firm's philosophy
	1970-1975-1980	1970-1975-1980
1) A business is responsible for making a profit and abiding by legalities	13.2- 0.1- 0.6	17.4- 2.2- 1.7
2) A business is responsible for making a profit and helping to solve social problems which a business may directly create (such as pollution)	23.1-16.1- 9.6	27.5-17.1- 7.8

In addition to making a profit, a
business should help to solve
social problems whether or not a
business helps to create those
problems:

3) As long as there is at least some short-run or long-run profit potential	24.2-23.5-21.9	21.3-26.5-26.7
4) Even if there is probably no short-run or long-run profit potential	31.3-46.4-46.6	28.1-41.5-46.1
5) Even though doing so may reduce short-run profit and no long-run profit returns are possible	8.2-13.9-21.3	5.7-12.7-17.7
TOTAL	100- 100- 100	100- 100- 100

*Predicted Opinion

THE FUTURE

The future of corporate social responsibility is not definite. New and innovative ideas must be developed and implemented, combining the wants and needs of both society and the corporations.

Code of Ethics

In "Ethical Management: A Growing Corporate Responsibility—Part 2," Robert Boulanger and Donald Wayland suggest a written code of ethics. This code includes responsibility for the community, firm, shareholders, superiors and peers, consumers, employees and trade unions, immediate families, suppliers, and competitors. All these groups should be considered by management in the decision-making process.

Boulanger and Wayland predict that there will be difficulties with implementing the new code: "Unless supported by concrete action, even the best code of ethics will achieve little."[14] The code of ethics must be supported not only by management executives, but by all employees of the corporation.

A formal written code of ethics is a reference tool for consistency; it puts into words an abstract idea; managers can justify ethical conduct if it is criticized; and it would ensure honest policy actions. However, for such a code to be useful it must be well written—concise, clear, not too rigid, dynamic, and flexible.

These requirements would be difficult to fulfill, especially in the initial stage of development. Management would probably be resistant to change and the change may be viewed as restructure.

The development of a formal code necessitates a method of enforcement. This leads to restrictions in the free enterprise system which the United States prides itself upon.

Since government intervention is usually viewed negatively, a different kind of relationship between government and business is needed. Some sort of business-government coalition should be established.

Need for Education

Buchholz suggests another way for corporations to deal with the corporate social responsibility issue. Corporations must be willing to acknowledge public issues in order to understand and fulfill the needs of society and corporations. Corporations must develop the "capacity to identify and research public issues, the willingness to debate these issues in the public arena, and the ability to work with other groups in society, particularly government, that have other ideologies and other incentives, to solve these problems."[15]

Another way to introduce corporate social responsibility into the framework of business is to teach it in schools. Schools should encourage future executives to take on values in line with what society expects. Boulanger and Wayland state that "schools of business administration should use every means at their disposal to help instill a sense of integrity and honesty in budding executives."[16]

The issue of corporate social responsibility is one that is prevalent in society and will continue to be in the future. The ideas for a social contract of business with society should be taught in schools. Once it is instituted at that level, young executives will have a base on which to make their decisions. The corporate social responsibility issue is still in its initial stages and people are still trying to devise a formal definition. After the scope of the issue is defined, definite steps to regulate the problems can be taken.

Need for Business/Academia Co-operation

Both the business community and the academic community act as social institutions which set ideologies and economic paces for individual freedom and democracy. Corporations are an integral part of society and depend on it for their existence, continuity, and growth. Furthermore, they must strive to coordinate their activities with the goals of the overall social system.

The business community and especially large corporations are major financial supporters of higher learning institutions. Between 1979 and 1981 their direct support of colleges and universities increased from $230 million to $870 million. Theoretically, in return, academic institutions provide services and resources. According to a university-industry relations study done by Peat, Marwick, Mitchell & Co. industry will not become a major source of R&D funds in the near future. Presently, despite the seemingly large support, industry provides only 3.5 percent of the total R&D funds to U.S. universities while the federal government provides 68 percent. Apparently, the business community does not realize the importance of the academic community as the main source of ideas that will become major policy positions in the future.

Legitimacy Needed

In order for a business to survive and grow, it must seek and maintain society's view of legitimacy. It has a economic rationale, a political rationale, and an intellectual rationale. Historically, society has had no qualms supporting its economic and political rationales. Unfortunately, business had not yet succeeded in developing a lasting level of interaction with the academic community, and consequently, lacks the intellectual rationale for societal legitimacy.

To spark the erosion of this legitimacy gap, this study closely examines the expectations of each contributor. The issue is not based only on what business expects of the academic community but also how the academic community sees itself and its expectations of the business community. Business needs academic support to narrow the intellectual legitimacy gap and to play a more effective role in public affairs. The conceptual framework presented analyzes the differences between the business community and academic community under three dimensions: core values, objectives and goals, and organizational structures. These are the roots of the strategies pursued by the two institutions. The business community's ultimate goal in building effective academic-business relations are:

1. To enter into the academic community for their ideas and viewpoints, rather than their financial support.

2. To develop an active and trusting relationship, rather than operating from an essentially inactive and mutually suspicious mode.

3. To bridge together business and various segments of the academic community by facilitating and encouraging an open exchange of ideas, attitudes, and experiences. Accomplishment of these goals would make it possible for the institutions to respect each other's values and achievement criteria and to work together toward a mutual goal for society's good.[17]

SETHI'S MODEL

S. Prakash Sethi developed an issue–environment matrix in which he divided the life-cycle of a social issue or problem into four stages: preproblem, identification, remedy and relief, and prevention. The social legitimacy of a corporation is determined in this environment.[18]

In the first stage, the problem is not widespread. There are a few isolated cases of a corporation cutting corners or doing something that has a negative impact on society. These isolated events do not cause a social issue. However, when similar acts are performed by a large number of companies and are continued over a long period, their cumulative effect is substantial. Most corporations respond at this stage by doing what is required by law.

The identification stage is a very critical stage in the life-cycle of a problem. During this stage the problem is defined and the source is determined if possible. Many times the source is difficult to determine because by the time the symptoms appear the cause no longer exists. Also, technology has changed thus making it more difficult to ascertain the source of the problem. A lack of data may also make it difficult. Public perception of corporate behavior during the preproblem and problem identification stages determines the extent of flexibility available to corporations in later stages.

During the remedy and relief stage, compensation and/or punitive damages are determined. Many things are taken into account before the decision is made, such as the economic impact on the industry, the workers, the owners, and the creditors. This period is marked by conflict as groups try to improve their respective positions. Often, the government is called upon to help pay for the damages in the form of a subsidy.

In the prevention stage, ideas and changes are discussed and activated in order to prevent the problem from reoccurring. Two things must happen in this stage. There must be a qualitative change in the value sets of the business and its government, and a modification of the social arrangements among various groups in the social system. At this stage, a business can destroy its social legitimacy by fighting every measure that is not favorable to it.

Business Response Modes

Businesses can respond in three ways to the problems they face, based on social obligations, responsibilities, and responsiveness. The social legitimacy of a business is determined by which of the modes a business uses to respond to a social situation.

When a business responds in the mode of social obligation, it adheres only to the economic and legal restraints—it does the bare minimum. A corporation acting in this way is acting defensively or in a proscriptive manner.

The social respnsibility mode is prescriptive. The business does not wait until it is told to do something. Instead the business recognizes the problem and seeks out ways to solve the problem. This behavior meets social expectations.

By acting in a socially responsive manner a firm is acting in a proactive manner. The business is not just responding to the problem, but is anticipating the problem. It is trying to prevent the problem before it even becomes a social issue. If the firm responds in the preproblem stage in a prescriptive or proactive way, it is likely that the public will react positively toward the corporation. If the corporation response is proscriptive and occurs late in the life-cycle of the problem, it will erode the business's base of social legitimacy.

Issue–Management Matrix

The issue–management matrix focuses on corporate strategies that will bring a positive response from academia. By working with each other, both the business world and the academic world will achieve more than if they work independently. The best strategy for the business community is to develop coalitions with the academic community when an issue is still in the preproblem stage. These issues will parallel the growth pattern of the industry. As the industry grows, so will the number and magnitude of the issues.

Relation to Business-Academia Issue

The business community should learn the current research interests of the academic groups that deal with the issues that are prevalent to the industry. Most of all, the community should build trust by not putting pressure on the academicians. They should accept the conclusions reached by the academic community. The businesses should provide data freely. This will create a greater exchange of ideas and will build trust which is beneficial to both. "No academia of reaching the academic community is likely to be successful if the corporation's general response mode is that of social obligation, and it is unwilling to change its own position in light of new findings."[19]

Corporate social responsibility has been debated for decades and probably will be for many more. There is no more correct definition of social responsibility. Between Milton's and Stone's opinions lie many different interpretations of social responsibility. Unifying these various views will not be easy, as demonstrated in our example with the business community and the academic community. However, Sethi proposes a business strategy where the business and the academic communities can work together to benefit everyone.

CASE STUDIES

The first case examined is that of Union Carbide. An accident occurred in 1984 in Bhopal, India, at the plant of Union Carbide India, Ltd. A chemical leak from a tank killed almost 2,500 people and injured between 30,000 and 40,000 people.

Union Carbide's chairman formed a crisis-management team to deal with Bhopal-related matters. The team arranged for relief for the victims and an investigation of the accident, as well as the disposal of the remaining chemical at the plant.

Union Carbide chose to behave in Sethi's stage of social obligation concerning the Bhopal incident. Union Carbide denied guilt in the accident on the basis that its affiliate, Union Carbide India, Ltd., and the Indian government were responsible for design of the plant. Union Carbide provided specifications for the plant and Union Carbide India Ltd. was responsible for construction. Materials, management, and inspections were wholly Indian. The transfer contract absolved Union Carbide of any responsibility should anything go wrong with the equipment, according to Union Carbide.

Because of the Union Carbide connection with the Bhopal plant, they maintained a degree of responsibility whether they acknowledged it or not. Union Carbide did not go beyond their social obligation. They denied responsibility for management and inspections of the Bhopal plant. Their transfer contract confirmed that denial of responsibility. India said Union Carbide was to blame because they had majority ownership in the plant and were responsible for the plant's faulty design. The socially obligated corporation does not violate laws, but neither does it go beyond what the law demands. The corportion in the state of social obligation is neutral where values and ethics are concerned. Union Carbide followed both of these behavior patterns.

The chairman of Union Carbide contends that the technology at Bhopal was sound and the plant well-designed. However, he cannot deny a March 20, 1985 statement he made acknowledging that the Bhopal plant should not have been operational under existing conditions.[20]

Although Union Carbide claimed they were not to blame, they tried to make a $350-million settlement with the victims. Union Carbide felt this settlement was very generous because compensations would have exceeded by far ordinary settlements in Indian courts.

The second case involves the Johnson & Johnson Corporation. In October 1982, the Tylenol tragedy broke out in Chicago, killing at least seven people. Extra-Strength Tylenol capsules laced with cyanide left users dead within minutes.

Johnson & Johnson's manufacturer, McNeil Consumer Products Co., recalled 264,000 bottles of Tylenol nationwide within minutes. The Food and Drug Administration warned Americans not to take any Extra-Strength Tylenol capsules. The product was pulled from the shelves of drugstores and supermarkets.

The Ashland Oil Company's spill of one million gallons of diesel fuel into the Monongahela River (Pittsburgh, Pa.) on January 2, 1988, is the most recent tragic event and has the issue of corporate social responsibility written all over it. It is tragic in the sense that it disrupted water services to hundreds of thousands of people spanning three states and in terms of the impact that the million-gallon leak of fuel will have on the environment.

How Ashland responded to the spill is the key. They immediately took responsibility. Ashland awarded a $250,000 grant to the University of Pittsburgh to study the effects of the fuel spill. They set up toll-free telephone numbers to try to settle claims related to spill damages. Many feel that Ashland Oil did not act in a socially responsible way because they let such a spill happen out of pure negligence. Others contend since they responded quickly to help eliminate the damages done to the environment and to society in general, that makes them socially responsible.

In the case of Johnson & Johnson, investigations all but ruled out the possibility that the Tylenol capsules were contaminated at the manufacturing plant. It was believed that the capsules were tampered with at some point in the distribution chain, although it could not be determined whether a disgruntled employee sabotaged the product or a madman tampered with the product from the store shelf. In any event, McNeil, the producer, offered a $100,000 reward for information leading to a conviction in the case. At no point did Johnson & Johnson deny their responsibility, as did Union Carbide, even though the extent of their involvement was that their capsules and packages were not totally tamperproof.

The Tylenol tragedy of 1982 did have some positive outcomes. Because of these deaths, Johnson & Johnson promoted a triple-seal package in hopes of regaining consumer confidence. Johnson & Johnson moved quickly to halt public distrust. All agreed that the company had earned its good reputation and deserved public support, as they were also the victim. Ultimately, these events led to changes in the packaging of drugs and the design of capsules. Stricter government standards were developed for over-the-counter items.

Johnson & Johnson acted in a socially responsible manner. A socially responsible firm accepts liability. Johnson & Johnson never denied that they were liable to individuals affected by their product. Johnson & Johnson compensated its victims in the absence of clear legal grounds. A socially responsible firm accepts responsibility for solving current problems and admits their deficiencies. Finally, Johnson & Johnson cooperated with the government in research to improve standards. The Union Carbide and Johnson & Johnson cases are familiar examples of corporate behavior in socially obligated and socially responsible firms, which further illustrate Sethi's model.

MANAGEMENT'S PERCEPTION OF CORPORATE SOCIAL RESPONSIBILITY

Interviews were conducted with members of management at three area firms and with one former management to explore management's perception of corporate social responsibility in the business world of today.

David Burford, personnel manager of Penreco, feels that corporate social responsibility means "to be a good neighbor and meet the social obligations to the community," as well as "the social needs of employees."[21] Burford states that there are no viable arguments against corporate responsibility. Arguing for the issue, he feels that Penreco should "see that we benefit as many social organizations in the community as possible, such as blood drives, volunteer fire departments and food cupboards."[22] Penreco's recent $4-million cleanup project is evidence of their stand on corporate responsibility.

The concept of corporate social responsibility, according to William Johnston, vice president of the First National Bank of Mercer County, involves extensive interaction between the bank and the community it serves. He contends that "the bank is more unique in its community responsibilities" than perhaps, production industries. "The bank has a responsibility," in his opinion, "to the community to reinvest in that community. Business development is a social responsibility of the banking industry, which includes bringing new business into an area and helping local entrepreneurs develop their own business. The banking officer is expected, and often required, to be actively involved in the community's civic organizations and functions, that is, Chamber of Commerce, United Way and boards of directors of charitable organizations."[23] When questioned as to what he felt was a suitable manner for measurement of social responsibility in a corporation, Johnston stated that a measure of a bank's social responsibility is the success of its involvement in the community. This involvement often creates or retains business for the bank. Ultimately, success for the bank means success for the community, and vice versa.

When asked about government regulations and agencies, Johnson stated, "incumbent on the leadership of the banking corporation are the regulation requirements, but the moral and civic requirements are to protect the assets of the corporation." "Government agencies have their purpose but their shotgun approach to creation and enforcement of socially and corporately related laws and regulations has penalized companies and cost them a great deal of money unnecessarily."[24] Johnston points out the redundancy of government jobs created to perform tasks that socially responsible banks perform on their own, although he feels that many people dealing with banks deserve some assurance that the bank is being watched. Governmental control or security for the public's benefit is a must in the banking industry.

Eric M. Scheid, district manager of Richman Brothers Clothing, feels that "responsibility is a broad term which can be applied in every sense of society—the business world especially. Richman Brothers gains a better image for the public by contributing toward corporate responsiveness." "We feel it is the duty of our corporation as well as other prominent retail firms to relay a sense of responsibility toward the various issues facing humanity. It is up to each individual to have a great concern for the many problems facing our society. By contributing corporately, the power to solve problems is greatly intensified. I feel corporate responsibility is needed to maintain a healthy culture in every sense."[25]

An interview with Kenneth Calhoun, a former employee of Alcoa, restates the feeling of current management personnel on corporate social responsibility. Alcoa is very much in the public's eye, and it is the intent of the company to promote a positive, upright image. Managers here are also urged to be active in the community.

Additionally, because of the increasing power of government regulation, Alcoa has staff exclusively to stay abreast of the state and federal legislation that will affect them. Their involvement with regulation allows Alcoa to make use of their lobbying efforts and to change their own procedures before compliance is forced upon them.[26]

Several interviews were conducted on the subject of corporate social responsibility. The managers interviewed feel that corporate social responsibility is imperative in the business world today. (Table 11.2 compares management's contrasting views on corporate social responsibility.)

Corporate social responsibility is an area of business operations that merits attention. More and more, corporations must face their responsibility to society. The business that accepts social challenge will be viewed in a more positive light than the company which waits to be mandated, regulated, or fined. Interviews with management personnel reveal management's support of the concept of corporate social responsibility in practice. The corporation of today must communicate to society as well as to stockholders.

CORPORATE RESPONSIBILITY IN THE INTERNATIONAL MARKET

Corporate social responsibility can be examined on two levels: the national level and the international. We will be concerned with exploring some of

Table 11.2
Management Perceptions

INTERVIEWEE	DEFINITION OF CSR	ATTITUDE TOWARD GOVT. REGULATION	MEASUREMENT OF CSR
Calhoun, Kenneth Former Employee Alcoa	Important concept of making sure image is upright and public has less to disapprove of.	Alcoa stays abreast of legislation and works with it.	Involvement in charity and community functions as well as the ability to keep up with the changing environment.
Johnston, William E. Vice President - First National Bank of Mercer County	Extensive interaction between the bank and the community it serves.	Government agencies have their purpose, but can penalize companies unnecessarily.	Success of involvement in the community.
Rumbarger, Kenneth - Manager Penreco	The extent to which social obligations of the community and social needs of employees are met.	Penreco does all they can without regulation. When government regulates, Penreco goes beyond.	The extent to which Penreco benefits as many social organizations in the community as possible, ie. blood drives, volunteer fire departments and food cupboards
Griffen, Audrey Employee, Penreco	Responsibility and obligation to the surrounding community, to the workers and concern for the environment.	At PENRECO, we go beyond government regulations and look to the future to see what future regulations may require.	PENRECO is responsible to the people in the community to insure them a pollution free community.
Scheid, Eric M. District Manager - Richman Brother Clothing	A broad term that can be applied in every sense of society-the business world especially- regarding issues facing humanity.	Regulation is good - it addresses the concerns of everyone.	The public's reaction to the business overall.

the main issues in the international realm. In so doing, we will study the Union Carbide disaster in Bhopal, India.

On December 3, 1984, history's worst industrial accident took place at Union Carbide Corporation's pesticide plant in Bhopal, India. A valve on an underground storage tank gave way under pressure, spewing a cloud of deadly gas over the sleeping city. This methyl isocyanate leak cost more than two thousand lives and it could be years before the long-term health effects on the residents of Bhopal are known. The Bhopal facility is one of fourteen Union Carbide plants in India. Union Carbide owns 51 percent of the plant and the rest is owned by the Indians.

The Bhopal case comes at a time when new rules are needed for international business and corporate international responsibility needs to be re-evaluated. Union Carbide chairman, Warren Anderson, stated that his firm had a "moral responsibility to provide aid,"[27] but he denied that they were criminally responsible for the accident. On the other hand, the Indians said that all the responsibility rested with the multinational, not the local subsidiary. Thus, the Indian government sued only the Union Carbide, not the Bhopal subsidiary. Their suit argued that "multinationals engaged in hazardous activities are not entitled to the legal shields that usually protect parent companies."[28] Is this notion of the parent company being responsible for its foreign subsidiaries so farfetched? Not according to supporters of social responsibility.

Not only has the degree of social responsibility of multinational corporations for their foreign subsidiaries been questioned, but so have their health and safety standards. In a survey conducted by *Business Week,* 49 percent of those surveyed were convinced that multinationals maintain lower health and safety standards at overseas factories.[29] This kind of performance damages the image of the multinational corporation and also the image of American attitudes. Such actions, as lower safety standards, are not examples of social responsibility. A socially responsible company will consider the effects of its actions—both national and international.

This disaster has raised concern over the way in which multinationals operate around the world, particularly in third world countries, and has prompted inquiry into health and safety standards in foreign subsidiaries. Many multinational corporations expand into foreign countries to overcome U.S. laws and restrictions, and to use the standard legal shields to insulate them from any liability. These actions of multinationals often appear unethical and unjust. We have come to a point where it is necessary to re-evaluate the tendencies of those multinational corporations who ignore their international social responsibility.

SUMMARY

American business executives today are deeply concerned over the loss of public respect for businesses and the loss of their ability to provide leadership in society. How can this be regained? Some executives feel that the first step is for businessmen to honestly reexamine what has gone wrong, why, and to what extent the business itself has caused public hostility. They should also look at the improper behavior and failure to address crucial problems facing society.

Americans still believe in the free enterprise system. They have no quarrel with profit making; but they do have a problem with unethical and questionable business practices conducted at the public's expense. What is to be done about companies that pollute our water and air and are indifferent to the hazards of pollution?

Corporations have no choice but to deal with the growing issue of social responsibility. The problem, however, lies in conflicting ideas about social responsibility. To stockholders, the social responsibility is to increase profits, whereas to environmentalists, it is to ensure safety to society through taking precautionary measures no matter how expensive.

Changes must occur now in order to avoid disasters in the future. Businesses must look beyond immediate self-interests and recognize the needs and demands of society. They will only hurt themselves by ignoring the pleas of the stakeholders, because without their loyalty, they will be left with a diminishing number of customers. Corporations must be concerned with fairness, justice, and rights, rather than profit and loss.

,A happy medium must be sought where the public as well as corporation interests can be promoted. Ends as well as means must conform to ethical principles accepted by society. Corporations can no longer make excuses or try to justify unlawful actions. Changes must be implemented now.

There are two different paths a corporation can choose to take. It can turn its back on the entire issue and continue as it has in the past. Small changes might occur due to government intervention but the corporation will operate strictly out of social obligation. Another choice is to take voluntary action making it unnecessary for the government to intervene. Corporations can develop substitute materials and products. They can consider redesigning or restructuring their organization. They might also accept the stakeholder approach to bring about necessary political and legislative changes. These are just a few voluntary actions a corporation can implement to assure the public that it is socially responsive. In the long run this will help the survival of corporations because they will gain public trust.

Corporations are leaning toward social responsiveness. Corporate social responsibility is not merely limited to companies in the United States, but justly includes all U.S. interests in the international realm. Due to the rising concern displayed by society, corporations are currently engaged in the quest to match their corporate performance with the expectations of society.

NOTES

1. S. Prakash Sethi, "A Conceptual Framework for Environmental Analysis of Social Issues and Evaluation of Business Response Patterns, *Academy of Management Review* (January 1979): 63.

2. Milton Friedman, "The Social Responsibility of Business Is to Increase Its Profits," *New York Times Magazine* (September 13, 1970): 33.

3. Ibid.

4. Thomas M. Jones, "Corporate Social Responsibility Revisited, Redefined," *California Management Review*: 22 no. 2, (Spring 1980): 60.

5. Ibid., p. 65.

6. Ibid.

7. Ibid.

8. Christopher D. Stone, "Why Shouldn't Corporations Be Socially Responsible?" *Business Ethics* (1984): 133.

9. Ibid., p. 136.

10. Rogene A. Buchholz, "Social Responsibility Revisited," *Journal of Enterprise Management* (1982): 2.

11. Richard T. De George, "Can Corporations Have Moral Responsibility?" quoted in Tom L. Beauchamp and Norman E. Bowie, *Ethical Theory and Business* (Englewood Cliffs, N.J.: Prentice-Hall, 1983), p. 58.

12. Ibid., p. 60.

13. Ibid., p. 63.

14. Robert Boulanger and Donald Wayland, "Ethical Management: A Growing Corporate Responsibility—Part 2," *CA Magazine* (April 1985): 52–53.

15. Buchholz, "Social Responsibilty," p. 6.

16. Boulanger and Wayland, "Ethical Management," p. 59.

17. P. Sethi, "A Conceptual and Strategic Framework for Understanding Schism Between Business and the Academic Community: Developing Effective Response Patterns by the Business Community," *University of Texas at Dallas* (1980): 4.

18. Ibid., p. 14.

19. Ibid., pp. 21–25.

20. "Anderson Reflects on Managing Bhopal," *Industry Week* (October 13, 1986): 21.

21. Interview with David Burford, personnel manager of Penreco, February 1988.

22. Ibid.

23. Interview with William Johnston, vice president of First National Bank of Mercer County, February 1988.

24. Ibid.

25. Interview with Eric M. Scheid, district manager, Richman Brothers Clothing, February 1988.

26. Interview with Kenneth Calhoun, formerly of Alcoa, February 1988.

27. Ted Gest, Kenneth Sheets, and Ron Taylor, "As Lawyers Move in on India's Tragedy," *U.S. News and World Report* (December 24, 1984): 26.

28. William B. Glaberson and William Powell, "India's Bhopal Suit Could Change All the Rules," *Business Week* (April 22, 1985): 38.

29. Stuart Jackson, "Union Carbide's Good Name Takes a Beating," *Business Week* (December 31, 1984): 40.

12

Business Ethics: The Ideological Background

One of the more common issues confronting business today is that of the environment. Historically, industry's track record for dealing with the environment in a responsible, conscientious manner is far from impressive. Many are aware of the underlying economic principles that led to the abuse of the environment by business. For instance, U.S. industry has often been appalled by the idea that measures must be taken to reduce their polluting activities and that they must become responsible for the costs of such actions. Political action taken to rectify these practices has become one of the most common issues facing business. Faced with this new pressure of accountability, industry has displayed some very predictable reactions. In this chapter we will discuss how business values have changed over the years and ethical considerations in business.

BUSINESS VALUES

If practices such as lying and stealing were accepted as the norm, business could not operate. In addition, there has developed over time an informal code of standards that dictates what is and what is not good business practice. However, there are several areas in which it is highly debated whether the business world has a duty to act in accordance with certain ethical principles. Examples of such areas are: free speech and trade secrets, worker safety, deceptive advertising, environmental responsibility, discriminatory hiring, and business operation in countries with corrupt governments. There are essentially three broad perspectives from which scholars and businesspeople have tried to reconcile business with these issues. The conservative position asserts that the only role of business is to maximize profit, and it neither has the responsibility nor the right to take on these other issues. The moderate position seeks to unite moral and social responsibility with the pursuit of profit. This is now the strongest and most widely accepted position on business ethics in the United States. Finally, the liberal viewpoint believes that it is the capitalist economic system itself that makes business and ethics incompatible. Each of these positions contains both strengths and weaknesses, most of which depend upon the social and economic structure of the country being discussed.

THE LIBERAL POINT OF VIEW

The first perspective that we will discuss is the liberal point of view. According to this viewpoint, business (in a capitalist economy) is in and of itself unethical. One of the strongest arguments for this position comes from the well-known Karl Marx. Marx asserts that private property in a free market economy is unethical for three reasons.

First, profit instead of need becomes the motive for labor. This occurs because exchange leads to overproduction which in turn creates what Marx calls selfish need. Thus production becomes self-centered in nature.

Second, a free market economy leads to deception and fraud within the society in which it operates. This occurs because the individuals who are parties to an exchange are acting out of self-interest, and an individual's self-interest will always attempt to outdo that of another or relative gain will be sacrificed.

In hypothetically describing this relationship between trading parties, Marx puts himself in the shoes of one and states, "My social relationship with you and my labor for your want is just plain deception, and our mutual reintegration is deceptive just as well. Mutual pillaging is its base."[1]

Finally, and most important, business and ethics are irreconcilable in a capitalist society because people are treated as means instead of ends. This is an absolutist argument in that no outcome justifies using another person. Furthermore, Marx asserts that under a capitalist system, an individual tacitly consents to being used for others' purposes, though he may think he is merely pursuing his own. "But each of you actually does what the other thinks he is doing. You actually made yourself the means, the instrument and the producer of your own object in order to appropriate mine."[2] Thus, in a capitalist society, there exists a fundamental conflict between an individual's self-interest and the effect it has on his fellow man. When such a conflict leads to blatantly immoral practices, the liberal asserts that any form of ethical corporate social responsibility would be next to impossible to achieve.

THE MODERATE POINT OF VIEW

The next perspective on business ethics is that of the moderate. In relation to the United States, the moderate essentially accepts the free enterprise system as it is, but seeks to integrate new values into business (primarily corporate) goals and policy.

The moderates see this strategy as most appropriate and timely in light of public pressure on business to adhere to more than just the broad rules of competitive economic behavior. One such change in the rules that will make business more ethical in the eyes of society is that the external costs of doing business will no longer be permitted to be thrust on the public. Examples of such external costs are: environmental contamination, safety hazards in products caused by cost cutting, and the like. By internalizing these costs, prices will naturally rise, and consumers will bear the burden of such reform. This in turn will lead to change in the relative market positions of both industries and firms.

According to the moderate, another area in which more ethical practice will be forced on business is that of equal opportunity. Business will be expected to fill positions of responsibility with both disadvantaged minorities and women.

One of the most important points stressed by moderates when speaking of such a redesign of business's social contract is the manner in which it is implemented. The moderate position views it as vitally necessary for private management to play an active part in conjunction with external groups and government to reshape the current contract. Melvin Anshen says, "There can be no greater danger than to permit the new rules to be formulated by either the small group of critics armed only with malevolence toward the existing system or the much larger group sincerely motivated by concern for ameliorating social ills but grossly handicapped by their ignorance of the techniques and dynamism of private enterprise...."[3] Anshen goes on to suggest ways that private management can make contributions to this quest. One way is by evaluating technology and making cost estimates for rectifying such problems as environmental contamination. Another possibility is to initiate programs within the existing corporate structure that will enable disadvantaged people to be better educated and rise to higher positions. One possible way of organizing this with the profit motive in mind would be to shift the idea of defense contractor to the nondefense sector. Companies would bid on contracts aimed at improving social ills created by external costs. This has already been implemented in such areas as housing, education, and urban systems analysis and planning. The important point here is that any form of ethical business reform must take place in the context of the current economic system and the profit motive must remain intact.

THE CONSERVATIVE POINT OF VIEW

Finally, the last position to be scrutinized is that of the conservative. This argument can best be portrayed by using Adam Smith's invisible hand argument as an example. His argument is essentially one for no interference with the free market system whether it be of a moral or any other nature. If each individual seeks to maximize his own self-interest, then the collective interests of all would be better served than with any form of intervention.

Milton Friedman asserts that beyond obeying the law, the main responsibility of a business executive is to maximize profits. Another argument from the conservative perspective for a laissez-faire treatment of business in regard to ethics is that by giving preferential responsibility to social issues, business would be violating its primary responsibility to shareholders. "The stockholders or the customers or the employees could separately spend their own money on any particular action if they wished to do so. The executive is exercising a distinct social responsibility, rather than serving as an agent of the stockholders or the customers or the employees, only if he spends the money in a different way than they would have spent it."[4] Furthermore, business executives are not elected officials and do not possess the necessary expertise to determine what is or is not beneficial to society. A concrete example of the conservative position toward business ethics lies in some of the actions of the Reagan administration. By decreasing regulation in environmental and safety standards, as well as antitrust regulation, Reagan is essentially freeing business of major ethical restrictions.

The pronounced presence of poverty, pollution, discrimination, fraud, and overall corruption throughout business in this country indicates that there is a need to rework the social contract with business in some way. In order for any moral worth to come out of such an alteration, the basis of it must be morally commendable and feasible.

A capitalist economy is not inherently unethical (and hence morally blameworthy) in and of itself. Human nature, however, is indeed self-seeking, and man cannot be held morally responsible if and when he does not act in the best interest of the group of which he is a part. Therefore, a system must be created in which an individual's promotion of his own self-interest also contributes to the well-being of the entire group. A centrally planned or communistic economy would not fulfill this requirement. Furthermore, it would not be feasible or even possible for such a system to be introduced in this country due to its history and values. If such a system were instituted, moral atrocities far worse than those occurring now would take place.

However, the solution to the current ethical problems related to business is not found in the conservative position either. By letting business run wild, powerful individuals and corporations will only grow stronger at the expense of the weak and disadvantaged. Furthermore, society cannot continue to bear the kind of external costs business has been placing on it in recent years. Not only is the environment deteriorating, but upward social mobility is stagnating, and honest, ethical business practices are becoming harder and harder to find. Hence, even a mild hands-off policy such as the one pursued by the Reagan administration has both moral as well as tangible detrimental effects.

Perhaps the only way to reconcile business with more ethically acceptable practices is by taking the moderate approach. The reason for this essentially lies in the fact that moral behavior can be linked to the profit motive. Since the American public generally accepts and values the free market structure in principle, it would be reasonable to merely alter or regulate those aspects of the system considered morally wrong and harmful. Regulations to prevent pollution can be made, antitrust legislation can be stiffened, and most importantly, incentives can be provided, in the form of the profit motive, for companies to alleviate or prevent social ills caused by external costs of doing business. As can be seen in the case of public demand for American business divestiture in South Africa, society can impose morality on business, and is especially threatening when the profit motive is used as a weapon. In addition, with business's cooperation in the restructuring of the social contract, far more effective solutions can be found to unethical business practices than if reform were instituted unilaterally. In fact, it is only right that business participate in rectifying the social damage it has done. Norman Bowie refers to this as the principle of contribution. "If one contributes to a social harm, then one has a proportional obligation to contribute to its alleviation. Since business clearly does contribute to social problems, it has at least some obligation to correct them."[5] Hence, this type of solution leads to the most constructive and feasible moral outcome, and is morally praiseworthy in and of itself. Finally, it must be taken into account that U.S. business is by far the most powerful in the world. The moderate approach to increasing ethical business practices seeks to choke off business's undesirable and immoral side effects, while at the same time allowing its positive aspects to thrive. Few in this country would argue with the asumption that the underlyung roots of our capitalistic system such as the Puritan work ethic are morally praiseworthy.

There is substantial evidence in recent years that business participation in restructuring the social contract and correction of its own adverse effects on society is not just rhetoric or wishful thinking. Over the last ten years, General Motors has been perfecting the development of emissions systems on cars in an effort to curb air pollution. GM has actually gone well beyond the standards required by the EPA in this area. In the area of water pollution, businesses are researching ways of restoring lakes and rivers that have already been significantly contaminated. Union Carbide undertook several projects in the late 1970s aimed at cleaning up bodies of water in the New York State area.

Another example of such initiative can be seen in Westinghouse's decision to clean up six hazardous waste sites in Bloomington, Indiana, even though at the time it dumped capacitators containing PCBs there, it was not illegal. The real shocker is that it planned to make this action profitable. According to the June 3, 1985 issue of *Business Week,* the company planned to build an incinerator to destroy the chemicals. "The Pittsburgh company expects its

Table 12.1
Comparison of the Three Main Views

CONSERVATIVE	LIBERAL	MODERATE
Believes there should be no interference with free-market.	Assumes Business to be unethical.	Accepts free enterprise-system.
Each individual try to maximize own self-interest.	Profit is the motive for labor.	Seeks to integrate public values into business goals.
Main responsibility is to maximize profit for shareholders.	People are self-centered and go after their own self-interest.	Seeks private mngt, gov't, and public to reshape ethical standards.
Business doesn't know what is best for public and can't solve it's problems.	People are treated as a means instead of an ends.	External costs of cleaning up society not to be put on public.
Believes in decreased regulation of business.	Conflict between individuals self-interest and fellow mans.	Companies can bid to clean up social ills caused by external costs.

Bloomington incinerator to become a demonstration of its disposal technology. . . . "[6] and will hence attract customers from other municipalities which are running out of landfill space.

Environmental issues are not the only ones business has attempted to tackle. Many companies have taken on training programs for the hard-core unemployed, especially minorities and women. Some receive subsidies from the government to undertake such programs. Montgomery Ward and Westinghouse are just two examples of companies with well-designed training programs. Finally, another area in which business has taken initiative to renegotiate the social contract is in quality-of-work life issues. Some practices that private enterprise has initiated to improve the quality of work life are: instituting a four-day work week, flexible daytime hours, cafeteria-style compensation plans, and the establishment of special services like alcoholic programs.[7] The point is that business can and does take initiative to reform certain aspects of the social contract in the hopes that it will be perceived as more "ethical" by the public. If successful, profits can only rise. Table 12.1 compares the three main views.

In conclusion, it has become obvious that U.S. business faces serious challenges due to increased social pressure for morally responsible business behavior. Business people and corporations may either ignore the challenges, counterattack by educating people about the benefits that flow from the free market system, or integrate new values into corporate goals and policy. The last of these options is indeed the only viable one. Americans have lost confidence in the morality of business and business leadership. Gerald F. Cavanagh says, "Only a small minority of Americans now have confidence in business and business leadership. Enlightened self-interest continues to be clung to as the business ideology even though its effects are undermining the very institutions it is designed to preserve."[8] In order to stop this erosion and reverse its effects, moderate reform must take place. Radical reform could wipe out the good with the bad, and no reform could allow U.S. business to destroy itself. According to Cavanagh, "in the traditional American pragmatic fashion of incremental change, there are signs of hope."[9]

NOTES

1. David Braybrooke, *Ethics in the World of Business* (New Jersey: Rowman-Allan-held, 1983), p. 25.

2. Ibid., p. 26.

3. Tom L. Beauchamp and Norman E. Bowie, *Ethical Theory and Business* (Englewood Cliffs, N.J.: Prentice-Hall, 1979), p. 146.

4. Milton Friedman, "The Social Responsibility of Business Is to Increase Its Profits," *New York Times Magazine* (September 13, 1970): 3.

5. Beauchamp and Bowie, *Ethical Theory,* p. 150.

6. Ken Miller, "Westinghouse Makes Clean-Up Profitable" *Business Week* (June 3, 1985): 44.

7. Fred Luthans, Richard M. Hodgetts, and Kenneth R. Thompson, *Social Issues in Business* (New York: Macmillan, 1980), p. 119.

8. F. Cavanagh, *American Business Values in Transition* (Englewood Cliffs, N.J.: Prentice-Hall, 1976), p. 169.

9. Ibid., p. 170.

13

Contemporary Views of Business Ethics

The concern of business and society with business ethics has been a matter of heated debate in recent years. It is apparent from national dialogue and opinion polls that the American people have shown a growing distrust of the behavior of U.S. businesses in general and the large corporation in particular. There also appears to be a considerable difference between public expectations about business behavior and the views that corporate leaders espouse about their own activities. The traditional position of business disallows the notion of ethics in its pursuit of the mandated obligation to achieve profits while efficiently allocating resources. This point of view contends that to take on the ethical and social responsibility role would be playing God in an area that is not properly the domain of business. The opposite point of view, and one more frequently expressed in business literature today, describes managers' concerns about the ethical problems with which they are faced. They recognize their responsibility to reform their behavior or risk having weighty and nonmanageable standards imposed from elsewhere, especially from government.

The problem is complicated by the absence of a specific body of ethics to which all individuals and groups might refer for the resolution of conflict situations in which morality is involved. Most community, area, and institutional groups follow significantly different moral and ethical norms. Business, then, faces the problem of harmonizing its operations and objectives with the prevalent ethical code and somehow establishing priorities for any area of conflict.

DEFINITION AND MEANING

The word *ethics* comes from the Greek word *ethos* and has to do with character. Ethics is a word with many meanings. In one sense, ethics can be defined as a branch of philosophy that concerns itself with the moral concepts of right and wrong. It is "the principles of conduct governing an individual or group."[1] Business ethics concerns itself with the relationship between business goals and practices and the good of society.

Vincent Barry (1980) defines ethics as the moral conduct or the code one follows. Morality is the property of an action by which it conforms to a standard or norm of human conduct. In this case business ethics would be the moral conduct or code one follows within a business and these ethics could vary from business to business or industry to industry.

Rogene A. Buchholz (1986) refers to ethics as a conception of right and wrong in relation to human behavior. According to this, business ethics refers to the right and wrong behavior in business decisions. Therefore, whether to hire or fire employees, the manner of treating employees, deciding on the type of advertising, type of products, pollution, stock pricing and accountability to society, and the like are ethical decisions. In these decisions the concern should be what is morally right and wrong.

Ethical consideration is not necessarily included in every business decision. But, whenever human judgment is called for, standards of right and wrong enter into the picture.

JUSTIFICATION OF BUSINESS ETHICS

In the eighteenth century John Wesley once expressed what seemed to him a curious dilemma. He said that religion makes a man frugal, and frugality begets wealth. Wealth makes a man indifferent to religion, so it seems religion destroys itself.[2]

Wesley's observation lies at the heart of the conflict between present-day promoters of the "social responsibilities" of business and corporation leaders. Social critics have pronounced lack of ethical direction as the cause of this strife. Marquis Childs states this best, holding that the businessman has a drive to seek wealth, "but beyond the limited wants of bodily comfort he has no real sense of why he is seeking it, and while he searches there is built up an accumulated resentment over the abuses he is helping cause."[3] These abuses come in the form of water and air pollution, unfair hiring practices, profiteering, and illegal payments, to mention only a few. Most of the strife is being caused by the conflicting groups' ideas of ethical rightness, inextricably tied to religious and philosophical beliefs, and the extent of societal consideration owed by corporations.

John R. Schermerhorn, Jr., defines an ethical dilemma as a situation in which a manager "must choose whether or not to pursue a course of action that, although offering potential gain, is unethical in a broader social context."[4] Under a credo of social responsibility, a business would be held to follow the course of action favoring society. However, it is doubtful that many corporations' behavior is congruent with prevailing societal expectations. Most firms merely guide their conduct by the social obligations imposed on them by legal statute. Fewer yet are socially responsive, focusing on preventative actions to avoid adverse social impacts from company activities.[5] There are many extreme views on the limitations of business's responsibility to society. In his *Theory of Moral Sentiments,* Adam Smith held that "the wise and virtuous man is at all times willing that his own private interest should be sacrificed to the public interest or order of society."[6] This is not to say corporate leaders today are not virtuous. Business leaders are now only one of many with leadership capacity in huge companies that often have little or no ethical directives for employees to follow. These same employees are then evaluated in monetary terms that are reported to their superiors, promoting the most positive economic action. Milton Friedman further defines this action taken by executives as a mere response to the business owners' desire, which generally is to make as much money as possible while conforming to the basic rules of society. Furthermore, Friedman believes that social responsibility is the area of individuals, not corporations.[7]

In contrast to Friedman's extreme pro-profit ethical actions, Fletcher Byron, chairman of the Koppers Corporation, relates that profits to a company are like breathing to a person—"but breathing is not the sole purpose of life, and profits are not the sole purpose of . . . business management."[8] It appears, therefore, that some executives recognize the pressure that society is placing on them. However, society must also realize that profit, the basis of America's free market, is not a "bad" aspect of big business. ATT's chairman, Frederick Koppel, states that "when someone asked me, which do you put first in your mind, service or profits, I said naturally I put service first, but we can only serve by earning money."[9]

Many authors provide justification for current moral decisions made by executives. One of the best known is A. Z. Carr's tenet that the ethics of business are separate from societal ethics based in religion.[10] He further states that in these "game ethics," the closer a businessman comes to telling the truth, the more respect he should deserve—but as an individual, not a businessman. In a slightly different vein, H. B. Acton describes competition for the businessman as a "jungle situation," providing an ethical justification based on the Darwinian survival principle in a market of limited consumers, suppliers, and raw materials, Strictly interpreted, any decision an executive makes is considered appropriate if it insures the long-term survival of the business, regardless of societal impact.[11] Furthermore, William E. Peacock relates that businessmen quickly apply wartime ethics to business situations.

These principles of war and trade can be recalled by using the acronym MOOSEMUSS. The first *M* stands for mass—concentrating strength against an enemy's weak point. The first *O* is for objective. In war or business you have to be clear on just what you want to accomplish. The second *O* represents offense—the notion that few competitions are ever won by being passive. *S* stands for simplicity—the importance of making your strategy clear to all employees. *E* represents economy of force. In business you use the fewest resources practicable to keep the operation functioning while concentrating on the objective. The second *M* is for the maneuver or strategy used—frontal assault, flanking attack, and the like. *U* stands for unity of command—pinpointing responsibility. The last two principles starting with *S* are surprise and security—the practice of timing while keeping your strategy secret.[12] Peacock, however, fails to address the rights of civilians-consumers ultimately affected by the corporations' "military academy" ethics.

ARGUMENTS FOR AND AGAINST BUSINESS ETHICS

Business ethics is concerned with the ways in which people conduct themselves in the day-to-day activities of an organization and the morals and values that are implemented in this process. It is a cause for concern among managers who must monitor and oversee the activities of the organization. Managers face obligations and moral dilemmas when making business decisions each day. In order to avoid the pressures of strict government regulation, it is important for managers to practice good business ethics. Businesses today are aware of increasing social responsibility and the implications of their actions. As a result, sound business ethics must be implemented in organization operations in order to fulfill the expectations of society and the consumer.

On the other hand, arguments against business ethics exist. First, the free market argument states that if the market is left alone and everyone pursues their own self-interests, then the good of society will follow as the end result. Second, the loyalty of managers and employees to the owners of the company is the justification for the pursuit of the highest rate of return possible regardless of what they must do to maximize profits. The implication is that individuals are absolved of any ethical responsibility because they are merely doing what they were told to do. Third, there is an argument which states that business operates according to a special set of ethical principles that are different than the ethics of society. Because business is the main area of competition in our society, it has become somewhat of a game of strategy in which the rules are set by government and in which its strategy is implemented only to maximize profits without regard for the ethical ideals of society.

ETHICAL THEORIES

The two major ethical theories from which ethical principles are derived are the teleological and deontological theories. These two schools of ethical theory basically differ in their approach to determining the moral rightness or wrongness of an action. Both are rather broad theories that are not specific to business; nevertheless, the principles presented in each have definite applications to business ethics.

The teleological arena has utilitarianism as its most accepted member. Utilitarianism was most precisely defined and developed in England and the United States by Jeremy Bentham, James Mill, and most notably John Stuart Mill. This theory has apparently had a more lasting effect in intellectual circles than most other consequence-oriented theories, making it worthy of consideration in the development of a personal business ethics structure. The theory has as its prime tenet the idea of the "utility" of an action determining its moral worth or rightness. Utility is defined as the capacity of an action to produce pleasure or happiness. Thus, the goal or objective of this theory is to take an action that would utlimately produce the greatest amount of happiness for the greatest number of people. Intrinsic to this approach is the idea of minimizing the pain or wrong that results from an action. To apply the theory is extremely difficult because it embodies a mandate to somehow measure the "happiness" and "pain" that result from an action. The nature of those two qualities make measurement almost impossible.

However, Bentham and others felt that one could exactly sum all the pleasures on one side and all the pains on the other. If this sum was in favor of the pleasures, then the action was ethically right. Contemporary advocates of this theory favor a more generalized approach to the weighing of the pains and pleasures. One criticism of this approach has to do with the determination of exactly what can be defined as pleasure and what should be categorized as pain. In light of the complexity and interdependence of our modern society, the exact classification of something as pain or pleasure is very difficult to accomplish. In summary, the theory seems to be a refinement of the old adage "the end justifies the means."

Deontology is also a very broad area of ethics theory. It has many subdivisions, but all embrace common elements. In general the theory focuses on the right or wrong of an act itself regardless of the outcomes. It highlights the concept of duty or the following of moral dictates as the judgment of the right or wrong of an action. Thus, the value of a specific act lies in motive, not outcome. W. D. Ross popularized a facet of this theory that provided for the overriding of a duty by another related duty to facilitate the situational aspect of most ethical actions. This gave the theory a more far-reaching application. In summary, this theory seems to emphasize the inherent rightness or wrongness of an act on the basis of higher standard than the consequences of the act (i.e., duty, honesty, fairness, etc.)

PUBLIC OPINION

The debate over business's social responsibility to consumers first emerged shortly after the stock market crash in 1929, but experienced a lull until the early 1970s. At this point, a series of events beginning with the illegal payments made to the Nixon campaign during Watergate shook America's trust in large business. The oil embargo during 1974 was also questioned by consumers as a possible profiteering scheme. Furthermore, political kickback activities in various foreign countries were discovered in 1975. For example, Exxon admitted to paying $46 million alone to Italian parties. Public opinion fell still another notch with the rapid inflation and deep economic slump of 1973–1975.[13]

Polls conducted during this period supported the massive drops in consumer trust of big business. The Harris poll showed that in 1966, 55 percent of the public had "a great deal of confidence" in the heads of corporations, but in 1973 only 29 percent did. This further dropped to 21 percent in 1974 and 15 percent in 1975. Even more dramatic were the results of the Hanhelovich survey which showed the percentage of Americans that thought "business strikes a fair balance between profits and public interest." In 1968 this proportion of the population represented 70 percent, falling to 20 percent in 1974.

More recent polls conducted by the Gallup organization demonstrate that both the general public and business executives think ethical behavior is declining in the United States. Sixty-five percent of the general public think the overall ethics in society has declined in the past decade while only 9 percent think they have risen.

There are many theories as to why businesses have resorted to using unethical measures. Gerald L. Cavanagh notes that "values of spending, consumption, immediate gratification, and self-fulfillment, and the professional manager's goals of short-term return have had a more recent and profound influence on the business system."[14] Cavanagh further notes less savings activity and thereby less funds available for investment, causing a decrease in industry growth rates and productivity. It may be inferred, therefore, that these new values have put managers into some dilemmas when faced with meeting growth requirements, profit goals, and the like.

Furthermore, individuals ushered into large corporation structures are often just one more of the masses and are governed by the corporate norms regarding ethical behavior. Theodore Quinn believes personal relations found in smaller businesses are lacking, being replaced by strict regimentation and subordination in the giant corporations. Quinn further characterizes the prevalent attitude as "utter inhumanity of man toward man when the corporate interest is involved."[15] There is not room for individuals to make a difference in corporate social procedures while in low to middle management positions. Therefore, by the time the employee has reached a top-level position he has learned "the club ethic which sees, hears, and speaks no evil of fellow members."[16] Surveys do not support a climate of improvement, either. Sixty-five percent of the students polled perceived the current business arena as unethical, 50 percent felt that they would have no alternative but to compromise their ethics in certain dilemmas. Many students seem "all too willing" to give in to ethical pressures on the job.[17]

Businessmen are divided when it comes to the relevance of charges concerning their reported lack of ethics. Walter A. Haas, chairman of Levi Strauss, epitomizes the faction that holds that business ethics are merely indicative of society's ethics:

> To me this concern about business credibility is only a part of a much wider concern I have about general morality today. It occurs at all levels...a lack of concern for other people, an attempt to get away with all that you can get away with. I see this in every facet of society.... That the doubt about business credibility is part of a whole malaise of society disturbs me very much.[18]

Not all executives are that defensive, but even those who are concerned over the state of business morals are kept from criticizing other businesses for fear of worsening the general public opinion.[19] Ethical issues, however, have been found to be tied to key relationships in the organization structure. For example, employees engaging in purchasing activities encounter relatively more ethical dilemmas than their salaries or positions would indicate, based upon their outside contacts with bidding suppliers.[20] This is important in determining corporate policies to cover individual positions.

Those managers who support improved social responsibility of business cite the advantages of improved public image, longer viability, better environmental conditions, avoidance of governmental regulation, and stockholder interests as factors that support a social program. Strong resistance, based in claims of a loss of profits, lack of appropriate skills, dilution of primary purpose, and lack of any support system are hard to battle, however.[21]

Business Efforts

Business has been making efforts to address the question of ethical "rightness" in certain social areas. Most business activities have been geared to creating adequate voluntary measures, mostly internal codes of ethics, to prevent government regulation. These codes, however, are quite variable and are not readily verifiable as to their effectiveness. Buchholz also cites the hesitancy of some corporations to even adopt a code based merely on the fact that "ethical behavior is not necessarily rewarded in the marketplace."[22] Furthermore, not only does government have influence on business through its regulatory bodies like the Environmental Protection Agency (EPA), Occupational Safety and Health Administration (OSHA), and the Federal Aviation Agency (FAA), but business also influences the political arena. Interpersonal contacts, public relations campaigns, lobbying, direct candidate support, and illegal acts are tools corporations may use to sway politicians to their side of the social responsibility issue.[23]

The "economic illiteracy" of public officials, the undermining of industry's independence, and the likelihood of increasing socialistic tendencies are reasons executives cite to avoid governmental regulation.[24] Steps corporations have taken to address the issue of public responsibility are increasing in scope.

The earliest recognition of the problem was the formation of huge public relations departments to deal with public inquiry. No doubt, Friedman would proclaim this as mere window dressing on the part of corporations done merely to appease social responsibility groups. However, even more focused attention has beeen drawn to the issue by groups such as the Conference Board on business credibility. Organized and attended by representatives from Allied Chemical, Bethlehem Steel, Exxon, IBM, Motorola, and fifty other major U.S. firms, topics that have hurt business as a whole were discussed.[25]

Another reporting mechanism designed to evaluate social accomplishments of business is what Schermerhorn terms a "social audit," whereby actions such as resource commitment and performance in such areas as consumerism, community service, environment, and equal employment programs would be done. These audits would then become a basis for public relations work for the corporations.[26]

Of significant note, however, is the lack of overall corporate commitment to form individual business or industry codes like those found in accounting, medicine, and law. A study done by Brenner and Molander showed that 25 percent of respondents favored no ethics code at all, 58 percent preferred one dealing with general precepts, while only 17 percent preferred one dealing with industries. Furthermore, the belief in the effectiveness of codes of ethics in altering human behavior was not widespread. Sixty-one percent believed that people would violate the code whenever they could avoid detection, and only 41 percent believed the code would reduce unethical practices.[27]

This response does not indicate conditions conducive to internal policing of ethical decisions made by employees. Buchholz concedes that codes are most successful in narrow areas where there is "general agreement that certain unethical practices are widespread and undesirable, but do not, however, offer executives much hope for controlling outside influences on business ethics...."[28]

The advantages of having a code of ethics are that management's attention on vital problems becomes more focused, a degree of legal protection is provided, a justification for decisions made in an "ethical" manner is now readily available for employees, and identification of penalties for broken policies limits an employee's temptation. Unfortunately, Schermerhorn notes that internal barriers exist that prevent insiders from exposing unethical procedures within a company. These include fear of violating strict chains of command, fear of rejecting group norms, and uncertainty caused by ambiguous priorities stated in the code.[29]

In response to society's demands, business has taken some limited actions as mentioned earlier. The appropriateness and effectiveness of these actions have been vague. Nevertheless, Childs is convinced that today's businessmen are more concerned with social responsibility than their predecessors. He names force, persuasion, and the separation of ownership and control in large corporations as the reason for the change in attitude.[30]

The force Childs spoke of may be directly related to the more harsh penalties given corporations by government in whistleblowing cases. No longer can companies remain oblivious to effects on employees and society. Clearly, business has had to adapt to numerous government regulations, costing itself and consumers billions of dollars.

Logically, it seems businesses should be scurrying to develop adequate public responsibility/corporate ethics guidelines to maintain an even balance between the corporate drive for profits and society's demand for fair, even if extra, services.

Jaspan holds that morality is a relative item in U.S. business unlike in some foreign countries where it is independent from societal constraints. However, his application of ethics concerns corporations in the United States, and with that limitation, there is a distinct chance to change the "rules of the game."

Therefore, since the "rules of the game can be changed through law to raise the moral level of business practices, then indeed business ethics are not separate from the ethics of society as a whole."[31]

The Future of Business Ethics

As to whether business will assume a larger social role in the face of the recent spotlight put upon it, Keith Davis feels the public will ultimately make that decision based on the strength and duration of its demands. In any case, the present situation is not unusual in a free, democratic society. In fact, Childs says these tensions will continue as long as the United States has a "mixed" economy in which "the tradition of freedom and the tradition of social responsibility are kept in a healthy balance. They will not be automatically resolved by permitting government to take over everything, no, alternatively, by seeking to free the economic system from all involvement with government."[32] In confirmation of this view, Childs, citing Niebuhr, concludes that dogmatic presuppositions, whether laissez-faire dogmatics, or socialistic dogmatics, make for injustice, and the best societies have a mixture of strategies that seek to guarantee freedom on the one hand and justice on the other.[33]

Clearly, social responsibility is an issue that will require much time and thought to solve. There are no easy solutions. Yet the ease with which business makes the transition to provide public services in a "responsible" manner will mandate new obligations for other servants of consumers.

A CASE STUDY: INSIDER TRADING

"Greed is all right, by the way. I want you to know that. I think greed is healthy. You can be greedy and still feel good about yourself."[34] This is a quote from an address Ivan Boesky gave at the University of California at Berkeley in 1985. Ironically, greed led Ivan Boesky to be the center of the biggest scandal to hit Wall Street since its collapse in 1929. On November 14, the Securities and Exchange commission revealed that Boesky, one of America's richest and savviest stock market speculators, had been caught in an ongoing insider-trading probe.

Ivan Boesky arrived on Wall Street in 1966, where he was taken with a specialized form of stock speculation called risk arbitrage. Ideally an arbitrager buys up target stock in hopes of backing a successful takeover. By buying up the stock, the arbitrager helps the "raider" by increasing the price of the stock. If all goes well, the "raider" will have found enough backing to make a takeover bid. This too will increase stock prices. The arbitrager will then wait until the takeover battle becomes very heated. When it reaches this point, and the prices of the stock peak, the arbitrager dumps his stock on the market at a tremendous profit. Of course, if the takeover bid fails, the arbitrager stands to lose a great deal of money. This may sound a little shady, but in actuality it is perfectly legal. If an arbitrager stays within these boundaries, he is all right. Unfortunately Ivan Boesky did not.

Boesky was indicted for insider trading, which is when a person uses confidential information, not available to the general public, to make capital gains on the market. Specifically, Boesky would use tips concerning potential takeover bids to get in on the deal at rock bottom prices. He would then sell his stock at the most opportune moment, thereby making a substantial capital gain. This has been compared to playing poker with a marked deck.[35] The big question for the SEC was: Where did he get his information?

The answer to that question actually started the whole Boesky scandal. The investment banker's covert role began to surface as far back as May 1985. An anonymous letter from Caracas to the Merrill Lynch investment house alleged trading irregularities on the part of two of the company's employees in Venezuela, both of whom have since left the firm. After some discreet investigation, Merrill Lynch found that their employees were receiving inside information from a broker in New York. The broker's information came from a source at the Bahamas branch of the Swiss Bank Lue International. Merrill Lynch became very suspicious and alerted the SEC in June 1985.

The SEC began to pursue this case diligently. Because of a constant barrage of questions from the SEC, the authorities agreed to divulge the name behind the account number: Dennis B. Levine. Levine was a young investment banker from New York. People involved with his account at the bank realized his ability to pick winning stocks, especially concerning takeovers. They even began to copy many of his investments, but eased up as suspicion of insider trading began to rise. On May 12, the bank turned over evidence to the SEC concerning Levine's activities. Levine was arrested on insider-trading charges. Levine was employed by Drexel Burnham Lambert, Inc. as a managing director and a merger and acquisition specialist. That is how Levine in turn named Boesky as the man he was getting paid by to supply information. "Boesky, Levine claimed, agreed to pay him about 2.4 million dollars as a percentage of profits in return for the inside information. But Levine was arrested soon after and didn't get the money."[36] Although Levine apparently was not Boesky's only source of information, he alone was willing to testify against Boesky. At this point it would seem Boesky was in a lot of trouble, but the SEC thought they could use Boesky to catch some bigger fish—and this is where Boesky made one of his biggest deals.

The deal was that Boesky would let the SEC tap his phone for a period of two months, and that he would testify against any individuals or firms indicted as a result of the conversations. "In exchange Boesky...agreed to put $50 million in escrow for the benefit of investors harmed by his illegal trading. He also agreed to pay the U.S. Treasury a $50 million fine, the largest ever in a securities case and an amount equal to nearly half the SEC's annual budget."[37] He was barred from the investment business in the United States for life, though given up to sixteen months to settle his operations, and he still faces a possible five-year jail term. This announcement hit Wall Street on November 14, sending it into a panic.

Believing that Ivan Boesky was the only person in New York profiting from insider information is equivalent to believing the earth is flat. Boesky, who many have claimed was hardly a financial wizard, drifting from three different colleges before finally earning a degree from the Detroit College of Law, was able to obtain and use insider information. Does one really believe that raiders such as Pickens, Icahn, and Bass were able to get where they are on just brains and luck, and of course within the boundaries of the law? Is anyone on Wall Street honest? These are the questions that most Americans are asking.

It is likely that the Boesky scandal may lead to many other revelations of fraud. One of the main targets of new inquiries seems to be Drexel Burnham Lambert, Inc., which came under strong suspicion because of the financial backing it provided for several of Boesky's ventures. As the probe into these insider-trading deals increases, so does the momentum of many people who would like to see stricter regulations enforced on the market.

Currently, the laws on insider trading are very obscure. Most traders see them as sort of a nuisance or a joke. At the most, the laws only make traders a little more careful of where they get their information. The question seems to be whether new laws would infringe upon our free market system. Already the market has seen a decrease in activity following the Boesky scandal. People have begun trading in relatively risk-free securities as opposed to the more high-risk, high-return junk bonds. Is the age of the raider "tycoon" over?

Ivan Boesky broke the law when he bought stocks of takeover targets on tips from Levine. But Boesky did no wrong when he sold $440 million worth of securities before the Securities and Exchange Commission revealed its insider-trading charges against him, knowing full well that the prices almost certainly would fall after the incident. How could Boesky be guilty of a crime in the first case and innocent in the other? Because the SEC said so.[38]

The continuing insider-trading investigation has arbitragers wondering whether the SEC is coming after them next. With insider-trading rules being so vague, it is often very hard to answer this question. Congress has never passed a law specifically prohibiting insider trading, let alone defining it. The only thing written about it is the Securities Exchange Act (1934) that prohibits fraud in connection with the sale of securities. Because this is such a broad statement the commission is constantly amending the rules as it goes along, sometimes defining a new kind of insider trading after it brings up a case. Unlike the Supreme Court, which has no arm of enforcement and rests alone on its prestige, the SEC is "judge, jury, and prosecutor."[39]

The way the SEC used to define insider trading was fairly simple. A person violated the law if he bought or sold stock on the basis of material nonpublic information about his company. Information is material if it is something a reasonable investor would want to know before he buys or sells. That basic definition was held up by the Supreme Court in a landmark 1968 decision on an SEC case against executives of Texas Gulf Sulfur. The Gulf officers loaded up on the stock before the news broke to the public.

The Supreme Court has held in other cases that an outsider also violates the law when he trades on information from an inside tipster. This is where Boesky comes into the picture. It also held that such a tipster was in violation of the law. This is where Levine enters the picture.

The rules have become considerably more complicated as the SEC has expanded the definition of insider trading to include investors who are not insiders and who trade on information that may not be material to the ongoing business of a company. "In 1980 the SEC adopted Rule 14e–3, which makes it illegal for anyone with inside information about a takeover to trade the target company's stock."[40] This means that an investor is in violation of the rule even if he does not get the information directly from an insider. He simply has to "know or have reason to know" that the information came from an insider.

Rule 14e–3 is just what Boesky violated. Levine gave him advance word on takeovers and Boesky bought stocks of the target companies. When the stocks went up, Boesky's "ship came in" with enormous profits. Boesky sealed his guilt by agreeing to share part of the profits with Levine, making it undeniable that he believed Levine was furnishing him with real inside information, not just Wall Street gossip.

"That son of a bitch is outrageous" stated one angry arbitrager when he received news of Boesky's scandal.[41] Though Boesky will plead guilty to a criminal charge that could put him in prison for five years, some Wall Street people say he got off easy. Boesky was allowed by federal law to liquidate at least $440 million in holdings. These include Time, Inc., USX Corp., Gillette Co., Holiday Corp., Copper Vision, Inc., and Public Service Co. of Indiana, all of which are known or rumored to be takeover targets. The proceeds have been used to reduce the margin debt of the fund, Ivan F. Boesky and Co., to $240 million from $680 million, according to the law firm of Choate, Hall and Stewart, which is acting on behalf of Boesky's investment partnerships.[43]

The SEC's review of the timely sales indicates the losses that Boesky's investment partners avoided were "substantially less" than some news reports of $40 million. In effect, Boesky avoided the market slump caused by the news of his own spectacular downfall. "This may be the best insider information he ever received," steamed one senior Wall Street trading executive.[43]

Boesky's case has brought horrendous losses for some stock market speculators, but it promises to bring a windfall for stock market lawyers. As the scandal reaches into Wall Street's top investment banks and law firms, white-collar criminal defense lawyers have been swamped with calls from prospective clients. Some people on Wall Street jokingly are referring to the Boesky scandal as "the Criminal Lawyer Employment Act."[44]

The 1980s have been a time of unusual activities on Wall Street. A new breed of traders constantly tries to take over other companies. Many new terms have come from these activities. The creation of junk bonds by raiders helps them to raise large sums of money and enables them to succeed in their takeover bids. There is also the practice of greenmail, which has become prevalent in many corners of the financial world. These practices may soon be a memory if new regulations are passed.

A final note concerning Boesky's scandal: three days before the SEC announced the indictment of Boesky, they permitted him to dump $440 million dollars of his portfolio onto the market, knowing that when the announcement came, the price of high risk securities would drop. Boesky got caught beating others out of profits, so the SEC let him get rid of $440 million before the bottom fell out of the market. In addition, he can write off nearly half of his $100 million fine on his taxes. Is it fair that when a person robs a liquor store for a few dollars and gets caught, he stands to go to jail for up to fifteen years, while Ivan Boesky, who made millions illegally, will go to jail for five years? Is this justice?

NOTES

1. Webster's New Collegiate Dictionary, 7th ed. (New York: Harper and Row, 1981), p. 468.

2. Marquis Childs and Douglass Cater, *Ethics in a Business Society* (New York: Harper and Brothers, 1954), p. 83.

3. Ibid., p. 86.

4. John R. Schermerhorn, Jr., *Management for Productivity* (Carbondale, Ill.: John Wiley and Sons, 1984), p. 663.

5. Ibid., p. 671.

6. Childs and Cater, *Ethics,* p. 121.

7. Milton Friedman, "The Social Responsibility of Business Is to Increase Its Profits," *New York Times Magazine* (September 13, 1970): 33, 122–26.

8. Leonard Silk and David Vogel, *Ethics and Profits* (New York: Simon and Schuster, 1976), p. 160.

9. *The Executive Opinion,* (New York: Doubleday, 1970); quoted in Silk and Vogel, *Ethics and Profit,* p. 161.

10. Albert Z. Carr, "Is Business Bluffing Ethical?" *Harvard Business Review* (January–February 1968): 143–53.

11. H. B. Acton, *The Morals of Markets* (London: Longman Group, 1971), p. 33.

12. Quoted in Silk and Vogel, *Ethics and Profit,* pp. 17–19.

13. Ibid., pp. 20–21.

14. Childs and Cater, *Ethics,* p. 90.

15. Norman Jaspan, *Mind Your Own Business* (Englewood Cliffs, N.J.: Prentice-Hall, 1974), p. 35.

16. John A. Pearce, III, "Newcomer's Need for a Code of Ethics," *Collegiate Forum* (Fall 1978): p. 12; cited in Schermerhorn, *Management,* p. 682.

17. Silk and Vogel, *Ethics and Profit,* p. 27.

18. Ibid., p. 25.

19. Rogene A. Buchholz, *Business Environment and Public Policy* (Englewood Cliffs, N.J.: Prentice-Hall, 1982), p. 91.

20. Schermerhorn, *Management,* pp. 671–72.

21. Buchholz, *Business Environment,* p. 88.

22. Schermerhorn, *Management,* pp.677–78.

23. Silk and Vogel, *Ethics and Profit,* p. 51.

24. Childs and Cater, *Ethics,* p. 99.

25. Schermerhorn, *Management,* p. 680.

26. Buchholz, *Business Environment,* pp. 98–99.

27. Ibid., p. 99.

28. Ibid., p. 99.

29. Schermerhorn, *Management,* p. 680.

30. Childs and Cater, *Ethics,* p. 98.

31. Buchholz, *Business Environment,* p. 84.

32. Keith Davis, quoted in Schermerhorn, *Management,* p. 673.

33. Childs and Cater, *Ethics,* p. 134.

34. Larry Martz, "True Greed," *Newsweek* (December 1, 1986): 40–50.

35. George Russell, "Going After the Crooks," *Time* (December 1, 1986): 52.

36. David Pauly, "The SEC Bags Ivan Boesky," *Newsweek* (November 24, 1986): 68.

37. Ibid.

38. Monci Jo Williams, "What's Legal—and What's Not?" *Fortune* (December 22, 1986): 36.

39. Ibid., p. 37.

40. Ibid.

41. Ford S. Worthy, "Boesky's Web," *Fortune* (December 22, 1986): 27.
42. Russell, "Going After the Crooks," pp. 50–56.
43. Ibid., pp. 48–56.
44. Powell, Bill, "Wall Street's Top Cop," *Newsweek* (March 2, 1987): 48–50.

14

The Foreign Corrupt Practices Act

The foreign payments controversy erupted in the early 1970s as a result of the Watergate investigations and the Securities and Exchange Commission's investigations into questionable practices of corporations with regard to payments in foreign countries for political or business purposes. During this period, a new awareness evolved in business ethics.

Ethics can be defined as the principles of conduct that govern a person or a group, enabling that individual or group to decide whether a certain act or policy is morally right or wrong. In most cases, this is an easy judgment to make. On the other hand, some ethical judgments are far more difficult. Values and priorities may provide a different scope of interpretation, even though a complete description of the situation is not always available, and stressors on the individual can lead to exaggerations, bluffing, and deceptions. Americans are almost compelled to cynicism and doubt with regard to controversial and ethical positions. Because it is often difficult to agree on ethical norms, individuals often put ethics aside.

Behind unethical or illegal acts is the desire to have results. Management is often under pressure to provide immediate results and short-term perspectives. Unethical behavior can be conditioned or encouraged by the organizational climate and expectations. One company survey reported that managers do feel pressure to compromise personal ethics to achieve corporate goals. Young managers may automatically go along with their superiors to show loyalty.[1] These managers, each functioning on a different corporate level, are concerned with one thing: getting the job done. Most companies give awards for achievement and accomplishment, for sales, growth, longevity, and loyalty, but none for honesty, compassion, or truthfulness.

A bribe is a payment made to induce the payee to do something for the payer that is improper and is an inducement to any person acting in an official or public capacity to violate or neglect his or her public duty. Bribes subvert the laws of supply and demand and result in free markets being replaced by contrived markets. The foreign payments controversy has many ethical implications related to honesty and fairness. Foreign payments were deemed unfair, unethical methods of competition. Honesty is essential to the moral foundation of a free enterprise system. This is why bribery is unethical and illegal.[2]

Our sense of ethics grows out of our past. We learn what is right and wrong early in life, and these notions mature as we gather new evidence and experiences. At each stage, we are heavily influenced by our environment. As with cultural values, so too with ethical values, it is easier for us to see the ethical blind spots of other people. This is also true of corporate bribery abroad, which will be the focus of this chapter.

In the aftermath of Watergate, it was discovered that many U.S. corporations had made questionable or illegal domestic and foreign payments in order to obtain or maintain business. In many cases these payments were concealed by falsifying records and maintaining off-the-book accounts.

The Foreign Corrupt Practices Act was enacted on December 19, 1977, in order to prohibit the maintaining of slush funds and the payment of bribes to foreign officials. In an era in which business ethics was a popular theme, it was the intent of Congress to use the act as a means of increasing corporate accountability.

The act's impact is much broader than its title suggests. There are two provisions: the accounting provision and the antibribery provision.

The accounting provision of the law amends the Securities and Exchange Act of 1934 to require companies, among other things to:

1. Make and keep books, records, and accounts, which, in reasonable detail, accurately and fairly reflect the transactions and disposition of the assets of the issuer
2. Devise and maintain a system of internal accounting control sufficient to provide reasonable assurances that
   a. Transactions are executed in accordance with management's general or specific authorization
   b. Transactions are recorded as necessary to permit preparation of financial statements in conformity with generally accepted accounting principles or any other criteria applicable to such statements, and to maintain accountability for assets
   c. Access to assets is permitted only in accordance with management's general or specific authorization
   d. The recorded accountability for assets is compared with the existing assets at reasonable intervals and appropriate action is taken with respect to any differences.[3]

This portion of the act is considered by members of the legal and accounting professions to be the most significant expansion of the Securities Exchange Act since its enactment.[4]

The provisions directly affect all U.S. companies that are registered or file reports with the Securities and Exchange Commission under the Securities Exchange Act of 1934. Over ten thousand publicly held companies are involved. In addition, the act applies to domestic as well as foreign transactions. The antibribery provision of the act makes it a criminal offense for any U.S. business to pay money or give anything of value to a foreign official, foreign political party, or any candidate for foreign political office for the purposes of influencing any act or decsion, including a decision to fail to perform official functions. However, the law does not cover facilitating payments (also known as "grease" payments). While payments to foreign officials are considered corrupt and illegal, payments made to clerks to facilitate are not illegal—or at least are not noted to be illegal under this act. Under this act, it is also considered illegal to offer money or anything of value to anyone while having reason to know that a part of all of the money or object of value will be used for the purpose of influencing an act, decision, or indecision.

REASONS FOR THE FOREIGN CORRUPT PRACTICES ACT

During the 1970s, questionable payments made to foreign government officials by U.S. corporations were being widely exposed to the government and the public. The Watergate scandal marked the beginning of several questionnaires and acts forcing corporations to expose all payments given to obtain or retain business. "Foreign payments are defined as any transfer of money or anything of value made with the aim of influencing the behavior of politicians, political candidates, political parties, or government officials and employees in their legislative, administrative, and judicial actions."[5] Most payments are used to obtain business over competition, avoid foreign governments, and reduce taxes on export or custom clearances. "In 1974, the Securities and Exchange Commission, (SEC), announced that any company which made illegal political contributions or other foreign payments should disclose that fact to its shareholders and to the commission."[6] Hundreds of corporations were subject to the jurisdiction of the SEC and a large percentage, approximately 527 U.S. corporations abroad, admitted to making payments to foreign officials for the purpose of influencing the flow of business. Bribery became a national scandal.

Large firms such as Lockheed and Exxon admitted to corrupt payments and were among the highest in payoffs: Exxon ($59.4 million), Lockheed ($55.0 million), Boeing ($50.4 million), and General Tire and Rubber ($41.3 million). These payoffs were made over a six-year period.[7] Through these bribes, corporations were able to obtain an unfair advantage over their U.S. competitors overseas. Corporations that played by U.S. standards found themselves excluded from foreign markets due to other U.S. corporations extending exorbitant monetary gifts to foreign officials that influenced markets.[8] Not only did bribery upset the foreign markets, but customs officials in other countries are paid low wages in the expectation that their income would be supplemented by payments from foreign corporations.

The American public felt that bribery tarnished American democracy in foreign countries and therefore was destructive to the best interests of foreign policy. Bribery was incompatible with American ethical standards.

In 1977, the Carter administration passed the Foreign Corrupt Practices Act (FCPA). This act makes it a crime for U.S. corporations to offer or provide payments to officials of foreign governments for the purpose of obtaining or retaining business. The act also required all publicly held corporations to keep appropriate records in order to make it difficult to conceal political payments. Although many firms have prohibited "grease" payments, the FCPA does not cover this form of payment. "Grease" payments do not influence decisions or create an advantage over competition. "Grease" payments may be advantageous to a corporation because they encourage recipients to perform normal duties. Corporations which violate the FCPA face enormous penalties. A corporation may be given a fine up to $1 million and the officers involved may be imprisoned up to five years with or without $10,000 in fines.

INITIAL RESPONSE OF THE PROFESSION

The immediate response of CPA firms was in keeping with the spirit of the law. For example, Arthur Andersen & Co. issued a subject file rider two days after the act became law, detailing the prohibition of payments to foreign officials, defining punishment for violators, and recommending the adoption of corporate codes of conduct and compliance with the law.[9] Although the accounting provisions were mentioned, no suggestions for their implementation were made.

In August 1977, before the FCPA became law, the American Institute of Certified Public Accountants (AICPA) had established a special advisory committee to develop criteria for evaluating an entity's system of internal control. The committee took on new meaning with the passage of the act. On September 15, 1978, the committee issued its preliminary report, urging companies to reexamine the accounting control procedures in place and to continue to do so on an ongoing basis. More explicit documentation of such procedures was emphasized. The committee urged involvement at the level of the board of directors and a strong control environment to discourage management overrides of the system. Increased utilization of internal auditors was also suggested.

EVALUATING INTERNAL CONTROLS

Many corporations turned to their auditors for assistance, and major CPA firms began to develop strategies to aid clients in the evaluation of internal controls. Their approach was one of education concerning the provisions of the act. Then the auditors produced revised audit procedures intended to examine internal control systems, identify weaknesses, and at the same time, document systems. This would allow the client some defense if the client should be called upon to demonstrate compliance with the FCPA.

These services went beyond those performed in the course of the normal audit. It was often to the advantage of the corporation to enlist the services of an independent auditor in such an evaluation because the auditor was already familiar with the corporation's system and developed a systematic approach to the problem. An example of a method of dealing with internal control is Haskins' & Sell's "control set," which consists of an internal accounting control questionnaire of forty-four double-width pages, an evaluation summary, a set of decision tables indicating possibilities for errors and irregularities, and suggestions for their elimination.[10] Flexibility is a necessary characteristic of any approach because of the diversity in operations and structure among clients. A survey of Fortune 500 companies indicated that 89 percent of the respondents had expanded their internal documentation effort to comply with the act.[11] However, since 1977, the FCPA has continually come under criticism by U.S. businesses because of its ambiguity. Many critics charge that the act discourages U.S. export trade because its provisions are difficult to interpret and enforce. As a result, many U.S. businesses avoid overseas transactions for fear of breaking the law, resulting in a much less efficient market.

As has been previously mentioned, the FCPA made it a criminal offense to pay bribes of any sort to foreign officials to secure or obtain business abroad. Since heavy fines, jail sentences, and accounting legislation were all incorporated into the act it made it virtually impossible to disguise such payments and enable U.S. corporations to maintain their business overseas. This legislation caused many side effects, the first of which is the ambiguity factor. Second, since the ordeal with Lockheed brought global bribery to the headlines in the post-Watergate era, many companies became quite conservative in their export efforts and adopted a policy of retrenchment to appease both management and stockholders. Third, the act placed U.S. firms at a distinct disadvantage in relation to their competition because foreign entrepreneurs would not even consider them unless a payment was involved. Next, investigation and prosecution on the part of U.S. firms often brought foreign officials and businessmen into the media spotlight which caused chagrin on the part of both parties in their respective countries. Finally, the act has also caused law-abiding firms to proceed with extreme caution, and many profitable and legitimate transactions were often avoided in order to insure that no violation of the act was committed. As a result of all these side effects that resulted in inefficiency, reduction of overseas contracts, and exports, U.S. businesses began to pressure Congress into reissuing the FCPA so that it provided more freedom for them.

In 1981, they received encouragement when the Reagan administration endorsed the Business Practices and Records Act, a bill that redefined the accounting standards and helped remove some of the ambiguity from the FCPA. The bill stated that "payments which are customary in the country where they are made and intended to secure prompt performance of a foreign official's duties would not be actionable."[12] However, "any payment for the purpose of getting a foreign official to act in violation of the recipient's legal duty as a public servant would be judged a violation of U.S. law."[13] The bill was also in favor of removal of criminal liability for failure to comply in the accounting standards, as long as they did not significantly alter the company. These stipulations along with the fact that many U.S. companies set up partnership arrangements with foreign companies so they could make the payments, have helped to increase business action abroad.

Although the Business Practices and Records Act was encouraging, it did not mean that Congress would continue to ease up on the restrictions of the original FCPA. Congress is very hesitant to take action on this act. Because of this, many critics feel that any loosening of the restrictions of the original FCPA are unlikely. The following section elaborates on this point of view, and also provides some different perspectives on this issue.

BUSINESS PERCEPTIONS OF THE FOREIGN CORRUPT PRACTICES ACT

The *Columbia Journal of World Business* conducted a survey in April 1981 to determine whether or not Fortune 500 firms felt the act should be repealed. The data was recorded by Suk H. Kim in "On Repealing the Foreign Corrupt Practices Act: Survey and Assessment," which appeared in the fall 1981 issue. The questionnaire was sent out by mail to all of the firms on the Fortune 500 Largest Industrial Corporations List. Two hundred and thirteen corporations returned the questionnaire, giving a response rate of 42.6 percent. This is relatively high and removes some of the risk of nonresponse bias. Through preliminary questions, the analyzers of the survey were able to determine how the questions were answered by relatively well-informed personnel. The results were as follows.

Sixty-four percent felt that the act should be repealed for various reasons that will be discussed further. Twenty-one percent felt that immediate action should be taken to change the act significantly, and 13 percent felt it should be retained.

The first reason firms found for the repeal of the FCPA was that the act puts U.S. companies at a competitive disadvantage. Eighty-three percent of the 213 firms felt that U.S. companies were at a disadvantage. Twenty-six percent claimed a loss of substantial foreign sales as a direct result of the act. These losses were estimated at 2 to 51 percent of total foreign sales. For example, in 1980, it was reported by the U.S. embassy in Muscat, Oman, that a U.S. firm lost a $20-to-30-million deal mainly because of lengthy delays while the application of the act regarding this transaction was being researched.

A second reason for the repeal of the act is the substantial increase in audit costs. Increases in the size of audit staff took place in 39 percent of the respondents. Eighty-nine percent had increased the internal accounting documentation in order to comply with the act which is very vague as to accounting responsibilities. In 62 percent of the firms, the "cost of compliance" far exceeded the "benefit of compliance."

National legislation on foreign payments was the third reason for the repeal. Business executives felt that their companies faced double-jeopardy. They were under the jurisdiction of both the SEC and the Justice Department. Seventy-two percent believed that such legislation and monitoring agencies only exist in the United States. In many countries, foreign payments are legalized and encouraged. The firms suggested "that to put the U.S. exporters on an equal competitive footing with foreign companies, Congress should scrap the act and seek an international forum to solve a world-wide problem of corrupt business practices."

Lastly, 69 percent felt that the SEC failed to clarify the act and instead used such vague terms as "reasonable assurance" and "reason to know." Bills have been introduced in Congress to clarify the act. Senator John Chafee's bill (S. 2763) introduced in May 1981, calls for the Justice Department to be the sole enforcer of the act and for the act to include a "materiality" standard in section 102. Chafee feels that the bill will not compromise the act, but clarify the confusion and ambiguity. The article concluded that the bills should be extended further to repeal the FCPA.[14]

Another article, "Foreign Corrupt Practices: A Manager's Guide," brings in a new view of the act. This study indicates that the act has not had a negative effect on U.S. trade. This article points out that the evidence used to support the opposite hypothesis has been found through opinion surveys of the executives. However, published trade statistics and other government reports of 1980 provide data to test the above hypothesis on "competitive disadvantage." The results of this test indicate that the FCPA has not negatively affected the competitive position of U.S. industry in the world marketplace.

During 1980, the Commerce Department consulted U.S. foreign service posts on their views, and responses were received from fifty-one embassies, representing countries accounting for 80 percent of total U.S. exports in 1979. Nineteen percent believed the FCPA put the United States at a competitive disadvantage due to uncertainty and the lack of clear guidelines. Based on the responses of the embassies, the fifty-one countries were classified into two groups. Group 0 consisted of the countries where FCPA was not seen as a disadvantage and Group I consisted of countries where the FCPA was listed as a disadvantage. This classification was double-checked with a geographical scheme and suggests that improper payments are more common in some countries than others. The Business Periodicals Index and the Wall Street

Journal Index were also consulted, thus adding reliability to the grouping classification.

Finally, the article stated that if bribery has no effect on the firm's competitive performance, then a law discouraging firms from using bribery will have no negative effect on their competitive performance. This study indicated that improper foreign payments were at the least unnecessary and probably counterproductive.[15]

THE AUDIT COMMITTEE

There are two types of audit committees. The first type is a functioning body; the second is a sham. An outcome of the FCPA and the "ethics movement" in general was an increase in the number of functioning audit committees and an expansion of their involvement in evaluation of internal accounting controls. A 1981 survey of audit committee activities revealed that 67 percent of audit committees reviewed their company's compliance with the FCPA.[16] Failure to do so might be viewed by the SEC as a weakness in internal accounting control under the act. It has become the practice of many audit committees to discuss internal controls with internal and independent auditors, review the findings of the auditors, discuss improvements with management, and review procedures for determining the effectiveness of the company's code of conduct.

COST-BENEFIT RELATIONSHIP

Critics of the FCPA have claimed that compliance with the act involves substantial increases in audit costs. Much of this increased spending has been in the area of internal auditing.

Independent auditors find that the initial cost of documenting the system involves a one-time additional expense. After that procedure has been completed, audit costs may even become lower, since the auditor is better able to rely on the system of internal controls, and may be able to reduce subsequent testing in the source of the audit.

The FCPA does not contain a materiality standard, which means that strict interpretation of the law will result in costs that are much greater than the benefits derived. This issue of accuracy versus materiality can make compliance with the act expensive. The legislative history of the act has supported the application of a cost-benefit relationship. The Senate Committee on Banking, Housing and Urban Affairs has recognized that this relationship is valid and urged accountants to use their professional judgment in evaluation of the systems maintained by issuers.[17]

CURRENT DEVELOPMENTS

There have been recent attempts to alter the provisions of the FCPA. Senator John Chafee has introduced a bill to include a materiality standard, recognize the cost-benefit concept of controls, and limit penalties to known violators. The AICPA generally supports such a bill. The Reagan administration goes beyond this position, to oppose the continuation of the accounting and record-keeping provisions. It is unlikely that such sweeping changes will be made, but the result has been a lessening of administrative efforts with regard to the act. The Reagan administration proposed the Trade, Employment and Productivity Act of 1987 which would clean up the unnecessarily vague "reason to know" standards, amend the FCPA to specify types of payments that would be exempt from the act, and clarify the FCPA requirements to keep books, records, and accounting obligations not separate but part of the overall obligation.[18]

SUMMARY

The Foreign Corrupt Practices Act has been in effect for ten years. It no longer champions a popular issue, and it lacks administrative support. The act is, in essence, a relic. However, the FCPA has been responsible for changes in the accounting practices of reporting corporations and revisions in the role of the independent auditor.

The act made section 320.28 of SAS a federal law. It required SEC companies to examine their accounting systems with particular emphasis on internal accounting control. CPA firms adopted the role of educator with respect to the accounting provisions, working with more involved audit committees to comply with the act. It gave auditors support in their encouragement of improvements in clients' control systems. Independent auditors frequently played a major role in the documentation of such control systems. The final result was a system that could be relied upon to reduce testing during the conduct of the audit.

FINAL REMARKS

The repeal of the Foreign Corrupt Practices Act is a matter of debate. One possible solution would be to seek an international forum to solve the worldwide problem of corrupt practices. The main problem with this solution is getting all countries to agree that corrupt practices are a problem. Not everyone will agree with the United States on this issue. A second possibility is to keep the act. If one goes by the idea that we should play by the rules of the country in which we are, this act is not applicable. The act as is carries too many ambiguities that are costing companies many, many dollars in their broad accounting practices. Although we tend to believe that firms should act within the law of the country in which they are doing business, we came to the conclusion that the repealing of the act is unrealistic. Senators are not going to repeal an act against bribery and have their constituents think that they are in favor of bribery. The solution seems to be what is already taking place. Bills should be passed that give strict, easy-to-understand guidelines that explain the needed accounting practices and the "reason to know" clause. If there must be an act, clarify it and put it under the jurisdiction of one judicial body.

NOTES

1. "The Pressure to Compromise Personal Ethics," *Business Week* (January 31, 1977): 107.

2. Rogene A. Buchholz, *Business Environment and Public Policy* (Englewood Cliffs, N.J.: Prentice-Hall, 1982), pp. 84–88.

3. Deloitte Haskins and Sells, *Internal Accounting Control—An Overview of the DH&S Study and Evaluation Techniques* (1979), p. 40.

4. Manuel A. Typgos, "Compliance with the Foreign Corrupt Practices Act," *Financial Executive* (August 1981): 46.

5. Buchholz, *Business Environment,* p. 84.

6. Ibid., p. 86.

7. "Business without Bribes," *Newsweek* (February 19, 1977): 63–64.

8. William Proxmire, "The Foreign Payoff Law Is a Necessity." *New York Times* (February 5, 1978): 16F.

9. Arthur Andersen & Co., *Subject File Rider—President Carter Signs Foreign Corrupt Practices Act of 1977* (December 21, 1977): 1.

10. Deloitte Haskins and Sells, *Internal Accounting Control,* p. 6.

11. Suk H. Kim, "On Repealing the Foreign Corrupt Practices Act: Survey and Assessment," *Columbia Journal of World Business* (Fall 1981): 18.

12. "Administration Backs Changed Bribery Law," *Time* (March 16, 1981): 22.

13. Ibid.

14. Kim, "On Repealing," pp. 16–20.

15. John L. Graham, "Foreign Corrupt Practices: A Manager's Guide," *Columbia Journal of World Business:* 89–94.

16. Coopers & Lybrand, *Audit Committee Guide, Third Edition* (1982): 23.

17. J. Michael Cook and Thomas P. Kelly, "The Foreign Corrupt Practices Act Has Made the Internal Accounting Controls of Public Companies a Matter of Law," *Journal of Accountancy* (January 1979): 58.

18. "Assuring America's Competition Preeminence," *Business America* (March 2, 1987): 6.

15

Business-Government Relationships

INTRODUCTION

In the past two decades, there has been a substantial increase in public concern over business behaviors and the protection of the environment. The first instance came in 1887 when the Interstate Commerce Commission (ICC) was formed to regulate U.S. railroads. The government has taken an increasingly active role in regulating the economy. The relations between government and business have never been easy, but in recent years their difficulties have increased as each has grown in power and complexity. A major change in the relationship between government and the private sector has taken place, with highly significant political, legal, social, and economic implications. Archie B. Carroll states that "in recent years . . . the depth, scope, and direction of government's involvement in business affairs have become hotly debated issues of modern times."[1] This chapter will discuss the relationship between business and government in order to provide a better understanding of the nature and scope of this relationship. To thoroughly describe such a complex relationship would require numerous volumes. Therefore, this chapter will focus only on the development of business–government relations in the United States, the regulatory process, the major problems, and the future of this relationship.

VIEWS OF BUSINESS–GOVERNMENT RELATIONSHIPS

According to Rogene A. Buchholz, the volume of the regulations affecting business is so great that it is difficult today to find an area of business that is untouched by government regulation. John P. Davis calls for less government

Table 15.1
Federal Regulatory Agencies Staffing (Fiscal Years, Permanent Full-Time Positions)

Area of Regulation	1984	1985	1986	(estimated) 1987	1988
SOCIAL REGULATION					
Consumer Safety & Health	55,521	54,395	53,764	55,155	54,592
Job Safety & Other Conditions	15,570	14,577	14,303	14,554	14,409
Environment & Energy	16,835	18,373	19,134	20,556	20,598
TOTAL-Social Regulation	87,926	87,345	87,201	90,265	89,599
ECONOMIC REGULATION					
Finance & Banking	9,697	9,763	10,972	12,828	13,854
Industry-Specific Regulation	5,715	4,969	4,792	4,927	4,930
General Business	8,841	9,026	9,136	9,167	9,654
TOTAL-Economic Regulation	24,253	23,758	24,900	26,922	28,438
GRAND TOTAL	112,179	111,103	112,101	117,187	118,037

Source: Center for the Study of American Business, Washington University. Derived from the Budget of the United States Government and related documents, various fiscal years.

intervention. He emphasizes that the best government is the least involved government. Neil H. Jacoby classifies the relationship between business and government as an "adverse relationship." He adds that government officials look upon themselves as probers, inspectors, taxers, and publishers of business's transgressions. Businesspeople view government agencies as obstacles, delayers, and constraints to economic progress, having much power to stop and little to start. Stiner (1980) states that it is a delusion held by many that government intervention in business is bad. There is no doubt that government regulations have achieved important benefits. Thus, any notion that regulations per se are opposed to the public interest is not worth considering. Business could not operate without certain types of regulations.

Government today is vast and complex. Within the legislative and executive branches there are many unelected officials. These officials are often subject to scrutiny by the public and the media. (Table 15.1 presents detailed staffing data for the major federal regulatory agencies and activities.)

THE REASON FOR GROWTH

The growth of the federal government can be seen primarily as a result of increases in the federal budget. The Depression-era programs such as those from the New Deal legislation, created huge increases in the budget. World War II alone raised the budget to astronomical levels. Government at that time was increasingly involved in the economy and introduced many new regulations in the business community. Along with these new regulations came numerous agencies to monitor them. These factors all caused further increases in the federal budget.

Reasons for growth in government are seen as a consequence of growing military expenditures. Most believe that the advent of big government occurred during World War II and the cold war era that followed. Government grew as the United States continued to expand as a world power and inherited more international responsibilities. Another era leading to growth in government was reflected in the period of the Depression. This period created areas of government spending that are still a part of society today. The government took action to reverse the economic slump and continued to remain active in the recovery of the economy. Even at the present time the government is part of the growing welfare system that originated during the Great Depression. This system currently absorbs the largest amount of the federal budget.

During the 1960s, government continued to expand by implementing new regulatory agencies or expanding current ones. The basis for much of this involved public policy and pressure to force businesses to conform to new and existing regulations. In this respect government growth is viewed as a result of public policy, whereby government controls an expanded number of functions, not the private sector.

Increased government functions are observed in retirement and unemployment pay, funds for construction of hospitals and schools, small business loans, minimum wages, and a host of other areas. In contrast, at one time, most of these functions were in the hands of the private sector, but now have been instrumental in expanding the size of government.

Other writers, such as Lawrence Hebron, see society's constant support of government intervention as the cause of growth in government, while that same society also complains about the size of government. The growth of government and its intervention in the economy are based on certain constitutional amendments. The big factor is the way these constitutional provisions are interpreted, which leaves much to be desired. In this respect these interpretations can either restrict or expand the growth of government depending on the desires of society. (Refer to table 15.2, which presents detailed administrative costs of federal regulatory agencies and activities.)

BUSINESS INFLUENCES ON GOVERNMENT

In attempting to influence the public policy process, business is exercising the same right as any other interest group in society. Indeed, this is the process by which public decisions in the United States are made.

Business has several major purposes in its efforts to shape public decision

Table 15.2
Administrative Costs of Federal Agencies (Fiscal Years, Millions of Dollars)

Area of Regulation	1984	1985	1986	(estimated) 1987	1988
SOCIAL REGULATION					
Consumer Health & Safety	$3,062	$3,195	$3,233	$3,567	$3,616
Job Safety & Other Conditions	836	860	823	892	978
Environment & Energy	2,671	2,976	2,793	3,656	4,078
TOTAL-Social Regulation	$6,569	$7,031	$6,849	$8,115	$8,672
ECONOMIC REGULATION					
Finance & Banking	$649	$620	$887	$759	$830
Industry-Specific Regulation	293	289	270	295	308
General Business	458	507	528	603	675
TOTAL-Economic Regulation	$1,400	$1,416	$1,685	$1,657	$1,813
GRAND TOTAL	$7,969	$8,447	$8,534	$9,772	$10,485

Source: Center for the Study of American Business, Washington University. Derived from the Budget of the United States Government and related documents, various fiscal years.

making, and it employs a variety of approaches to achieve these ends. Among the many goals that business hopes to achieve in its struggle with government are to:

1. maintain an environment favorable to business
2. inject rational thinking into government
3. counterbalance union power and influence
4. promote political interest of managers
5. counterbalance the power of groups with objectives contrary to those of business (e.g., consumerists, environmentalists)[2]

Influencing Government Decision Making

Lobbying. A lobby is defined as "a political interest group . . . whose shared activities include attempts to influence decisions made within the public policy-making system."[3] Lobbying can take many forms, such as groups of a general nature that have lobbying as one of their common interests. Examples of this are the National Association of Manufacturers and the Chamber of Commerce of the United States. A lobby might also represent groups of more specific or limited interests as is the case with individual companies, trade associations, and the National Federation of Independent Business. However, lobbying in any form constitutes one of the most significant influential activities of business on government.

Electoral Process. This refers to the activities that business can use to influence the election of candidates through contributions to election campaigns. Although the federal criminal code forbids business contributions to candidates in federal elections, there are a number of permissible actions a firm can take to shape the electoral process:

1. Encourage stockholders and employees to register and vote, although the firm may not suggest how they should vote.

2. Permit candidates to tour company premises to meet or greet employees. If the firm does this, however, it must grant all candidates the same privilege.

3. State its position on public issues affecting its well-being, including legislation currently pending.

4. Communicate information to employees and stockholders concerning candidates for office, including voting records of members of Congress.

5. Provide political education programs for employees. A firm can promote on a nonpartisan basis its employees' voluntary involvement in direct political action on their own time. Also, an employee may be granted a leave of absence without pay to work in a political campaign.[4]

The 1974 campaign law opened the door for further legitimate business involvement in elections by permitting establishment by corporations of political action committees (PACs). These committees can make periodic presentations to company officials and stockholders on behalf of particular candidates and can collect campaign funds.

There has been some criticism of PACs. Current statistics indicate that PACs are, indeed, multiplying rapidly. In 1978 there were an estimated 525 PACs, and some enthusiasts predicted that as many as 1,500 other companies would set up such committees in 1978–1979.

It does not appear that business has excessive political power. This is a difficult issue because management techniques of power are simply not very sophisticated. The exercise of political power should not necessarily be viewed with disdain, as it represents the dynamic process by which a pluralistic society works. Business, along with labor, education, farmers' associations, and most other groups in society are politicized in that they attempt to influence public policy. As Jacoby has said, "In a pluralistic society, every institution has a right—if not a duty—to do what it can to survive. Pressure upon government for this purpose is a legitimate expression of a fundamental drive."[5]

Advocacy Advertising. Advocacy efforts are an interesting aspect of the adversary relationship in coping with social problems. Business firms are now running paid advertisements taking sides on many public issues. Such "advocacy advertising" is highly controversial. Critics demand that it be regulated to prevent it from becoming deceptive propaganda, while proponents regard it as an indispensable form of communication under the right to free speech.

Business has found in advocacy advertising an aggressive technique to combat criticism. This is in contrast to the traditional ways of ignoring criticism or reacting defensively to attacks one at a time. The effectiveness of such techniques is hard to measure. At best, we have only opinion polls on both sides of the issue. Advocacy advertising reflects the business view that the media does not adequately portray accurate or balanced views. Critics hold that such means are not readily available to opponents, who may not have the resources to engage in advertising efforts. S. Prakash Sethi holds that advocacy advertising as carried on by many large firms in recent years is of questionable value and of doubtful effectiveness on economic, sociopolitical, and ideological grounds, but that it can serve to enlarge public debate on issues normally dealt with only in academic journals or in legislative halls.[6]

GOVERNMENT INFLUENCES IN BUSINESS

Since government represents the people in the political arena, there is common agreement in all countries about government intervention in business affairs. This enables government to influence business in different ways. In the United States government affects business through both nonregulatory influences and regulatory influences.

Nonregulatory Influences

The government might use many ways to control the behavior of business in order to achieve social objectives. Carroll presents the approaches of moral suasion, voluntary standards, subsidies, the tax system, and financial policy.[7]

Moral suasion is sometimes called "jawboning." Jawboning is a generalized form of government appeal. An example is for business in general or specific industries to hold down prices or for labor to be restrained in wage demands. Jawboning usually begins with the president of the United States calling for business's cooperation for the public's interest.

Voluntary standards or guideposts represent a more specific governmental effort to control business. Government sets standards and then appeals to business to comply voluntarily.

In subsidies and procurement contracts, government spells out the goods and services to be delivered along with requirements that must be met (hiring and training minority groups, favoring depressed areas or small business, etc.).

A tax system can be used to provide incentives for business to comply with government's wishes, such as hiring certain categories of people (unskilled, minorities) or encouraging investment in capital goods.

The financial policy of government helps steer business behavior in directions that achieve national objectives. Three programs can be used for this purpose. First, direct loans are made by federal departments and agencies. Second, loans are guaranteed and insured by federal departments and agencies. Third, loans are made by federally sponsored agencies such as the Federal National Mortgage Association. These approches may be supplemented by various forms of government pressure or coercion, which can range from public chastisement of individual organizations to veiled threats to terminate government contracts or other benefits.

Regulatory Influences

Regulation is one of the most important tools that government can use to directly influence businesses to consider social objectives and interests along with business objectives. The regulation of business by the federal government has become so pervasive and comprehensive that

no business, large or small, can operate without obeying a myriad of government rules and restrictions. Costs and profits can be affected as much by a directive written by a government official as by a management decision in the front office or a customer's decision at the check-out counter. Fundamental entrepreneurial decisions such as: what lines of business to go into, what products and services to produce, which investments to finance, how and where to make goods, how to market them, and what prices to charge are increasingly subject to government control.[8]

This growth of regulation has been referred to as a second managerial revolution with a shift of decision-making power from the managers of corporations to a vast number of government regulators who are influencing, and in many cases controlling, managerial decisions of the typical business corporation. These types of decisions, which are increasingly subject to governmental influence and control, are basic to the operation of a business organization. Murray Weidenbaum describes some of these decisions:

1. What lines of business to go into?
2. What products can be produced?
3. What investments can be financed?
4. Under what conditions can products be produced?
5. Where can they be made?
6. How can they be marketed?
7. What prices can be charged?
8. What profit can be kept?[9]

The volume of regulations that affect business is so large that no corporation in the country can comply with all the laws and regulations to which it is subject. The National Council on Wage and Price Stability, for example, conducted a study in 1976 that listed 5,600 regulations from twenty-seven different agencies with which steelmakers must comply. In 1976, a total of eighty-three federal agencies were regulating business.

Some argue that the tremendous growth in the cost or volume of government regulation might reflect a failure of the market system to achieve national goals. Government regulation does not evolve in a vacuum, but as a political response to problems that do not seem to be solvable by market forces alone. The net consequence is that government is thrust deeper and deeper into what were originally private business decisions.

THE EVOLUTION OF FEDERAL REGULATION

Federal regulation arose out of public concern and the government's need to control the behaviors of businesses. Considering that businesses were unstable, the government formulated regulations to help stabilize society.

Regulation evolved in four phases. Each has its own characteristics that have resulted in the establishment of government agencies. These are:

1. The arousal of the people—the driving force to utilize the regulatory process. Certain circumstances compelled people to urge the government, through complaints and lobbying, to force businesses to follow the regulatory process.
2. The need for regulatory process and enforcement agencies.
3. The methods employed by the regulatory agencies.
4. The penalties imposed for violation of the regulatory rules and the butting in of regulatory agencies in decision making.

In respect to federal regulation, society and businesses must first accept that government regulation has evolved and that the government will interfere in decision making. Second, we must be aware that government regulation is a societal response to actual and perceived problems in the private sector. In other words, it is society that sees the need for federal regulation. Third, there is the establishment of federal regulation agencies that still control business decisions. Fourth, it is "public interest" that keeps all the agencies concentrating on one basic idea—whether legal, political, or ethical. Fifth, these agencies can use the media to disclose publicly any news that will influence society's views.

THE INTRODUCTION (EXPERIMENTAL) STAGE (1887–1929)

A greater public sector role in private sector economic decision making took place in the years 1887–1929. Until this time, the free enterprise market system was generally accepted as the appropriate avenue for satisfying public interest. Government intervention prior to the twentieth century was limited to a role of helping the market succeed.

Societal involvement emerged because of the public's concern about problems that were not being addressed in the market. For instance, federal regulatory laws were enacted to administer guidelines for factory safety and also worker's compensation. "Private monopoly" corporations emerged during this time, called by historians the progressive era. These corporations were the public services or utilities. Thus, the significant legislation of this time was prompted by society's insistence that private sector institutions operate for the public good. As a result, legislation was passed which included:

1. the Interstate Commerce Act (ICC) (1887)
2. the Sherman Act (1890)
3. the Clayton Act (1914)
4. the Federal Trade Commission (FTC) Act (1914)

The ICC was the prototype for all subsequent regulatory commissions, including the FTC. The ICC was designed as an independent public body with power to oversee those private operations pertaining to the public good (originally the railroad industry). The ICC combined executive, legislative, and judicial power in one agency, which is contrary to the federal system's concept of "separation of powers." The ICC has the authority to issue regulations (a legislative function), the right to enforce its own regulations (an executive function), and the power to sit in judgment on business utilities which violate its regulations (a judicial function). This was justified on the grounds that there were controls over the agency in the form of presidential appointments to the commission, Senate conformation of appointments, and reviews of agency decisions by the Supreme Court, which insured that no misuse of agency power was committed.

Reasons Behind Government Involvement

These regulations were of two types: industry regulation and regulation of competitive behavior (also called antitrust). The industry and antitrust policies evolved in response to an unwanted side effect of the industrial revolution: market control by corporations using unfair business prctices. Monopolies, as they came to be known, could control the price of a product by changing the quantity that was sold. It appeared that a completely unregulated economy was going to be dominated by one or a few companies in most industries. This has pushed government toward regulation of these businesses in order to preserve the competitive structure of the U.S. economy. The passage of antitrust legislation preserved America's commitment to competition and the spirit of free enterprise.

According to Rogene A. Buchholz, there are theories with respect to the development of industry regulation and the antitrust area: (1) it was the result of a strong populist movement that was fearful of the power of big business combinations; (2) business people supported these policies in order to rationalize the system by establishing rules of competition that everyone had to follow; and (3) it was because the invisible hand of the market was replaced by the visible hand of management. The government has to fill the gap by regulating business in the public interest.[10]

Evaluation of Antitrust Policies

Since 1890 when antitrust policies first came into being, they have been both praised and criticized, yet remain and still influence businesses in the United States today. Though antitrust policies were formed to be beneficiary to business, not all businesses see antitrust this way and regulation has met with opposition. Supermarkets are one case in point. In 1957 Safeway supermarkets entered into a consent decree that barred predatory pricing (selling below cost to drive out competition). Management at the time was concerned with whether this was the right decision. The regulations resulted in Safeway becoming rather docile in the industry; so by 1983 Dale L. Lynch sought to have the decree lifted. Lynch's efforts were successful and by 1985 Safeway's profit margin matched the industry average of 1.2 percent of sales which demonstrates that Safeway is possibly gaining back some of the strength it lost previously.

Another supermarket chain affected by antitrust was A&P which, of all supermarket chains, suffered the longest. The company closed over 1,400 stores before being rescued by the West German Tengelmann Group in 1979.[11] The antitrust action imposed on A&P was restriction from making acquisitions for a number of years. The effect on the company was detrimental and not until the last few years has A&P shown any signs of regaining vigor.

Both demonstrate the effect of antitrust policies on business, and also took place before the Reagan administration. After Reagan took office antitrust has been an issue of prime importance. His administration gave considerable attention to the issue of whether antitrust policies are necessary to businesses or whether they in fact, constrain businesses. The Reagan administration seemed to dismantle the nation's antitrust laws according to William Shepherd in his article, "Bust the Reagan Trustbusters." The economy became more competitive during the 1970s and since antitrust laws are now being questioned this new competitiveness may be threatened. The Reagan administration attempted to explain its view toward antitrust in a rather simplified manner:

1. Competition is so pervasive throughout the economy that true monopoly can exist only with the active support of government.

2. The apparent instances of monopoly power merely reflect the superior efficiency of a few companies.

3. Such power has few harmful effects. One group of scholars even claims that the mere threat of competition is enough to force a monopolist to charge competitive prices.[12]

THE ECONOMIC STAGE (1930–1960)

During the Great Depression and the subsequent New Deal of the early 1930s, significant legislation regarding the relationship of government and business was passed, including:

1. the Securities and Exchange Act (1934)
2. the Wagner Act (1935)
3. the Full Employment Act (1946)

The onset of this phase stemmed from the public belief that the free enterprise system had failed to meet the public's needs as evidenced by high unemployment and the general low state of the economy during the Depression era. All agencies established during the economic phase under the New Deal Administration of Roosevelt were modeled after the ICC. Such agencies included the Federal Radio Commission, the Federal Power Commission, the Securities and Exchange Commission, and the Civil Aeronautics Board. The major concerns of these agencies focused on the control of the markets served, rates charged for services, and the obligation to serve the public.

Thus, the federal regulatory process was no longer limited to telling business what they could *not* do. Certain behavior was now mandated by these agencies and they acted as arbitrators between the conflicting demands of business entities. The agencies of this economic period were responsible for balancing the interests of both the public and the industry.

THE SOCIAL STAGE (1960–1970)

In the 1960s and the 1970s, our nation and our business environment entered into a new era: the social phase. This phase brought about a different regulatory process; it was one of more interest groups with the main objective of regulating activities on behalf of the public. These public interest groups used the power of the media to get their point across to state and federal governments. During this time, many new regulatory bodies emerged, including the Equal Employment Opportunity Commission (EEOC), the Occupational Safety and Health Administration (OSHA), and the Environmental Protection Agency (EPA), just to name a few.

This new social dimension of regulation showed great concern for the quality of goods and services with a desire to decrease damage to society.

These agencies were in charge of regulating many processes in the business world and society as a whole. Some examples of these constraints were setting minimum safety standards at the workplace, regulating the pollution output of some industries, and stopping employee discrimination. If companies fail to adhere to such regulation standards, they may be subject to fines, their business could be closed or shut down completely, and in some cases they could be sent to jail.

The new social regulation has caused much controversy over the years, and has given the federal government a much bigger role in the management process. The government hopes to establish a healthy, clean, and safe environment by means of these agencies. It also hopes to bring political and economic powers to society (the public sector) so they do not stay "locked up" in the private sector. They want to establish a set of values, such as a "humanistic" social policy for the good of the public.

The idea of social regulation is indeed a fine one, but as always, there is a price to pay. In order to keep the environment cleaner, employees happier, and products safer, the business world has to raise prices on their goods and services. This is usually done in the form of taxation, which in turn will decrease the production and use of products and reduce the benefits they could offer.

Social regulation involves all of us, from those who produce the goods to those who purchase them. In our society, people always look for more, want more, and expect to get more (the promise of a better future or the best is yet to come). Government agencies, the business world, and the public must work together to uphold the principles of our society.

THE RE-EVALUATION STAGE OF FEDERAL REGULATION

One of the major themes of Ronald Reagan's campaign for the presidency of the United States in 1980 was to reduce significantly the size of the federal government and also the corresponding growth of government spending. Reagan, the champion of conservative America, surprised few when he initiated massive cuts in agency activities. The public mood in favor of major reform of government regulation and "regulatory reform" was one of the issues of the 1980 political campaign. For example, Ronald Reagan included regulatory reform as part of his plan for the economic recovery of the nation. Reagan gave his speech in Youngstown, Ohio, in October 1980 to promote changes in government regulation:

We must help protect the health and safety of workers and consumers, and the quality of our environment. These are areas where federal regulation is not only appropriate, but necessary. But we must recognize that many regulations impair the ability of industries to compete, reduce workers' real income, and destroy jobs. Therefore, we must have a balanced regulatory approach in which we recognize that regulations have costs as well as benefits. We must ensure that regulations are limited to those necessary to protect health, safety, and environment.[13]

With the election of Reagan, the impulse for reform was translated into government policy. Regulatory reform was one of the top priorities of his administration.

The growth of federal regulation can be traced back to the Industrial Revolution, with dramatic growth occurring during the Depression era. However, the people of the United States have generally frowned upon excessive regulation due to their inherent concern over excessive centralized authority, especially when there is no perceived society emergency. This concern in essence was the cause of America's struggle for independence.

Another reason for the re-evaluative phase is the possible impression on society that ingenious solutions for current problems are not enhanced by constant regulation. The initiative needed to remedy the concerns of society may well be hindered by the very tool put in place to address those particular concerns: the tool of government regulation.

The concern over the role of government regulation is a real one. There is probably no clear way to answer these concerns; this is clear from the conflicting platforms the two main political parties of the United States preach during the campaign for the presidency of the United States.

THE FEDERAL REGULATORY PROCESS

Government today is vast and complex. Within the legislative and executive branches there are many unelected officials. These officials are often subject to scrutiny by the public and the media alike.

With this in mind, managers must remember that in responding to government regulation, the government does not act as a unified entity on one specific interest. Decisions are made by small groups or by key legislators. Their decisions are made largely on a legal basis. Managers are often confused by governmental regulation and often require advice from a legal consultant.

The decision process is further complicated by competition within the government's system of checks and balances. Once a new regulatory commission or program is established, the function of running this group is split between the House and the Senate. These two groups may not agree all the time which can slow down the regulation process. Another point to consider is the allocation of budget money. There is another group that must approve the money for the agency to function. Next the new group must be given a direction to work toward on behalf of the executive department of the United States.

There is such great depth within government that it hinders the creation of regulatory groups. Not many are created unless there is a great demand from the public. Getting everyone involved to agree on the desired decision is difficult and potentially extremely time-consuming. This could hinder an important law that would help the nation.

Once a program is created it is difficult to eliminate it because the people that work within the agency do not want to lose their jobs. They will push with everything they have to remain where they are.

Government must be sensitive to the interests of the public. It must realize where the nation is going and where it would like to be in the future. In order to arrive at this point, the standards of the government should become more uniform. This will help alleviate any problem that may come up dealing with some of the regulations.

The government has become vast due to the demand of the people. Since we demand better quality and prices along with higher salaries, we are forced to look for control which can only come from the government. The only way that we can control this country is to have an interactive government, but we must deal with some of the problems that will arise.

THE COSTS OF REGULATION

There has been a growing feeling that the public sector is not solving societal problems any better than the private sector. The public has expressed concern about the costs of government, direct as well as indirect. It is felt that the cost of government exceeds the benefits to society and creates new and more serious problems than it solves (Refer to figures 15.1 and 15.2, which present the trends in regulatory expenditures and agency staffing during the Reagan years.)

Free market economists have been in the forefront of regulatory reform proposals designed to bring these costs under control. This has been the main reason for deregulation of the airline industry and in partially freeing the trucking industry from government control.[14] The public policy debate in this area has largely been in terms of economic policy and the degree to which the nation can and should rely on market forces. Four kinds of costs associated with government regulation can be identified and will be discussed below.

Administrative Costs

Administrative costs include the actual budgetary costs for operating the federal regulatory apparatus. It was estimated that by the end of the 1970s there would be more than eighty regulatory agencies and about one hundred thousand government workers whose operating expenditures would exceed $10.0 billion.[15]

Compliance Costs

Compliance costs include those expenditures attributable to regulation incurred by firms. The Business Roundtable sponsored a study that showed

Figure 15.1
Trends in Regulatory Expenditures

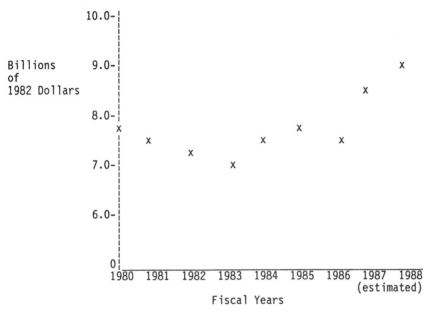

Source: Center for the Study of American Business, Washington University. Derived from the Budget of the United States Government and related documents, various fiscal years.

that the forty-eight firms which responded to the study incurred incremental costs of $2,621,593,000 in 1977 to comply with the regulation of six regulatory agencies.[16] (These agencies are the Environmental Protection Agency, Equal Opportunity Employment Commission, the Occupational Safety and Health Administration, Department of Energy, the Employee Retirement Income Security Act, and the Federal Trade Commission.) The magnitude of these costs can be measured against selected 1977 financial data for the forty-eight firms included in the study:

Incremental costs of regulation (six agencies)	$2.6 billion
Total capital expenditures	$25.8 billion
Total research and development costs	$6.0 billion
Net income after taxes	$16.6 billion

Transfer Costs

Transfer costs are costs that are placed on one segment of society for the benefit of another societal group. For example, efforts by OSHA to produce

Figure 15.2
Trends in Regulatory Staffing

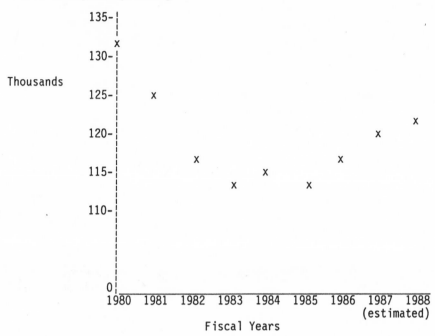

Source: Center for the Study of American Business, Washington University. Derived from the Budget of the United States Government and related documents, various fiscal years.

permissible levels of cotton dust in workplaces will confer environmental benefits on cotton industry workers. These costs, estimated at $808 million in 1976, ultimately will be paid by customers using cotton products in the form of higher prices.[17]

Inefficiency Costs

Inefficiency costs include costs from misallocation of resources as a secondary effect of regulation. It is estimated that regulation of safety in the coal mines has reduced labor productivity by 50 percent. The nation's productivity growth was reduced by nearly 20 percent due to increasing environmental controls and health and safety regulations imposed on private firms.[18]

Economic Benefits of Regulation

According to Regulatory Reform Act S.1080, the economic benefits of regulation are substantial. For example, air pollution benefits range from five to fifty-eight billion dollars annually. Automobile safety controls saved over 28,000 lives in an eight-year period. Seat belts alone reduced injuries by 34 percent and deaths by 28 percent. In the consumer product area, crib safety standards have reduced injuries to infants by 44 percent since 1974, and up to 60,000 lost work-day accidents and 350 deaths were avoided in 1974 and 1975 due to OSHA regulations.[19]

External Benefits or Costs

Some people think that government regulation is a necessity in modern society. Some functions cannot be adequately performed by market-oriented organizations because they involve external costs or benefits. For example, disposal of chemical wastes into rivers or streams that also provide drinking water for communities causes nonmarket costs of living in those areas where these water resources are being polluted.

The societal response to this kind of problem, particularly in the 1960s and 1970s, has been zoning controls and environmental pollution statutes and regulations. The main purpose is to place external costs on the private sector organizations generating them, so they are reflected in the market prices.

The present public policy concern has been whether the regulatory process has been successful in transferring these costs in an efficient and effective manner with proposals to moving from a command-and-control environmental approach to market incentives.

Invisible Benefits

Economists call these benefits "collective goods." As soon as such a good is created, it benefits every person whether he has paid for it or not and regardless of how many are also benefiting at the same time. Examples include national defense, police, and fire protection. Traditionally these types of benefits have been considered a proper function of government and reform movements have largely been designed to generate efficiencies in the regulatory process.

Market Deficiencies

The principal rationale for public safety intervention in the private sector was because of instabilities and deficiencies of the market system. The current debate is concerned with whether market forces are really more successful in the long run in correcting such deficiencies than government intervention. Reform in this area has largely focused on getting the government off the backs of its citizens by eliminating agencies or severely curtailing their function.

PROPOSALS TO IMPROVE REGULATION

Direct Control

Procedural improvements and streamlining are mandated by statutes. This may offer some slight advantages. Certainly elimination of the multiple administrative roles of legislators, enforcers, prosecutors, and judges combined in one agency would make the process more fair and probably more efficient. But procedural change will do little to lessen the regulatory burden.

Regulatory impact statements require each agency to evaluate costs and benefits before promulgating a major regulation. Some people believe that this will not change anything. It is like asking a barber whether you need a haircut. Agencies will be happy to do this since it increases their workload and therefore their need for staff and funds. Such people think that neither their agency nor the regulated industry should weigh both economic and social costs and benefits of existing and prospective regulatory activities.

Sunset laws terminate the existence of each agency after a specified number of years unless further existence is authorized by Congress. Some people question if the federal government would have the time and resources to do this and the agencies will direct undue time and resources to preparing justification for their continued existence. This will cause even less concern about results and more intent on image.

Review of agency action by Congress is not realistic. Congress is not in a position to review much regulation or to review any very carefully. Otherwise, it is the best alternative that is now a practical possibility.

Performance standards are to replace structural specifications and operational requirements as the main thrust of regulatory statements. Some think that this will improve the quality of regulation and will not affect the quantity.

Indirect Control

Economic planning and exhortation to comply is an old approach. President Gerald Ford tried this with his "WIN" (Whip Inflation Now) campaign, and President Jimmy Carter tried it again with wage-pricing guidelines. Some think these efforts are almost never successful, and when persuasion fails it leads toward coercion as demonstrated in the Carter experiment.

Compulsory disclosure and reliance on public opinion have been reasonably effective in the securities field, but have had little impact on the cigarette industry. Such mixed success creates doubt as to its general applicability.

Government ownership (following the European model) sometimes causes the competition to become monopolistic. Many government enterprises in our economy have already achieved varying degrees of monopoly, including Amtrack (National Railroad Passenger Corporation), TVA (Tennessee Valley Authority), and CPB (Corporation for Public Broadcasting).

Deregulation and reliance on legislation appears to be the least burdensome and the most effective alternative.

THE REFORM BILL OF 1982

This bill requires all agencies to follow certain procedures in making policy decisions in the following ways:

1. The bill increases the fairness and effectiveness of the regulatory process by requiring agencies to examine carefully the economic and noneconomic effects of all major rules before their adoption.

2. Agencies are required to issue agendas of all rule-making activities and the president is required to publish a governmentwide calendar of all major rule-making activities. This is done in order to facilitate public participation in agency decision making and to prevent duplicative and conflicting rules.

3. The bill requires agencies to review within ten years all existing major legislation so that an agency can update such rules when necessary or appropriate.

4. The bill standardizes the procedures followed by agencies for issuing subpoenas in ajudications.

5. It provides for more diversified selection of members to the administrative conference of the United States.

Cost-Benefit Analysis

Cost-benefit analysis is intended to bring rationality and order to the regulatory process. By quantifying benefits and costs, it is hoped that the regulations that survive this economic test will be more effective and those which are not on balance cost-effective will never be promulgated. Murray Weidenbaum, a principal advocate of this analysis, states that: "The aim of requiring agencies to reform benefit-cost analysis is to make the government decision-making process more effective, and to eliminate regulatory action that, on balance, generates more costs than benefits."[20] Cost-benefit analysis is merely an attempt to apply the principles of welfare economics to public policy proposals. Its rationale is the concept of a potential "Pareto" improvement. That is a reallocation of resources in which the gains may be distributed in a way that makes everyone in the community better off.[21] It started in the United States in the 1930s as an administrative method owing nothing to economic theory and adapted to evaluate federal water projects.[22] However, the present purpose of this analysis has spread to encompass most areas of the public sector, ranging from fuel policy and industrial project evaluation to health and social services.

Measuring Benefits and Costs

Everyone would agree that benefits derived from public projects ought to exceed their costs. The use of an investment criterion is essential in cost-benefit analysis simply because any project incurs future costs and creates a time stream of benefits. These future benefits and costs might be known and measurable in monetary systems. Extending this economic theory to regulatory areas is fairly obvious.

One common type of cost-benefit analysis attempts to measure and quantify all costs and benefits associated with a particular regulatory measure. Then total costs are compared to the total benefits. If the total benefits exceed the costs, it will be adopted. Otherwise, it will be rejected. It is rarely employed in this pure form.

A second type of cost-benefit analysis is to identify costs and benefits, but not necessarily assign dollar values to all elements of the equation. This avoids many of the problems of the debt-credit approach, because quantification is avoided. Once all the costs and benefits are identified, the decision maker must decide whether the proposal is worthy of adoption.

A third type of cost-benefit analysis deals with analyzing alternatives. Rather than starting with a specific proposal, the regulator compiles an array of regulatory alternatives for consideration. This form of analysis is called cost-effectiveness analysis.[23] Under this type of analysis, costs and benefits of each alternative are identified, and to the extent possible, quantified. Then, one by one, each is considered on its own merit, and the best is selected for adoption. This type is particularly useful in analyzing regulation in which either the total cost to be incurred is fixed or when the desired level of protection is given. For example, if the goal of the regulator is to reduce deaths due to automobile accidents to one-half of the current rate, the regulator could conjure up a whole set of possible ways to accomplish this, such as:

1. reduce speed limits significantly
2. strengthen drunk driving laws
3. require the use of seatbelts
4. mandate the installation of airbags
5. step up enforcement of current traffic laws
6. subsidize mass transit transportation

This shows the alternatives that could be analyzed and the least expensive alternative could be chosen to achieve the 50 percent reduction in highway deaths.

Another use of cost-effectiveness analysis is when total costs are known. The regulatory process is somewhat restricted by how much of society and money (regulatory budget) is to be spent.[24] With this fixed amount, the regulator investigates various regulatory types in order to achieve maximum benefits with this fixed budget. For example, Congress could mandate that the National Highway Traffic Administration could spend only $100 million of the GNP on reducing deaths on the highway. The agencies could analyze the benefits which can be expected from various regulatory alternatives within these constraints. The one expected to provide the most total benefits would be adopted.

These analysis criteria require that benefits exceed costs for their adoption. But in some social areas, certain social benefits are desirable regardless of cost. For example, rights guaranteed by the Constitution should not be subjected to cost-benefit analysis. By viewing the guaranteed right as a regulatory goal, it could be implemented in the most cost-effective manner possible. Therefore, the cost-effectiveness approach provides the analyst, who does not insist on benefits exceeding costs, with a means for applying quantitative methods to achieve regulatory efficiency.

Problems with Cost-Benefit Analysis

"The limitation on the usefulness of cost/benefit analysis in the context of health, safety, and environmental regulatory decision making are so severe that they militate against its use altogether."[25]

Quantifying benefits. Opponents and advocates of cost-benefit analysis recognize the problems with this approach. For cost-benefit analysis to be used in its purest form, somehow the value of these benefits must be quantified. The problem of how to value nonmarketed goods is probably the largest single shortcoming of this approach. Since the goods are not tracked directly in the marketplace, attempts to value them appear arbitrary (human life, for example).

Identifying costs. The second problem with cost-benefit analysis is the difficulty analysts encounter when they try to estimate costs associated with a particular regulatory proposal. In many studies on cost-benefit analysis, different costs are used by different analysts for the same problem. This results in different conclusions in terms of whether a proposal is worthy for adoption. However, cost-benefit analysis provides a means for exercising judgment based on a more complete understanding of the implications of the negative and positive aspects of a proposed rule.

Recognizing cost and benefits can move regulation making from the field of intuition and ideology to a more rational and intellectual plane.

THE FUTURE DIRECTION OF THE FEDERAL REGULATORY PROCESS

The regulatory process seems to be going in a direction in which both the private business sector and society will benefit through less costly enforcement mechanisms.

Table 15.3
Changes in Regulatory Spending During the Reagan Years (Fiscal 1980–1988, Millions of 1982 Dollars)

Area of Regulation	1980	(estimated) 1988	real % change 1980-1988
SOCIAL REGULATION			
Consumer Safety & Health	$3,205	$2,949	-8%
Job Safety & Other Conditions	873	798	-9%
Environment & Energy	2,553	3,326	30%
TOTAL-Social Regulation	$6,631	$7,073	7%
ECONOMIC REGULATION			
Finance & Banking	$419	$677	62%
Industry-Specific Regulation	324	251	-22%
General Business	411	551	34%
TOTAL-Economic Regulation	$1,153	$1,479	28%
GRAND TOTAL	$7,784	$8,552	10%

Source: Center for the Study of American Business, Washington University. Derived from the Budget of the United States Government and related documents, for fiscal years 1988 and 1981.

President Reagan's new regulatory philosophy has forced administrative agencies to issue regulations only when essential, and in the least costly approach. All actions that the federal regulators undertake must take into account not only what is necessary to achieve the maximum benefit for society, but also the condition of the particular industries to be affected by the regulations. (Refer to tables 15.3 and 15.4, which present the changes in real regulatory spending and the changes in the regulatory staffing during the Reagan years.)

Through "controlled trading" reforms, it is hoped that the societal aim of clean air and business' aim of economic growth will come about. There are three main programs under the controlled trading policy. The emission offset policy will permit plants to be built or expanded in areas that do not meet federal standards for clean air, by cutting back on the emission of preexisting plants. The "bubble policy" establishes uniform emission standards for the whole plant, not just certain stacks or vents. Finally, the emission reduction

Table 15.4
Changes in Regulatory Staffing During the Reagan Years (Fiscal 1980–1988, Permanent Full-Time Positions)

Area of Regulation	1980	(estimated) 1988	real % change 1980-1988
SOCIAL REGULATION			
Consumer Safety & Health	66,016	54,592	-17%
Job Safety & Other Conditions	18,201	14,409	-21%
Environment & Energy	19,621	20,598	5%
TOTAL-Social Regulation	103,838	89,599	-14%
ECONOMIC REGULATION			
Finance & Banking	9,649	13,854	44%
Industry-Specific Regulation	7,365	4,930	-33%
General Business	9,390	9,654	3%
TOTAL-Economic Regulation	26,404	28,438	8%
GRAND TOTAL	130,242	118,037	-9%

Source: Center for the Study of American Business, Washington University. Derived from the Budget of the United States Government and related documents, for fiscal years 1988 and 1981.

banking policy allows firms to curb pollution beyond what the new law requires and to "bank" these extra reductions for future use or sale.

SUMMARY

This chapter began with different views of business–government relationships. Over the past few decades, there has been increased public concern over business behaviors and the protection of the environment. The relations between government and business have never been easy, but in recent years their difficulties have increased as each has grown in power and complexity.

Government has grown immensely throughout history. This can be attributed to many factors such as increases in the federal budget, growth in military expenditures, addition of new regulatory agencies, expansion of existing agencies, increased government functions, and society's constant support of government intervention.

Business and government can exert pressure on each other in a variety of ways. Some examples of how business influences government are lobbying, influencing the electoral process, and advocacy advertising. Some of the ways government influences business are moral suasion, voluntary standards, subsidies, procurement contracts, tax systems, financial policy, and regulatory influences.

The evolution of the federal regulatory process can be broken down into four stages: the experimental stage, the economic stage, the social stage, and the re-evaluation stage. There are also costs associated with the regulatory process. These costs can be broken down into administrative costs, compliance costs, transfer costs, and inefficiency costs. The cost of regulation should be a concern of society as a whole, not just the affected businesses.

Federal regulation also reaps many benefits. These benefits range from cleaner air for us to breathe up to fewer lives lost on the highways each year.

Like anything else, there is also room for improvement in the federal regulatory process. This can be accomplished through either direct or indirect control. Another method is to include a cost-benefit analysis approach in the process.

The future of the regulatory process seems to be going in a direction in which both the private business sector and society will benefit through less costly enforcement mechanisms.

A CASE STUDY: DEREGULATION

Over the last eight years, the airline industry, the telephone industry, the railroad industry, and the trucking industry have all experienced deregulation which has greatly changed the way they carry out their planning, organizing, staffing, leading, and controlling.

Deregulation is an economic process used to reform an industry by making its market competitive. Under deregulation, protective regulatory rules are dropped and competition becomes the driving force of the industry. Deregulation makes industries define their place in the market rather quickly. Survival of the fittest—adapt or be abolished—is the name of the game. Companies must lower their prices in order to compete with new companies that are entering the market.

Deregulation is not a new process, but it has experienced its most prominent use over the last decade. Deregulation touches all facets of the business world. It not only affects the business sector but it eventually overflows into all sectors. The deregulation process took a long time to be recognized and put into effect, but finally by the 1960s it began getting recognition. Some say deregulation is the first successful redirection process to be attempted in U.S. industry in the last half-century since it has revitalized the three major U.S. industries of finance, telecommunications, and transportation.

Deregulation has met with both support and opposition. Supporters believe that it stimulates innovation in technology by adding the element of competition to a market. Others support the presumption that it lowers prices and gives the consumer more choices. By lowering costs, the inflation rate slows down while labor productivity increases. On the other hand, the opposition believes deregulation forces small companies either to sell out to firms in the industry or to exit the market altogether. In some cases it has hurt the unions and left high-cost industries virtually unprotected.[26]

Certain U.S. industries are drastically changing because of deregulation. Most of the industries that are experiencing deregulation were once regulated by the government or some other regulatory board. The airline industry is a fine example.

The airline industry was under the control of the Civil Aeronautics Board (CAB) until the Airline Deregulation Act was signed into law on October 24, 1978, by President Jimmy Carter. This was the first such act in a long time where a whole U.S. industry had been deregulated by the government. Deregulation of the airline industry meant many changes, some good and some bad. Airlines would now be able to experience true competition while offering the consumer more services coupled with lower fares.

In the short run, the benefits of deregulation seem to outweigh the losses, but in the long run it is difficult to say which ones will prevail. One of the major effects of airline deregulation is the disbandment of the CAB which for years has set fares and given out route assignments. Under the deregulation act, the CAB is to be dissolved completely within two years. Now each major carrier is allowed to independently choose one new route each year for three years and also to apply to the CAB for an unlimited number of additional routes. They can cut or raise prices within a range on routes where they have under 70 percent control over the traffic.[27]

Another effect is the change in the train of thought of the airline industry. Instead of each airline trying to retain its specific image by serving only important cities in a certain area of the country, they are diversifying by serving smaller cities in a larger range. For example, Eastern Airlines which for years flew only on the East Coast has added flights to the State of Washington and overseas. Also, airlines are now taking more risks, especially the larger ones like United and American. These airlines with substantially large balance sheets are spending a lot of money to update and increase their supply of equipment. Another plus for the airlines with large balance sheets is that it allows them to dominate the fare wars because they can afford to lose some of their assets without endangering their financial position as a whole.[28]

Some airlines, on the other hand, are acting a bit more cautiously. Instead of flaunting their assets they are focusing attention on cutting costs. Many airlines cannot afford to update their carriers so they are increasing flying time on each plane and better utilizing what they have. Others are decreasing their staffs both on land and in air, and their employee-to-passenger ratio is increasing. Still others have demoted their in-flight service by offering snacks instead of meals and getting rid of first-class seating. The elimination of first-class sections not only increases the availability of low-cost coach seating but also helps the airlines attract business customers who are more stable travelers in comparison to seasonal vacationers.[29]

Deregulation can be directly linked to various negative effects such as bankruptcy, employee layoffs, and fare wars. Deregulation caused Braniff Airlines to file for bankruptcy and was responsible for nearly $1.5 billion in losses between 1980 and 1982. Employee wages have drastically changed since deregulation. For instance, Continental has cut wages by nearly 50 percent and at the same time increased the number of hours in the employee work week. American regrouped its pay scale into two tiers with high wages for its veteran employees and very low wages for new employees. Finally, the fare wars caused the airlines to lower fares as much as 50 percent over the last ten years which weigh heavy on their balance sheets. Many smaller carriers were forced to fold because they could not sustain the economic pressure. One vice president said, "It's no longer a question of being productive to make money, but a question of being productive to survive."[30]

Deregulation has also injected fear in the minds of many—fear concerning safety regulations. Many feel that deregulation will mean that less attention will be paid to safety regulations. They believe that the airline's main objective will be earning more money at the expense of safety. This is a valid concern, since we have seen many airlines struggling to survive.[31]

Despite these negative effects and the fear of safety being jeopardized, airline ticket sales are booming. Many times, misfortunes for the airlines are blessings for the consumers. Deregulation has increased the number of routes and flights to smaller cities by adopting a hub-spoke system that supplies more connection between more cities. This has therefore increased the price range and quality of service that the consumer can choose from. Airline travel has now become more accessible to a larger portion of the population. Another bright side to deregulation is the increase in airline productivity.[32] Airlines have been able to achieve a higher output by using less input (resources). They can now serve more cities with the same number of planes while at the same time cutting their expenses. "The entire industry provided 19 percent more output with fewer than 1 percent more employees."[33]

It is easy to see the radical changes deregulation forces on an industry. These changes, however, are difficult to categorize as either good or bad since many have a bittersweet effect. In other words, what is favorable to the consumer is not always favorable to the industry. The airline industry is still at odds over whether deregulation has truly helped the industry; in fact some are asking for a return to regulation. The question of whether the airline industry will re-regulate is still unanswered. However, it is not likely that deregulation will soon become obsolete for it has become a trend of the 1980s, and an example of how we are constantly changing. Sam Coats said it best when he stated, "We would much rather have the opportunity to succeed or fail in a free-market environment."[34] Therefore, it is likely that deregulation will continue to have a powerful influence on U.S. business for years to come.

NOTES

1. Archie B. Carroll, *Business and Society: Managing Corporate Social Performance* (Boston: Little, Brown and Company, 1981), p. 99.

2. George A. Steiner, *Business and Society,* 2d ed. (New York: Random House, 1975), pp. 382–85.

3. Carol S. Greenwold, *Group Power: Lobbying and Public Power* (New York: Praeger Publishers, 1977), p. 14.

4. Ibid., p. 15.

5. Neil H. Jacoby, *The Business-Government Relationship: A Reassessment* (Pacific Palisades, Calif.: Goodyear Publishing Company, 1975), p. 7.

6. S. Prakash Sethi, *Advocacy Advertising and Large Corporations* (Lexington, Mass.: Lexington Books, 1977), pp. 20–21.

7. Carroll, *Business and Society,* pp. 106–7.

8. Murray L. Weidenbaum, "Government Power and Business Performance," in *The United States in the 1980s,* edited by Peter Dunigan and Alvin Robushka (Palo Alto, Calif.: Stanford University, Hoover Institution, 1980), p. 200.

9. Murray Weidenbaum, *The Future of Business Regulation* (New York: AMACOM, 1979), p. 34.

10. Buchholz, pp. 94–95.

11. Bill Saporito, "When Antitrust Hits You, You Stay Hit," *Fortune* (September 1, 1986): 64.

12. William G. Shepherd, "Bust the Reagan Trustbusters," *Fortune* (August 4, 1986): 225–27.

13. President Ronald Reagan, speech in Youngstown, Ohio. October 1980; quoted by the Regulatory Reform Act, S. 1080, November 1981, p. 8.

14. William Lilley, III, and James C. Miller, III, "The New Social Regulation," *Public Interest* (Spring 1978); reprinted in S. Prakash Sethi and Carl L. Swanson, *Private Enterprise and Public Purpose* (New York: John Wiley and Sons, 1981), pp. 143–52.

15. Marvin H. Kosters, "Counting the Costs," *Regulation* (July–August 1979); reprinted in S. Prakash Sethi and Carl L. Swanson, *Private Enterprise and Public Purpose* (New York: John Wiley and Sons, 1981), pp. 181–89.

16. "The Regulatory Revolution," *First Chicago World Report* (January–February 1978): 1–5.

17. Arthur Anderson & Company, *Cost of Government Regulation Study for the Business Roundtable* (March 1979).

18. Irvin Kristol, "The Hidden Costs of Regulation," *Wall Street Journal* (January 12, 1977): 14.

19. Regulatory Reform S.1080, p. 18.

20. Murray Weidenbaum, "Weidenbaum Analysis Benefit-Cost Analysis," *Across the Board* (Fall 1982): 62.

21. M. F. Drummond, "Welfare Economics and Cost-Benefit Analysis in Health Care," *Scottish Journal of Political Economy* (June 1981): 125.

22. Christopher Nash, David Pearce, and J. Stanly, "An Evaluation of Cost-Benefit Analysis Criteria," *Scottish Journal of Political Economy* (June 1975).

23. James C. Miller and Bruce Yandle, *Benefit-Cost Analysis of Social Regulation* (American Enterprise Institute, 1979), p. 5.

24. Lawrance J. White, *Reforming Regulation* (Englewood Cliffs, N.J.: Prentice-Hall 1981), pp. 222–27.

25. U.S. House of Representatives, report by the Subcommittee on Oversight and Investigations of the House Interstate and Foreign Commerce Committee, *Federal Regulation and Regulatory Reforms,* U.S. Government Printing Office, Report No. 96, p. 132.

26. "How Deregulation Puts Competition Back in Business," *U.S. News and World Report* (November 25, 1984): p. 51.

27. Rush Loving, Jr. "How the Airlines Will Cope with Deregulation," *Fortune* (November 20, 1978): 38.

28. Ibid., pp. 39–40.

29. Ibid.

30. "Deregulating America," *Business Week* (November 28, 1983): 83.

31. "How Deregulation Puts Competition Back in Business," p. 52.

32. Rogene A. Buchholz, *Business Environment and Public Policy: Implications for Management and Strategy Formulation* (Englewood Cliffs, N.J.: Prentice-Hall, 1986), p. 193.

33. "Deregulating America," p. 86.

34. "How Deregulation Puts Competition Back in Business," p. 52.

16

Closing the Gap

Today's society is confronted with the challenging task of re-evaluating and redefining ethics. The course for such a cumbersome task is prompted by the increasing concern for the perceived deterioration of ethical behavior and practices in the broader society as well as in the business world. As a result of the widespread concern, several studies have been made with astonishing results.

PUBLIC OPINION

A recent Gallup poll conducted for the *Wall Street Journal* concluded that 65 percent of the general American public felt that the level of ethics has declined in the last ten years.[1] Ethical practices within the business society are perceived to have fallen by 49 percent of the general public and by 23 percent of business executives.[2] The overall sentiment regarding the lowering of ethical standards among businesspersons is related to the overall acceptance by society of such a decrease in standards. A prevalent response toward decaying business practices is: "American business has to lie to survive due to imminent competition, production pressures, and government regulators. A more permissive behavior has become a norm within the business society in order to keep their heads above water."[3]

There is obviously an ambiguity between what is accepted moral behavior in business and what is accepted moral behavior in the broader society. There appears to be different meanings and parameters for ethics as one moves from the broader societal sphere into the business sphere. A question which must be addressed is: What are ethics? This question is omnipresent. In order to narrow the gap between society's definition of ethics and business's definition, an overall working definition must be established. One such definition of ethics is that it is the set of values that discern good from bad and right from wrong and the moral obligation one has toward others.[4]

This definition leaves many areas open to attack and manipulation. Several questions must be raised: Who decides what is morally right and wrong? When is an individual not morally obligated to others? Vernon Henderson, an ethics consultant to the Arthur D. Little consulting firm states, "In a society like ours, who's going to decide what's right and wrong?"[5] There are numerous factors that must be taken into consideration when forming the answers to those questions. First and foremost, the fact to remember is "that ethics are developed or formed; ethics are not something we are born with."[6] Since ethics are developed and several factors affect the development of moral behavior, we must realize just how difficult it is to wrestle with the issue at stake.

CORPORATE VIEW

Corporations seem to view ethics much differently than the broader society. They are at opposite ends of the spectrum. Corporations take ethics very lightly, as if they are not even applicable. For most the attitude is that "ethics is ethics and business is business."[7] Corporations have exonerated themselves from ethics because of the obstacle it presents. It must be realized, however, that the present corporate attitude is in direct conflict with society's ideal virtues. Business must take into account its dependence upon society for survival, for business is only one of many factors which make up the larger framework of society. Bearing this in mind, corporations ideally could not consciously partake in unethical practices knowing that they will undoubtedly affect the broader society. The practice of unethical behavior contradicts the moral behavior taught by the family, church, and culture.

Corporations deny that their behavior deleteriously affects and is solely responsible for the decline of moral standards. In order to substantiate their argument, corporations assert that the use of unethical business practices to the general decline of ethical and moral standards in the broader society is, in effect, a mirror image. Thus, it is no wonder businesses resort to unethical behavior when it is perceived as being condoned and prcticed on a larger scale.

Since a large percentage of the American public thinks ethics in general have declined, an analysis of other factors in the broader societal sphere must be closely examined. Traditionally, children are exposed to a set of values. Along with the paycheck, fathers bring home externally relevant values from the "real world." Mothers, on the other hand, are responsible for educating children in regard to domestic and familial values. Parents work as a team to prepare children for the ethical and moral decisions confronting them later in life.

THE FAMILY

Today's family is highly complex. There is a higher divorce rate and a higher percentage of two-income families, leading to a higher percentage of latch-key kids. The U.S. Census Bureau reports that 2.1 million school-age children come home to an empty house. It is also true that parents with high incomes, a high level of education, and professional employment are more likely to leave their children home alone.[8] If parents are too busy, who should instill the proper moral values in the following generation? These are two questions that remain in limbo as we struggle to take responsibility for ethical education.

THE MEDIA

The "me" society of the 1980s leaves many children unattended. As parents seek fulfillment and identity outside the home, they are replaced by the television. Human values are replaced by television's reflections on society, which undoubtedly have an impact on viewers.[9] Children as well as adults subconsciously internalize acts of violence and corruption which are then used as methods to get ahead. The idea of being ruthless in order to get ahead is most prevalent among businessmen and businesswomen portrayed on television. Some exemplary television shows are "Dynasty," "Dallas," "Knots Landing," and "Falcon Crest," in which the characters "are egotists driven by the most banal motives of power and profit."[10] These television shows display rich, crooked businessmen (like J. R. from "Dallas") as successful and admirable. This reinforces the idea that successful businessmen are crooked ones. Moreover, it says that it is all right to be crooked.

The film industry has even begun to act as a reinforcement in the portrayal of the so-called businessman. In *Wall Street,* two businessmen are portrayed: one a hardened arbitrager and the other a corruptible young stockbroker. *Less Than Zero* is a film about the children of West Coast affluence and their money-besotted nihilism. We can assume that the cinematic equation of capital and corruption will continue in the future.[11]

What can be said about the way sex is portrayed on television? Is it morally right for an executive, or anyone, to be married and still have an affair with his secretary? Maybe this is a cause of sexual harassment on the job; people are beginning to feel it is accepted in society.

Many advertisers paint an unreal picture of the world. They are "creatures of dissatisfaction." Many commercials portray the ideal people as people who have nice cars, expensive clothes, and no worries. Advertisers create unattainable expectations for some people. These people might feel they need to achieve these ideals and they will go to any length to achieve them, even unethical ones. It seems as though many advertisers feel they are value free.

EDUCATION

Are the values, or lack thereof, reflected in our schools? Perhaps the lack of values in business stems from the education that prepares us for these careers. William Scott and Terrence Mitchell reduce the origin of unethical practices in both the business organization and management schools to the individual. Simplified, "corrupt individual behavior supports and is supported by organizational norms."[12] Exanding upon this idea, they see management as a whole to be manipulators of employee values, "without respect for human dignity."[13] The individual is but an instrument for attaining the goals of the organization. Robert H. Hayes and William J. Abernathy of the *Harvard Business Review* cite the cause of ethical failure as a failure of business education to emphasize sufficiently creativity, sociability, and interaction. Too much emphasis is put on instrumental techniques which tend to dehumanize the entire leadership process. Regardless of how autonomous an organization considers itself to be, it is within the confines of a democratic society that we must live. Management schools are not living up to their obligation to teach good business ethics and to motivate modern moral development. According to Scott and Mitchell, "expectancy and manipulation" have been substituted in institutional curricula for "trust and human dignity."[14]

According to a 1986 survey conducted by the Ethics Resource Center, 89 percent of all accredited business schools claim to teach ethics "in some manner" but only 21 percent provide a separate ethics course. The rest say it is integrated into other classes. There has been debate about whether ethics should be taught as a separate class or integrated into the curriculum. However, if ethics is taught separately students get the idea that it is divorced from subjects like marketing and finance. David Vogel, who himself taught ethics, says that, "rather than examining past ethical dilemmas or attempting to guess what scandals may lie ahead, ethics teachers would do better to get students into the habit of seeing an ethical dimension to every business situation they come across."[15]

The problem of eroding managerial ethics can be solved in a number of ways. First, the question of managerial values can be raised and wrestled with through increased group discussions and overall improved communication. Second, there should be more involvement among business institutions and the professional world. Finally, business schools should promote community involvement to create better communication in the public, academic, and business communities. A congruency of values between these sectors should aid in equalizing our individual, moral, and ethical goals.

POLITICS

Another factor that needs to be dealt with when considering ethics is politics. Gary Hart, running on the Democratic ticket as a 1988 presidential contender, admitted to being unfaithful and having an affair with Donna Rice of Miami. Does something of this nature not have an impact on society and how they will view ethics? Hart insisted that he had done nothing immoral. If this is the case, then what is immoral? Hart was the best known Democratic name in the presidential race. His views on foreign and domestic issues were thoughtful, detailed, and out in the open. People, however, are less interested in his ideas and more interested in his character. It is also now known that John F. Kennedy shared a girlfriend with a mobster. Is this morally right? If society would have known this at the time of his presidency, they probably would not have accepted him.[16]

RELIGION

America's evangelical scandals have also had an impact on the decline of ethics. The Bakker scandal and the Roberts' extravaganza hit the headlines around March 1987. Oral Roberts shut himself up in his prayer-tower claiming that God would "call him home" unless people contributed $8 million to his Oklahoma headquarters by March 31.[17] Jim Bakker confirmed allegations of an extramarital affair with a church secretary seven years previously. The woman, Jessica Hahn, confirmed that she had had an affair with Bakker at the time. Bakker said he had paid more than $115,000 in blackmail money to Hahn to keep her from going public with the affair.[18] A Harris opinion poll found that 69 percent of its sample thought that electronic preachers did more harm than good. More to the point, 41 percent of viewers of religious television programs agreed. When asked whether electronic preachers were in the business mainly for the money culled from their followers, 54 percent of those followers answered yes.[19] It is obvious these scandals have had an effect on society, and that they have an effect on America's view of ethics.

CONCLUSION

As one can see from the aforementioned arguments, ethics is an issue that is difficult to examine clearly. This difficulty originates from the ambiguity and plurality of a standard working definition of "ethics." Ethics encompasses a myriad of factors which, unfortunately, have several different meanings to many different people. Since a large percentage of the American public thinks ethics in general have declined, an analysis of the other factors in the broader societal sphere must be closely examined. The family plays a major role in the instillation of moral values. As previously mentioned, ethics are developed, not innate. The value of the family are more likely bestowed upon the individual at an early age by the parents (if the parents have a substantial role in the child's preteen environment). If the root of ethical awareness lies outside the home, it would certainly seem to be the responsibility of academic institutions to teach good ethics. Business ethics evolve from ethics in the societal sense. Without a strong ethical sensitivity for our lives as a whole it is impossible to foster a firm ethical awareness in our professional lives. The question of who is responsible for ethical education remains unanswered. The gap of ethical and unethical behavior can only be narrowed if we begin to see the range of responsibility between the family unit and the business community. What starts in the home can only be strengthened by today's corporate culture.

NOTES

1. Roger Ricklefs, "Executives and General Public Say Ethical Behavior Is Declining in the United States," *Wall Street Journal* (October 21, 1985): 2.

2. Ibid.

3. Roger Ricklefs, "On Many Ethical Issues, Executives Apply Stiffer Standards Than Public," *Wall Street Journal* (November 11, 1985): sec. 2, p. 31.

4. Tom L. Beauchamp and Norman E. Bowie, *Ethical Theory and Business* (Englewood Cliffs, N.J.: Prentice-Hall, 1979), p. 1.

5. "Executive Life," *Fortune* (December 8, 1986): 65–66.

6. Beauchamp and Bowie, *Ethical Theory,* p. 2.

7. Ibid.

8. *Phi Delta Kappan* (April 1987): 638.

9. Hamman and Alkhafaji, "Business Schools," p. 2.

10. Ibid.

11. Ron Powers, "Businessmen Wear Black Hats," *Business Month* (December 1987): 70.

12. William A. Scott and Terrence Mitchell, "The Moral Failure of Management Education," *Chronicle of Higher Education* (December 11, 1985): 35.

13. Ibid.

14. Ibid.

15. "The Business Ethics Debate," *Newsweek* (May 25, 1987): 36.

16. Stephen H. Wildstrom, "A Risky Tack for Democrats," *Business Week* (July 20, 1987): 22.

17. "Praise the Lord and Pass the Loot," *Economist* (May 16, 1987): 23.

18. "TV Ministries Enveloped in Infighting," *Broadcasting* (May 30, 1987): 60.

19. "Praise the Lord," p. 23.

PART FOUR

The Restructuring of U.S. Companies

17

Mergers and Takeovers

A new war is presently raging in corporate America. It is a war of mergers, takeovers, and leveraged buyouts. A flurry of media articles document the battles of this blitzkrieg style of warfare. The corporate world has entered into an era of rapid change, and threats to established corporate procedures are on the rise. Attacks are being leveled almost daily against America's traditional business environment as never before. In fact we have reached the point where, as *Forbes* magazine states in reference to businesses, "no one is safe."[1] This virtual whirlwind of activity has caused business to center much of its time and energy on preventing external takeovers.

Changes in the stock market, governmental activity, corporate inactivity, America's trend toward high technology, and the increased threat of takeovers are forcing modern business to reshape its thinking and approaches connected with the running of its firms. This chapter will focus on the activities of takeovers and mergers: the reasons for them, associated problems and benefits, and present trends.

A study of these concepts is of vital importance to any student of business. Unless business managers at all levels learn to adapt to this changing environment they run the risk of becoming a takeover target for an enterprising entrepreneur or another company.

This unit concentrates on the three main areas of acquisition: takeovers, mergers, and buyouts. All of these involve different activities, but they all have the common goal of realigning a corporation. This chapter will focus on the activities of mergers and takeovers. The following chapters will address the concept of buyouts.

TAKEOVERS

Trends and Facts

Almost any corporation can be the target of a takeover. A takeover occurs when an outside force gathers adequate finances to purchase enough stock in a company to gain control. These unwanted overtures are aptly dubbed "hostile" takeover attempts. In the past two years alone nearly 240 U.S. companies, each valued at over $100 million, have been targets of hostile takeover attempts.[2] Most of these takeovers are instigated by one individual who has enough influence, financial capacity, and corporate savvy to threaten and indeed take over another company. People like T. Boone Pickens, Carl Ichan, Sir James Goldsmith, Brian Beazer, and Irwin Jacobs have gained wide notoriety as "corporate raiders" in reference to their constant attempts to enlarge their financial empires through hostile and friendly takeovers.

Another trend has surfaced in recent times. Declines in the stock market along with a weakening of the junk bond market have triggered the involvement of corporations themselves as takeover artists. For example, Eastman Kodak acquired an unwilling Sterling Drug Inc. in an agreement involving $5.1 billion.[3] Other recent corporate and individual takeover bids are listed in figure 17.1.

Reasons for Takeover Activity

A variety of factors feed the desire in corporate raiders to take over companies. Many of the takeovers involve brash, determined personalities who are not afraid to spin off unproductive divisions, restructure the company, and liquidate the assets of the companies they acquire. They are more than willing to make the sweeping decisions they feel are needed to make a company productive. Many "raider" opponents feel this fast action approach often ignores the importance of long-range goals and growth.[4]

A second reason for the rash of takeover attempts is the diversifying activities undertaken by many firms in the 1960s and 1970s. This diversified structure facilitates an ease of liquidating many subsidiary companies for profit. The parent company is often left intact but many holdings are sold, providing a raider with funds to pay the debt incurred in the takeover. This divesting of nonessential divisions in a large company is a major concern to any target company of a takeover attempt.

Finally, almost all takeovers and takeover attempts have resulted in a sizeable profit to the raider, whether or not they succeeded. Most takeovers begin with the raider purchasing large chunks of a target company's stock. This drives the stock value up. Thus, if a takeover fails, the raider can resell his holdings at the higher price. Some gains are rather impressive, as illustrated by the unsuccessful takeover attempt of the Goodyear Tire Company. Sir

Figure 17.1
Corporate Takeover Bids

SUITER	Target	Value
Eastman-Kodak	Sterling Drug	$5.1 billion
B.A.T. Industries	Farmers Group	$4.2 billion
American Brands	E II Holding	$2.7 billion
Bryan Beazer	Koppers Company	$1.7 billion
Paul Pilzerian	Singer Company	$1.06 billion
T. Boone Pickens	Diamond Shamrock Corp.	$300 million
Prime Computer	Computer Vision	$435 million

Source: *Wall Street Journal* (January 25, 1988); *New York Times* (February 1, 1988).

James Goldsmith initiated the takeover, but decided for a number of reasons that he could not complete the acquisition. Goodyear then repurchased his holdings in their company, affording Goldsmith greenmail in the amount of $90 million.[5]

Varying combinations of these and other factors have led to increased takeover activity. The most common motivational factor seems to be a desire for quick financial returns, often at the expense of the target company.

Financing of Takeovers

The takeover of another company, whether hostile or friendly, demands a sizeable outlay of capital, often running into the billions of dollars. Where do these people come up with that kind of money? The first and most obvious source is a bank loan. Many raiders simply disclose their plans to a lending institution. When the bank is convinced that the raider can make a profit from the venture and repay the loan, the funds are granted.

A second and highly popular method is through the issuance of junk bonds. By issuing so-called junk bonds, which are not rated by investment services and typically pay up to 3 percent more interest than less risky securities, a takeover artist can tap a virtually limitless source of cash.

Two other possible sources of capital are investment firms and other raiders. For example, the investment company of Shearson, Lehman Brothers and fellow raider T. Boone Pickens, Jr., recently provided $355 million and $150 million respectively to help raider Paul Bilzerian in his bid to take over the Singer Company. With this financial aid, Bilzerian successfully completed the Singer takeover. To repay these loans, he was forced to partially dismantle the company.[6]

Resisting Takeovers

How does a company resist a takeover? Businesses have initiated a variety of resistance tactics. The first way is by paying more attention to the stockholders. "It is likely that there would be fewer challenges to the existing managers of companies if more boards acted with day-to-day concern for the interests of their shareholders."[7] The stockholders' voices are affecting corporate governance more than ever before. Many companies are hiring outside directors so as to guarantee an impartial view of the company and keep the stockholders' interest in mind. The best way to protect and aid the stockholder is to resist any takeover attempt. By doing this one drives up the price of stock and gives the stockholder a much better return on investment while keeping control of the corporation.

Another method of defense against acquisition is restructuring. Many companies are doing this with a vengeance. One of the most popular forms of restructuring is a stock buy back. By repurchasing stock, a company can increase its capitalization, making it much harder to acquire. The best way to repurchase stock is through a leveraged buyout. "By transforming a public company into a private one, a CEO can take direct responsibility for something they actually own."[8] The only problem with restructuring is an increase in debt, which managers do not mind in this case, because a debt-ridden company is unattractive to takeover artists. Other restructuring involves the divesting of any unprofitable divisions of a parent company and a reinvestment of the generated funds. This limits the possibility of a takeover artist taking the same action to benefit himself financially.

Another defense mechanism used is that of "poison pills," or making a company unaffordable. This can be accomplished in many ways. Offering special low-priced stock purchasing plans to present stockholders if a takeover reaches a "trigger percentage" of total outstanding stock often deters a potential takeover.[9] Furthermore, many companies have already placed golden parachutes on their upper management personnel. According to Thomas Murray in *Dun's Business Monthly,* nearly half of the largest five hundred American firms pack golden parachutes to break the financial fall of the top executives. Recently, ousted chairman Sam Armacost received a $1.7-million package from Bank America Corporation as a golden parachute settlement.[10] A similar plan is presently growing in popularity which affords lower-level workers some degree of severance pay. The Herman Miller Company, a $531.6-million Michigan-based office furniture company, has installed a plan that would assure one year's severance pay to employees with two to five years of service who within two years of a hostile change of control are either fired or quite voluntarily.[11] Employees with more seniority would receive two-and-one-half years compensation. This type of poison pill has been dubbed a "tin parachute."

Other strategies often used are Pac Man ploys and pleas for friendly takeovers by another firm with guarantees of a continuation of existing employment status. (See figure 17.2 for takeover terminology)

The negative aspects of hostile takeovers (i.e., drastic company restructuring, sweeping management changes, divesting a corporation of its subsidiaries, etc.) call for a heightened awareness of the present-day economic environment. Modern management must be knowledgeable of defensive strategies a company can use against such hostile actions.

Legal Developments

Paralleling the increase in takeovers and mergers is a move to provide legal defenses against such actions. Twenty-seven states have enacted laws to limit shareholders' rights, thus strengthening management's ability to resist takeovers. Even the federal government is considering legislation to restrict takeover activity. Minnesota, Indiana, and, most notably, Delaware have passed legislation that seriously handicaps corporate raiders. Indiana's anti-takeover statute was upheld in 1987 by the Supreme Court in *CTS Corporation v. Dynamics Corporation of America*. Since then, more than a dozen states have enacted takeover laws. Some corporations in states lacking takeover legislation have threatened to relocate unless they too are afforded protective statutes. Delaware, being the "home" of half the companies listed on the New York Stock Exchange, has been the center of a heated controversy.[12] Corporate raider T. Boone Pickens mounted a campaign against their impending anti-takeover legislation by using news conferences, full-page newspaper ads, radio spots, and mailings to forty thousand of the state's five hundred thousand residents.[13] In spite of the campaign and a statement from the chairman of the Securities and Exchange Commission, David Ruder, that the bill was "too favorable to management," the bill was approved in the legislature by a 101 to 24 margin. (See figure 17.3 for a more detailed explanation of the contents of the bill.) Predictably, the bill was immediately challenged in the courts by Campeau Corporation and Black and Decker Corporation, both of which were attempting takeovers of other Delaware corporations.

State governments will no doubt continue to address the takeover issue unless the federal government intervenes with its own legislation, and

Figure 17.2
Takover Terminology

```
********************************************************************
*                                                                  *
*    The  fast  moving  takeover tactics of corporate raiders      *
*  and recently "Corporate Buyers" has  prompted  a  colorful      *
*  array  of  business  terms used by the media and corporate      *
*  personnel.  A sampling of these highly  descriptive  terms      *
*  includes:                                                       *
*                                                                  *
*  Corporacy:  Defined  by  corporate  raiders as entrenched       *
*  management,  guided by self-interest and ignoring the  best     *
*  interest of shareholders.                                       *
*                                                                  *
*  Golden  Parachute:  Hefty  payments  guaranteed  to  top        *
*  executives of a company if a takeover succeeds.  The exact      *
*  terms of these agreements vary widely and the amounts  can      *
*  be as large as $10 million for the CEO of a large company.      *
*                                                                  *
*  Greenmail:  Resale  of  the  shares of a company held by a      *
*  corporate raider, (usually at a high  profit),  in  return      *
*  for a promise to drop a takeover bid.                           *
*                                                                  *
*  Junk Bonds: So called because of the low credit ratings of      *
*  the  issuers.  They  usually  pay  a  higher-than-average       *
*  interest  rate  as a reflection of the increased risk, and      *
*  are often used  by  corporate  raiders  to  finance  their      *
*  takeovers.                                                      *
*                                                                  *
*  Pac  Man  Defense: Named after the popular video game "Pac      *
*  Man".  A  risky  maneuver  used  to  thwart  a  potential       *
*  takeover  in  which the target company turns the tables on      *
*  its pursuer and attempts to buy  them  out.  This  ploy         *
*  worked  for  American  Brands  Inc.  and Martin  Marietta       *
*  Corporation to avoid recent takeover attempts.                  *
*                                                                  *
*  Poison  Pill: A measure taken by the target of a potential      *
*  takeover in which the target company  makes  the  takeover      *
*  prohibitively   expensive.   Tin   parachutes,   golden         *
*  parachutes, and most  notably,  the  issuance  of  special      *
*  stockholder  securities  or purchasing options that can be      *
*  exercised if a takeover succeeds, are examples  of  poison      *
*  pills.                                                          *
*                                                                  *
*  Tin Parachutes:  A  poison  pill  that  is  increasing  in      *
*  popularity.  It  is  an  expanded  version  of the golden       *
*  parachute.  It guarantees generous severance  benefits  to      *
*  blue collar workers in the event of a takeover.                 *
********************************************************************
```

Source: Corporate Board (September–October 1985).

Figure 17.3
Delaware Takeover Legislation

```
*
*  The basic components of the Delaware Legislation are
*  summarized below.
*
*  Lacking prior approval from a target company's board, an
*  acquirer of 15% or more of the target's voting stock would
*  have to meet one of the following two tests to complete a
*  subsequent merger:
*
*     A.  It could purchase at least 85% of the target's stock.
*     (Stock held by directors who are also officers and by
*     certain employee stock plans would not be included in
*     determining whether the 85% level had been reached.)
*
*                          OR
*
*     B.  If the acquirer gained control of the target's board
*     but fell short of the 85% threshold, it could complete the
*     merger within three years if it got the approval of
*     two-thirds of the target's voting shares excluding the
*     shares already held by the bidder.
*
*  Companies would have 90 days to choose to "opt out" of being
*  covered by the law.
*
*****************************************************************
```

Source: *New York Times* (December 21, 1987); *Wall Street Journal* (January 5, 1988).

preempts all existing state-level statutes. The basis for such legislation would be the charge that many state laws "represent an unconstitutional interference with interstate commerce."[14]

Problems and Benefits of Takeovers

The hostile takeover of a company is a traumatic experience at all levels of the target company. Concern and worry over the situation cut deeply into the company's morale and stability. The most unsettling concern is for the company's future state. A takeover often results in loss of jobs, employees, and subsidiaries. This fear permeates a target company from corporate head-quarters to production line employees. Many stakeholders (suppliers, buyers, communities) are also interested in the action as it could easily affect their lives and jobs also.

A second problem associated with takeovers is the high debt level that a raider often leaves a company with. This debt load weakens the firm for the future. Added to this debt is the cost most companies incur trying to fend off a takeover, which may run into the millions of dollars.

A final problem with takeovers is a shift away from long-term goals, many of which are society-oriented. Many corporations presently spend millions of dollars on environmental concerns, safety programs, and community projects. It is felt that takeovers seriously jeopardize this type of expenditure. Robert Mercer, chairman and CEO of the Goodyear Tire and Rubber Company states that "a raider's idea of a clean environment is that, after swapping paper back and forth in a frenzy, you sell out at the last minute and stash the money in a Swiss bank account. This perversion of financial instruments has no redeeming social value and certainly creates no real wealth."[15]

The flip side of the takeover issue also exists. Advocates of takeovers cite the 8.4 percent average increase in the value of a business after a takeover, as documented in a study for the Twentieth Century Fund.[16] Of course, one would expect this as the goal of most takeovers is to generate capital quickly. The true impact of takeovers, though, cannot be ascertained until a study is done on the long-range returns of companies acquired through takeover tactics.

Another argument often used to support takeover activities is the need to perpetuate the entrepreneurial heritage that is a vital component of our culture. The American free market economy is based on the principles of open access and free competition. Thus, laws that severely limit the activities of modern-day entrepreneurs run counter to this heritage. Takeover artists claim U.S. business needs to encourage this spirit, not repress it.

Stockholders often benefit from a takeover or a takeover attempt, as such actions usually drive up the value of the target company's stock. A variety of studies reported gains between 16 and 34 percent in takeover situations. Between 1984 and 1985 alone takeovers generated $75 billion in premiums for shareholders.[17]

MERGERS

A merger occurs when two companies decide harmoniously to join together as one company. A merger differs from a takeover in that during a takeover there is little or no regard for the target company; in a merger a joint decision is made. Like takeovers, mergers have become quite common in corporate America. "In one sense, the wave of mergers sweeping America today springs from the same motive as others in the past—corporate managers egged on by financial wizards, think they can make more money together than separately."[18] The scope of the merger movement is evidenced by the fact that the number of mergers in 1984 was about 2,500 with nearly $54 billion transacted.

Companies merge with the hope that they will become more diverse and gain more shares of different markets. This may have been true in the past, but in corporate America today most of the mergers have been of companies that are similar in nature. A prime example of this type of merger occurred when Philip Morris acquired General Foods in 1985. Although Philip Morris is mainly known for its production of cigarettes, it did have smaller food companies under its parent name. Worried that lawsuits may eventually hurt the tobacco industry, Philip Morris decided to expand its share in the food industry through the purchase of General Foods. This merger between two similar brand names helped Philip Morris to expand their share of the market in another industry.

Most companies merge to achieve vertical and horizontal integration. A large company may find that the supply expense for one of its inputs is too high. Instead of paying the high price, the large company will instead merge with a company that manufactures the parts. "IBM has already purchased 17.5 percent of semiconductor maker Intel Corporation."[19] By doing this IBM is working to lower its costs of inputs.

The mergers that have worked quite well over the years have some striking similarities. In most cases the successful mergers involved industries in similar businesses. These mergers are financed by swap of stock or cash, and there is no borrowing of money. "The price does not include a lofty premium, and the management of the acquired company usually stays on to run the business."[20] Mergers have gained in popularity because they do not seem as ruthless as takeovers, but they accomplish the goal of acquiring another company.

Problems of Mergers

One of the main problems that arises when one company merges with another corporation is that some serious internal problems are often inherited. Once a merger has been completed, the acquiring company has the acquired company for better or for worse. A good example of this is if a corporation acquires another corporation which is in food production. "A series of bad crops and economic developments beyond the control of food companies could send costs soaring and eventually squeeze margins."[21] The parent company is now forced to deal with losses it never foresaw when the original merger was made.

Many times during an acquisition, the parent company gets caught in a *synergy trap*. This is "an assumption by executives that the skills honed in one business can be readily applied to another."[22] Many times the management skills in one industry cannot mesh with the management skills in another industry. The problem is that many of the corporate buyers do not take enough time in considering the management skills which will be needed in order to attain profits from the target company. In the end there is great difficulty in meshing the cultures of the two corporations. It is this difficulty that makes synergy a trap in the merger game.

Legal Considerations

Once a buyer and seller begin to negotiate the details of a proposed merger, they should be alert to specific problems which may arise in the legal areas and which may influence a proposed merger. They should also consider what effect the transition may have on other interested parties. Due to the nature of our society and legal institutions, other parties in addition to the buyer and seller may have an important stake in the proposed merger. The public, the creditors of the buyer and seller, and the stockholders of both may have vested interests in the transaction which may not be violated.

Legal securities problems in mergers may involve many areas of the law. If a seller requires the approval of its stockholders to sell its business, the seller may be required to prepare and file with the Securities and Exchange Commission proxy material to hold its stockholder meetings. The problem involved with the preparation of the proxy material for approval of the sale may be more involved than preparing such material for a regular annual meeting. Some of the stockholders of the seller may run into problems of short swing profits under section 16b of the SEC Act of 1934. Security law problems of this nature normally do not threaten the successful completion of the merger.

When a buyer intends to buy a seller for stock or securities, a basic problem may arise under the Securities Act of 1933 which may cause collapse of negotiations and failure of the proposed merger unless the buyer and the seller find a solution satisfactory to each.

Rules promulgated by the Security and Exchange Commission under the act seek (1) to inhibit the creation of public markets in securities of issues which have not disclosed material information about themselves in appropriate filings with the SEC;[23] and (2) to permit the sale of ordinary trading transactions of limited quantities of the securities of issuers which are making such filings, where exceptions are not otherwise available.[24]

There are three federal acts which are in retrospect of the Clayton Act dealing with acquisitions. Section 7 of the Clayton Act takes in a broad scope of antitrust laws. Three federal acts make up the major body of these laws.

The first is the Sherman Act, which provides that "every contract, combination in the form of thrust or otherwise, or conspiracy in restraint of trade commerce, is declared to be illegal," and further "that every person who shall monopolize or attempt to monopolize, or conspire to monopolize any part of commerce shall violate the act."[25] The first of the trust-busting statutes, the Sherman Act prohibits price fixings, boycotts, and allocation of territories through contracts of actions by competitors. The Sherman Act also attempts to reduce the power and activities of corporations with monopoly or near-monopoly positions.[26]

The Federal Trade Commission Act is the second major act and provides that "unfair methods of competition in commerce and unfair or deceptive acts or practices in commerce are unlawful."[27] This act also prohibits false advertising and unfair methods of competition that might enable a company to achieve a monopolisitic position.

The third act which is grouped among antitrust laws is the Robinson–Patman Act, which is an amendment to the Clayton Act. This act "prohibits discriminations in prices where the probable consequences of such discrimination would either be a substantial lessening of competition or a tendency to create a monopoly or to injure competition between third party and the person granting or receiving discrimination."[28]

Section 7 of the Clayton Act provides "that the act is violated when a corporation acquires assets or stocks in another corporation and the effect of the acquisition may be substantially to lessen competition, or tend to create a monopoly."[29] What this act says is that it need not actually be demonstrated that the acquisition has or will definitely lessen competition. This requires that there be a reasonable probability that the undesirable effect on competition will result. The main objective is to maintain a competitive business community.

Also covered in section 7 of the Clayton Act are four basic elements. (1) *Acquisition*. The presence of this element is the easiest to establish. There must be an acquisition of all or part of the assets or stock of another corporation. The acquisition may be made directly or indirectly by the acquiring company. (2) *Line of Commerce*. The lessening of competition under the statute may take place in any line of commerce. This has given the enforcement agencies an opportunity to restrict and broaden relative product lines to attempt to prove possible lessening of competition. (3) *Section of the Country*. The tendency of lessening competition need occur only in any section of the country, not the country as a whole. Government agencies have the leeway of attempting to prove possible lessening of competition throughout the country or in localized sections. (4) *Tendency to Lessen Competition*. The acquisition must substantially lessen competition or create a monopoly. The effect of the competition therefore does not have to be immediate. A reasonable probability of a substantial lessening of competition is all that is required to violate the statute.

There are also notification requirements which must be followed in a merger. Under a Federal Trade Commission requirement, there must be a sixty-day notice prior to the consummation of the acquisition by a buyer with assets of $250 million or more, of a seller of $10 million or more. The notice must be given within ten days after the agreement in principle has been reached. The same notification requirements apply to a buyer with less than $250 million in assets who proposes to acquire a seller with $10 million in assets or more, where the resulting corporation would have assets exceeding $250 million.[30]

These are only a small number of laws that govern corporate acquisitions and mergers. For each separate merger, there are many laws to look into. All mergers and acquisitions are unique. The many laws that would cover all mergers are beyond the scope of this chapter.

SUMMARY

Mergers, takeovers, raiders, junk bonds . . . what do these mean to business today? What influences does "acquisition fever" have on the functions of business in America today? The true impact of the "takeover" philosophy has yet to be measured. With state and federal governments involved and many companies developing their own defense strategies the arena will be dust-filled for some time.

To be sure, corporations have become quite sensitive to their internal economic health and stability. Many bold decisions are being made in corporate headquarters today that might not have been considered only a few years ago. There is a move on the part of many companies to divest or improve the performance of unprofitable divisions, increase their own overall efficiency, and in general, become more responsible managers of the stockholders' invested capital. As Richard Madden, CEO of Potlach Corporation, who recently defended the company against a hostile takeover, stated: "More than ever we have to change. A well-run company with a good stock price is a lot more raider proof than a poorly run company with artificial defenses."[31]

A CASE STUDY: MERGERS AND REGIONAL ANTITRUST LAWS

A Transportation Department administrative law judge has recommended that the merger of U.S. Air Group, Inc. and Piedmont Aviation, Inc., the two smallest of the major carriers, be disapproved because it would reduce East Coast competition and hurt consumers.

The decision by Judge Ronnie A. Yoder questions many of the economic assumptions used by the Transportation Department in evaluation of airline merger cases and the antitrust assumptions used by the Justice Department.

Analysts believe U.S. Air and Piedmont will enhance the merger's chances if they compromise to allow the merger's principal opponent, American West Airlines, Inc., to gain access to U.S. Air's and Piedmont's strongest market area, which is east of the Mississippi and north of Florida.

When merged, U.S. and Piedmont would be the nation's fifth largest carrier. In the Eastern U.S. submarket, where U.S. Air and Piedmont are centered, the merger would give them a 50 percent or greater enplanement share at thirty-eight points. The two carriers now compete in twenty-one nonstop city-pair markets and serve fifty-seven common points. Nine of the nonstop city-pair markets are served only by them and six are not served by other turbojet carriers.

As a result, the merger would substantially reduce competition in numerous city-pair markets, including those served by slot-constraint airports at Washington National. U.S. Air is said to be trying to dominate this particular market.

Administrative law judges' recommendations usually carry greater weight. This particular rejection is hoped to be overruled so the merger can take place.

This particular case of airline merger is one of the many corporate mergers which is attempted each year. This shows that although each company may have the financial backing and the corporate names, that not all mergers will be successful.

This particular rejection was based in part on the Clayton Act. Section 7 of the Clayton Act is directly related to this case. It states that any acquisitions which lessen competition or create a monopoly are illegal. In the case of U.S. Air, it was undertaking this merger for the purpose of lessening competition.

NOTES

1. Peter Newcomb, "No one Is safe," *Forbes* (July 13, 1987): 121.

2. Robert Mercer, "Raiders Might Be after Your Company Next," *Industry Week* (June 29, 1987): 14.

3. Brian Burrough, "Back in Action," *Wall Street Journal* (January 25, 1988).

4. Andrew Sigler, "Takeovers: The Economic Cost," *Corporate Board* (September–October 1985): 5.

5. "The Raiders: A Quick Fall From Grace", *Newsweek* (December 8, 1986): 66.

6. "But Can He Handle An Ax?", *Business Week* (January 25, 1988): 35.

7. Murray Weidenbaum, "The Best Defense Against The Raiders," *Business Week* (September 23, 1985): 21.

8. Anthony Bianco, "Deal Mania—The Tempo Is Frantic and the Prosperity of the U.S. Is at Stake," *Business Week* (November 24, 1986): 75.

9. Ruth Simon, "Of Pots and Paintbrushes," *Forbes* (November 3, 1986): 110.

10. Thomas Murray, "Here Comes the 'Tin' Parachute," *Dun's Business Monthly* (January 1987): 62.

11. Joani Nelson-Horchler, "A Catchall Parachute," *Industry Week* (February 9, 1987): 17.

12. "Compromise Near in Delaware," *New York Times* (December 21, 1987): D2.

13. Laurie Hays, "Pickens Impels Blitz to Topple Measure on Hostile Bids," *Wall Street Journal* (January 14, 1988): 32.

14. C. Yang and J. Weber, "Is Delaware about to Harpoon the Sharks?" *Business Week* (January 25, 1988): 34.

15. Mercer, "Raiders," p. 14.

16. Doug Bandow, "Are Hostile Takeovers Good For The Economy?" *Business and Society Review* (Fall 1987): 47.

17. Ibid.

18. "How the New Merger Boom Will Benefit the Economy," *Business Week* (February 6, 1984): 42.

19. Ibid., p. 46.

20. Joan M. O'Connell, "Do Mergers Really Work?" *Business Week* (June 3, 1985): 88.

21. Zachary Schiller and Amy Dunkin, *Business Week*, "New? Improved? The Brand Name Mergers," *Business Week* (October 21, 1985): 110.

22. O'Connell, "Do Mergers Really Work?" p. 89.

23. Earl Kinter, *Primer on the Law of Mergers* (New York: Macmillan, 1983), p. 147.

24. Ibid., p. 129.

25. Charles A. Scharf, *Acquisitions, Mergers, Sales, and Takeovers* (Englewood Cliffs, N.J.: Prentice-Hall, 1971), p. 128.

26. Ibid., p. 129.

27. Ibid., p. 130.

28. Ibid., p. 132.

29. Ibid.

30. Kenneth Clarkson, Roger Miller, and Gaylord Jantz, *West's Business Law* (New York: West Publishing Co., 1986), p. 129.

31. Kathleen Weigner, "To Make Your Company Raider-proof, Run It Right," *Forbes* (November 3, 1986): 110.

18

The Buyout

This chapter will discuss the buyout phenomenon: why it became increasingly popular in the 1980s, types of buyouts, the international aspect, and a framework showing the transaction process of the buyouts of the parties involved. "In 1986 some 4,000 of America's largest companies . . . will spend nearly $200 billion to transform themselves. That is four times the amount spent just three years ago, and the crest keeps rising."[1]

TYPES OF BUYOUTS

There are various types and combinations of buyouts, each of which has its own advantages and/or disadvantages to the specific company which is seeking an organizational or financial structural change. The first and most popular method of making a company private is leveraged buyouts (LBOs). LBO refers to the way in which the deal is financed. In such ventures, the purpose price is financed mostly through debt. A group of investors, led by an investment banking firm specializing in such financial deals, usually contributes about 10 percent of the total purchase price. The remainder of the purchase is financed by loans secured from banks and even insurance companies. This debt is charged or leveraged against the company's assets.[2] This chapter will focus on LBOs.

The second method of restructuring is known as management buyout (MBO). MBO occurs when the existing management of a company, with the help of financial institutions, buys back the company and creates a private entity. MBOs may refer to the purchase of the entire company itself or just a subsidiary in which a relationship would exist between the company and the subsidiary. MBOs can be rather complex and some form of leveraged financing usually occurs in this method.

Another type of restructuring is referred to as a spinoff. This occurs when employees of one company choose to establish a new firm, utilizing previously acquired skills and capital. Like the MBOs involving a subsidiary, a spinoff will usually maintain a relationship with the previous employer. Spinoffs may occur in industries which are easily penetrable and suitable for such entrepreneurial ideas or where subcontracting and reliance on similar firms is common.[3]

The final type of buyout is known as Employee Stock Ownership Plan (ESOP). This allows employees to assume a direct role in corporate governance. An ESOP is a trust set up for employees which borrows money from banks in order to buy back stock from the company. The company then contributes money to the fund which is used to pay off the debt, free of tax. Of the five thousand companies which have ESOPs, only five hundred have been estimated to be actual LBOs.[4]

LBO DEVELOPMENT

Although LBOs in their current form first appeared in the 1960s, they have become increasingly popular over the past ten years. In 1960, many corporations decided to merge or to acquire new businesses, some of which were not in the same industry. This strategy was mainly to reduce the risk of busines failure and to spread it over diverse groupings of the business entity. Most of these mergers however, were not very successful.

The impact of inflation upon the economy has undoubtedly increased the appeal for leveraged financing. The presence of inflation benefits debtors because it reduces the payment which is fundamental for the success of LBOs.[5] This inflationary economy usually benefits debtors because they will be paying less. Corporations involved in LBOs, therefore, are helped by inflation to pay off the debt incurred in financing the acquisition.[6] The amount of money involved in LBOs sharply increased from $636 million in 1979 to $10.8 billion in 1984. Ellyn Spragim states that "a few years ago it cost 9 to 10 times a company's earnings to buy it but now it takes 14 times the earnings or more."[7]

According to Alexander Taylor, in 1979 there were only sixteen LBOs while in 1983 there were thirty-six buyouts involving several billion dollars.[8] Susan Harding, Leon Hanoville, Joseph C. Rue, and Ara G. Volkan stated that almost one-half of all corporate acquisitions in 1983 were transacted as leveraged buyouts.[9] The estimate for 1984 and beyond was even higher. In the first quarter in 1983, sixty-two LBOs occurred, valued in excess of $4.9 billion, while in 1984, there were 250 LBOs which were worth $18.6 billion. This represents six times the rate of 1981 when only ninety-eight LBOs took place.[10]

It can be seen that the appeal and significance of the phenomenon has grown at an incredible rate and shows no signs of slowing down.

CHARACTERISTICS OF COMPANIES

Although LBOs have been known to encompass many diverse industries and have been attempted in companies which range in size and market strength, investors look for a company that has some basic characteristics. Leonard Shaykin belives that consistent past profits, predictable future profits, and quality management control are vital for the initiation of an LBO in a particular company.[11] LBOs are usually associated with mature companies in stable industries. The reasons are obvious for such a stipulation. Banks would not loan the enormous capital required for such deals to relatively new or emerging companies. In most cases, the managers demonstrated an aggressive entrepreneurial style. This should come as no surprise, because it is a necessary attribute in conducting a buyout. There are many problems that can arise during a buyout, and managers must be willing and able to face them. They must be true risk takers. Their first obstacle is to raise the money to finance the debt. Along this line, they must convince their external stakeholders that their company can still exist. Such was the case with Blue Bell. "We knew that the numbers (the cost of the buyout) would scare our major suppliers,"[12] stated CEO Edward J. Bauman. Also, the managers must have definite ideas regarding what they want to do with the company once it is private. Finally, the managers may meet some opposition from one or a group of stockholders in the early stages of the buyout. Unless they are aggressive and tenacious, the buyout may never materialize.

The condition of a company before a buyout is usually one of little or declining growth. The reason for this is because companies undergoing tremendous growth require a large amount of cash for ongoing projects, such as the hiring of more employees and R&D expenditures. A buyout would simply be more feasible in a low-growth company, so cash can be generated to help finance the debt. However, this is not to say that the company does not have potential. Albert J. Dunlap achieved great success for Lily-Tulip Inc. after being appointed president following a loss of $11 million as a result of going private. Dunlap cut out $50 million in overhead. At the same time, they reduced the debt, upgraded the product, and received a profit of $8 million.[13]

A company that is involved in a buyout is usually cash rich. For example, Beatrice, at the time of the buyout, had approximately $125 million in cash and $5 billion in current assets.[14] Only a small portion of this is needed for operating purposes. In addition, some of the assets can be liquidated in an emergency. This cash is very helpful in the payment of the acquisition price. It enables the managers to reduce the amount of borrowing needed for the company they acquire. For example, management of Macy's decided to sell off nine of its shopping malls for approximately $500 million. The money obtained from the sales was to help finance the debt incurred in the $3.7-billion buyout.[15] In addition to this maturity, companies must maintain market stability in regard to demand for their product. A stable demand rate will ensure the cash flow necessary to meet the interest payment and thus reduce the large debt.

Levi Strauss and Company, a prominent leader in the jeans market, had trouble adapting to the declining market as a whole. After having enjoyed great success in previous years, their earnings were down 80 percent in 1984. Donna M. Hostetler of Crowell, Weidon, and Company believed that the cycle was right for a LBO. Levi Strauss is a prime example of a company ready for the private ranks again. It had remained private for 120 years before it decided to enter the public market. However, fifteen years later, it recognized the need to return it to the status of a family affair.[16]

Although the future of LBOs can only be estimated, it is easy to see that the best bet for such enterprising ventures is relatively low growth and mature companies.

REASONS FOR BUYOUTS

There are several reasons why a LBO takes place: (1) Management concentrates on cash flow and does not concern itself with stock market pressures and short-term earnings being reported. Thus they concentrate on long-term growth and profitability. (2) Management become their own bosses. They can run the business the way they want to, reviving their entrepreneurial spirit. (3) Because of the financial structure that exists, management can pay off their debt and re-enter the public market for an enormous profit, usually in about seven years. (4) Shareholders receive an above-market price for their stock. For instance, the shares of Levi Strauss were bought back from common stockholders for $50 per share, which was higher than the current market price of about $30 per share.[17] (5) An LBO prevents hostile takeovers and corporate raiders. Thus the interests of management and employees will be protected. For example, Uniroyal Inc. went private in a LBO to escape a takeover bid by Carl C. Icahn.[18]

Tax Advantages

The U.S. tax code is very conducive to LBO activity because it permits investors to deduct interest on debts. This deduction decreases tax liability so that cash which would have been used to pay taxes prior to the LBO may be used to reduce the principal of the loan. Most companies pay little or no tax in the first few years following an LBO. The tax advantage of Norris Industries amounted to a $76 million decrease in taxable income. If we assume a tax rate of 50 percent, this leaves Norris with a $38-million savings. That amount was more than 60 percent of its interest payments in 1987.[19]

The accounting procedure for such an acquisition of a company's assets reflects a tax savings as well. The value of the assets can be increased from book value to their approximate market value on the acquisition date. Because this value is increased, depreciation is increased and in turn decreases the company's taxable income and tax liability.

Prior to the Tax Reform Act of 1986, the seller of the company also benefits greatly. If the sale qualifies for capital gain treatment, that is, the asset sold must have been a capital asset that was held by the seller for at least six months, the seller is liable for taxes on 40 percent of the gains recognized. The leniency of the tax code permits debtors to use IOUs as tax shelters and charge part of the cost to the federal government. As Benton Malkiel of Vale suggests, "our tax laws clearly encourage this kind of activity."[20] Capital gains now are treated as ordinary income.

BENEFITS TO THREE MAJOR STAKEHOLDERS

For the purpose of this study, stakeholders are defined as those groups which have direct economic interest in the buyouts. Without their approval the buyouts would not be completed. These include investment bankers, management, stockholders, boards of directors, employees, major creditors, major suppliers, and major consumers.

LBOs are a money-making bonanza for almost everyone involved. We have chosen to include only three major stakeholders—investment banking firms, management, and stockholders—in discussing the attraction of LBOs due to the fact that these groups are the major ones which must sit down and negotiate the deal. As John Greenwald suggests, buyouts are hotter than ever because, so far, they have produced countless winners and few if any losers.[21]

LBOs have become increasingly popular due to the lucrative financial opportunities which they afford. These deals have proven that everyone who participates can become a winner. The changes made in the federal reserve regulations in 1981 have allowed investment banking firms to arrange financing for the acquisition of stock in public companies. Since that time they have become havens for companies contemplating LBOs. It is evident why investment bankers have turned toward LBOs. Wall Street's fastest-growing investment banking firm, Drexel Burnham Lambert, has the ability to raise billions in leveraged finance. The profit that they have received from Beatrice's LBO by Kohlberg, Kravis, Roberts, and Co., another investment banking firm, has exceeded $86 million while KKR received only $45 million.[22] LBOs can produce enormous profits as returns on equity on these deals have been up to 50 percent annually. An investment firm participating in an LBO in which the new company decides to divest its subsidiaries may collect a fee from each spinoff. Eventually the bankers will underwrite its re-entry as a public corporation after the LBO has reached full cycle—usually after six or seven years. The substantial returns have also encouraged investment banks to get into the action using their own capital and assuming some ownership. An example of this technique is shown in the LBO of Beatrice by KKR. KKR has assumed much of the debt and management will own 12 to 15 percent of the company. Norman Kravis outlines his plan for continued growth and his confidence in the management team: "We will continue to grow Beatrice. There will be a stronger, more efficient, streamlined Beatrice 3 years from now and 8 years from now.... They (management) have the same interest we have, to maximize return on invested capital. They will run the company for the long run."[23]

It is evident that the interests and goals of investment bankers and existing management coincide in this case; however, some cases do not reflect such an attitude. Top-level and possibly middle-level managers who seek to control the company must take on the greatest personal liability in comparison to other eager investors. However, many managers seek to maximize their personal satisfaction through running the company their own way. In order for the management to demonstrate to the financial lenders a total and responsible commitment, managers often take out second mortgages on their homes in order to raise capital and assume a significant role in the LBO. This action shows that management is reliable and wishes to obtain a large stake of equity in the enterprise. John Oren, president of Eastway Delivery Service Inc., is a fine example of the entrepreneurial spirit that has shunned the layered bureaucracy of public companies. He believes staying private is the only way to achieve his entrepreneurial goals. "Having total control of my life is where I am at. The company is a reflection of that."[24]

In contrast to the enormous financial and entrepreneurial benefits that are part of LBOs, the manager must sacrifice some luxuries that he has enjoyed in the public company. Dennis Sheehan, CEO of Akia, believes that management must take personal pride in reducing unnecessary expenses in order to streamline the company in hopes of long-term growth. Therefore, we can see that management stands a lot to gain from such a venture while risking a great stake, but the track record has been very good so far. In addition, stockholders, the final major participants in this game, clearly come away from the deal with a substantial gain and no risks or binding obligations involved. Viacom International Inc. accepted a takeover bid from a management-led investing group that will give shareholders $2.35 billion, in a combination of cash and convertible preferred stock, and a 20 percent stake in the new company. The deal, heavily financed through loans, was finally negotiated after Viacom rejected a previous offer which did not provide for the shareholders to receive any stock in the company. Terence A. Ellses, president of Viacom, feels that this transaction is in the best interest of Viacom, its shareholders, and its employees.

THE PROBLEMS WITH LBOs

LBOs have become prevalent in business today. LBOs free companies from scrutinizing stockholders, let them escape from takeover bids, and allow them to concentrate on growth. However, these pleasures are not without financial risks. When a company engages in a LBO, they are assuming risks. One such risk is a possible economic downturn. If the company's respective business fluctuates with the economy, a subsequent recession would severely retard the company's earnings, thereby making it difficult to meet their financial obligations. Another risk is the rise of interest rates not anticipated at the time of the buyout. When the market rate increases, an increase in the company's interest obligations on the original terms of the loan will also occur.[25] A company which is only barely meeting its debt obligations may have some distinct problems in paying the increase in interest payments. A final risk deals with legal matters. Shareholders who are against the buyout may take the buyers to court if they feel they are being treated unjustly. For this reason, the buyers must make sure they take careful steps, and that everyone is happy during the buyout process. While LBOs are supported by many, they also have their share of critics. These critics deem LBOs more of a hindrance than a blessing and have many reasons for this feeling. The first criticism is that LBOs are not holy endeavors. They do not create jobs (often there is a "clearing of the house"), they do not increase productivity, and often they do not help America compete in the business world. For example, the United Food and Commercial Workers Union (UFCW) has forced Safeway Stores Inc., a nationwide food chain, to recognize and discuss the effects an LBO would have upon its unionized employees. This follows management's decision to join forces with KKR and raise $4.1 billion for a LBO—a deal which the UFCW feels will force Safeway to sell off some of its assets and thus cut employment. George H. Cohen suggests that unions are looking for new ways to protect themselves and force management to respect their voice in LBOs.[26] In April 1987, Safeway announced the closing of many of their stores in Texas, and many employees were laid off. Another criticism is that the LBO is inimical to progress. A typical LBO target is not the company in trouble. It is usually a company which has a large amount of assets, low debt, and achieves relatively consistent profits. Therefore, a company might elect to increase dividends or bonuses instead of upgrading factories, simply to avoid a takeover attempt. In the end all this will hurt the competitiveness of U.S. businesses. Finally, LBOs are diminishing the entrepreneurial spirit in America. Entrepreneurs used to search for new and innovative methods of business. However, LBOs have turned the spirit into a big money game. In doing this, progress can be severely depressed. Instead of developing new companies and practices, the "raiders" strive for large amounts of money to take over already existing companies. Again, U.S. business is hurt in the end.

FINANCIAL INSTITUTIONS' ROLE IN THE BUYOUTS

Institutions are willing to help finance LBOs due to the fact that the risk is much lower than the financing of new ventures. The institutional lenders

are aware of the fact that entrepreneurs are likely to be educated and knowledgeable about the field into which they are buying. Major investors are also
more likely to be wealthy, thus reinforcing their success as entrepreneurs
and reassuring the lender. Institutional lenders feel safer about investing their
money in an LBO when the entrepreneur himself is making a large contribution. Another characteristic of institutional lenders is that they are likely
to provide long repayment periods. This is due to the confidence that lenders
gain in the LBOs. They do not feel the need to demand the money in a short
period of time because the company is unlikely to have any great cash flow
in the starting stages. Financial institutions provide such tremendous funding
for various reasons. First, the management buyer has the assets and the
reputation of the company for a sound collateral. However, as valuable assets
for banks, the earnings of a buyout are also reasons for investing. Buyouts
are also very attractive because of the front and fees. Usually, in order for a
buyout to commence, banks require a significant "service charge" for their
enormous loan. Furthermore, banks are attracted to the interest rates. Since
buyouts are encouraged by the government, financial institutions are able to
charge an interest of about five points above the prime interest rate. Finally,
the lending institutions participate in up to 20 percent of all profits. With
these incentives, lending industries are flooding corporations with buyout
opportunities. Many regard the financial support as beneficial to the economy,
as well as to the particular company. First, the capital provided may help with
the restructuring of a company so it may be more efficient in operations.
Furthermore, some believe that with the added funds, introduction and development of product lines would be singificantly improved. Finally, companies would probably be future-oriented, which would increase the value
of the company (so debts could be paid easier in the future).

On the other hand, many regard the financial support as an omen. Even
though dividend payments are not a factor of the revenue, interest paid on
the loans are factors. In fact, some companies can be so burdened, that their
main objective is to meet interest payments, to the neglect of the re-paying
of the debt. Furthermore, some believe that inappropriate buyouts are being
financed and therefore straining the funds from useful investments. Generally,
the debt incurred from buyout deals can only be managed by those companies
able to economize, increase revenues, and increase profits relative to interest
and debt payments.

Even though financial institutions are presently lending to a wide range of
buyout clients, these institutions do have restrictions and guidelines. The
financiers always forecast financial downswings that could affect the success
and payment levels of businesses. Furthermore, predictions of interest levels
are always a grand factor in deciding the buyout deals. Notwithstanding, the
status of the company before acquisition is an important factor. For example,
competition, business structure, outstanding debts, and managerial competence are all aspects of the company's status. Therefore, even though it may

appear that lenders are providing all companies with buyout funds, financial institutions are applying strict criteria for their deals. One of the major investment banking firms in New York City is that of Forstmann Little & Co. They have financed such buyouts as Revlon, Dr. Pepper Co., and Allen-Bradley Co. It is lending companies such as this that help out LBOs. In order to feel even safer about their investment, they often seek to secure loans with personal guarantees, especially when the amount is substantial. As well as personal guarantees, another characteristic of institutional lenders is that they charge a much lower interest rate than that charged to nonentrepreneurial BLO investors. This is due to the previously stated facts that lenders are confident because of stable industry, established companies, and respected investors. Institutional lenders find it more profitable to invest in LBOs than in new ventures. It is an advantage for them to know the history of the entrepreneur in order to ensure the safety of their money. This is sort of a reciprocal arrangement because lenders are confident in their investment in LBOs while entrepreneurs receive the loan with a low interest rate.

LEVERAGED BUYOUT ON THE INTERNATIONAL LEVEL

The idea of LBOs is not only a domestic phenomenon, but also has become widely international. Many countries are experiencing the growth of LBOs.

Great Britain is experiencing a rise in LBOs, as 124 buyouts worth a total of £100 million were arranged in Britain last year, but it still remains far behind the United States in total monetary amounts. One of the largest buyouts Britain has experienced as of yet is with the Stone-Platt Industries. When the company went under, some divisions were sold to its managers, who in turn created a higher profit than it had experienced prior to difficulties in the company. For example, its electrical division was sold for $15 million to managers led by Robin Travener, chief executive of the Stone-Platt group. This division made £4.3-million profit before interest and taxes in 1980. The finance for this buyout came from the managers, banks, pension funds, insurance companies, and specialist finance companies.

Another major buyout in Britain was that of Thorn EMI. The primary objective of this conglomerate, stated by Sir Graham Wilkins, was to raise operating profit, which shrank 9 percent the previous year, to £171.7 million ($216 million) on sales 14 percent up at £3.2 billion for the year up to March 1985. Sir Graham's plan for this objective is to reduce the company to four product groups, rather than seven, so that the efforts for increased profitability could be more directed toward these four remaining divisions. The LBO took place when the three groups were bought out. The major advantage of this buyout was lessening the risk of three groups, while increasing the profitability of the other four groups. It is slightly easier for Sir Graham to hold four golf umbrellas than seven, but not a lot. The major disadvantages were failure to increase profitability, and failure to cover losses of sales revenue of the other three companies. Therefore, it is quite obvious that LBOs in Great Britain are on the rise.[27]

In France, LBOs are being strongly supported by the French government, which is lowering taxes in order to promote these buyouts. A major problem, however, has been identified by the two major financial groups (Compagnie Financiere de Suez and the Paribas groups): the need for managers to set up a company of their own, with outside backing, to buy the firm they work for. However, these buyouts are difficult under present French law. New owners are seeking new laws, which would allow them to use tax write-offs. The groups who seem to be benefiting most from the LBOs in France are foreign-owned subsidiaries and family-owned firms, because of the government's new emphasis on entrepreneurship and small business.[28]

Finally, a major LBO took place in Canada in 1972, which in turn has inspired action toward other LBOs. CIP, Inc., a Canadian pulp and paper manufacturer, was bought out, with a major part of the financial backing coming from the provincial government ($13.5 million in loans, grants, and preferred shares), while the federal government contributed $4.4 million in grants and $6 million in loans, private investor funds ($200,000), and also the employees ($425,000). The closing of CIP, Inc. would have left over 700 laborers unemployed, but the new company, Tembec, has been very successful ever since the buyout.[29]

Based on the previous examples, it is rather evident that the idea of LBOs is expanding to the international level, and is becoming quite successful.

THE PROCESS

The LBO transaction, in general, goes through the following steps:

1. The buyouts would be either by the management of the companies (in this case called MBO), investors outside the company (in this case called LBO), an employee of the corporation through the employee stock ownership plan (ESOP—in this case called employee buyouts), or a combination (in this case again called LBO). These groups present a proposal to the acquiring company.

2. This proposal must be supported by a financial package. This package usually includes the name of the bank(s), insurance companies, pension plans, and so on, supporting this proposal with financial details. The finance package represents the agreements between the different financial parties who consent to finance the LBO deal.

3. This deal usually is presented to the board of directors of the acquiring companies. The BODs are the stockholders' representatives. If the BODs feel that the deal is an attractive one, then they will present it to the stockholders for approval.

4. When the stockholders accept the deal, especially if the offer price is higher than the market price, then the stockholders sell their stock to the purchasing group at the agreed-upon price.

Table 18.1
The Buyout Process

PURCHASING GROUP	TYPE OF BUYOUT	FINANCIAL SUPPORT	CORPORATE GOVERNANCE	NEW COMPANY
MANAGEMENT	MBO	COMMERCIAL BANKS, INSURANCE CO. SPECIALIST FINANCE	STOCKHOLDERS	NEW COMPANY EMERGED
INVESTORS	LBO	COMPANIES PENSION FUNDS SMALL BUSINESS	BOARD OF DIRECTORS	
EMPLOYEE	ESOP	INVESTMENT CO. VENTURE CAPITALIST OTHERS	MANAGEMENT	
COMBINATION	LBO		EMPLOYEES	

5. The final stage after the stockholders' agreements is the formation of a new business entity. (These stages are presented for illustration in table 18.1.)

6. Sometimes employees enter into the picture by demanding an agreement with the new purchaser, especially if the employees were unionized.

THE FUTURE

1. Although it is questioned if LBOs actually result in increased motivation and productivity on the part of management and employees, they offer a future for up and running companies that might otherwise be liquidated or absorbed by conglomerates.

2. As long as LBOs involve a great profit motive when the company goes public again, many managers and investors will continue to take the opportunity.

3. Many people are willing to invest in LBOs, since there have been very few failures of buyouts. Therefore, the trend will continue to grow.

4. With a strong economy, declining interest rates, and low inflation, there will continue to be a large number of LBOs. However, any investor knows that financial fads may fizzle out.

5. Will the large debt taken on by these companies help or hinder the economy in the long run?

Even though it is hard to assess this question at this time because buyouts have not been around long enough, we think that it will help more than it will hinder. We think it will stimulate the economy, encourage the spirit of being an entrepreneur, and circulate the money that will keep the economy prospering. It will also hinder the economy through the loss of jobs, the stress that will be placed on the employees and the managers to be more efficient, and the pressure on those who want to double their money in a short time.

NOTES

1. Bruce Nussbaun, *Business Week* (November 24, 1986): 75.
2. Clemens P. Work and Manuel Schiffres, "Leveraged Buyouts—Are They Growing Too Risky?" *U.S. News and World Report* (November 18, 1985): 50.
3. Sue Birely, "Success and Failure in Management Buyouts," *Long Range Planning*, 17, no. 3 (1985): 32.
4. Rogene A. Buchholz, *Business Environment and Public Policy: Implications for Management and Strategy Formulation* (Englewood Cliffs, N.J.: Prentice-Hall, 1986), p. 247.
5. Susan D. Harding, Leon Hanouille, Joseph C. Rue, and Ara C. Volkan, "Why LBOs Are Popular," *Management Accounting* (December 1985): 51–52.
6. John Greenwald, "The Popular Game of Going Private," *Time* (November 4, 1985): 54.
7. Ellyn E. Spragins, "Leveraged Buyouts Aren't Just For Daredevils Anymore," *Business Week* (August 11, 1986): 50.
8. Harding, Hanouille, Rue, and Volkan, *LBOs,* p. 51–52.
9. Harding, Hanouille, Rue, and Volkan, *LBOs,* p. 51–52.
10. Gary Weiss, "ABC's of LBOs: What Makes Leveraged Buyouts Popular," *Barrons,* (August 19, 1985).
11. Greenwald, "Popular Games," p. 55.
12. Maggie McComas, "Life Isn't Easy," *Fortune* (December 9, 1985): 44.
13. Ibid., pp. 46–47.
14. *Moody's Industrial Manual,* 1985, p. 2609.
15. "Top Executives Offer to Buy Macy's," *New York Times* (October 22, 1985): A1.
16. Joan O'C. Hamilton, "Levi Strauss Wants to be a Family Affair Again," *Business Week* (July 29, 1985): 28.
17. Ibid., pp. 28–29.
18. Zachary Schiller, "Uniroyal: The Road From Giant to Corporate Shell," *Business Week* (July 14, 1986): 29.
19. Harding, Hanouille, Rue, and Volkan, *LBOs,* p. 52.
20. Ibid., p. 52.
21. Greenwald, "Popular Game," p. 55.
22. Abbass Alkhafaji, Jeff Dubois, Patty Hunter, and Jim Morgan, "A Current Perspective on Leveraged Buyouts," *Industrial Management Magazine* (September–October 1987): 30.
23. Ibid., p. 30.
24. Ibid.
25. Harding, Hanouille, Rue, and Volkan, *LBOs,* p. 55.
26. Aaron Bernstein, "A Union's Novel Attempt at Shaping a Buyout," *Business Week* (September 8, 1986): 31.
27. Harding, Hanouille, Rue, and Volkan, *LBOs,* p. 51–52.
28. Greenwald, "Popular Game," p. 54.
29. Spragins, "Leveraged Buyouts," p. 50.

19

Management Buyouts

THE CONCEPT

Management buyouts are similar to leveraged buyouts in many respects. In fact, many people use these two concepts interchangeably. In this chapter we will discuss management buyouts and give some examples showing how these buyouts take place.

Management buyouts have become increasingly popular over the past ten years as an alternate form of ownership. They have evolved from joint ventures, subcontracting, licensing, franchising, and spinoffs. A management buyout occurs when "the existing management of a subsidiary, usually with other investors, purchases the company from the owner."[1]

METHODS OF MBOs

Buyouts can be accomplished in several ways. The first is in the form of a cash purchase. In this case the management and investors purchase the company with cash. Another way a buyout occurs is when management stakes their own personal assets in conjunction with the business's assets as collateral for the loan. Leveraged financing is also used in the process of management buyouts. In these transactions, a group of investors who are purchasing the company will use the firm's assets as collateral. Therefore, the loans for the leveraged buyout are backed by the company not the investors.

The increased popularity of management buyouts may be due to a more aggressive style in upper and middle management. There is a great desire among managers to have a controlling interest in their business. Today's managers are more willing to take risks because they have increased confidence in their ability to guide their company into the future. Since managers often want to form their own separate entity, management buyout gives them an opportunity to become entrepreneurs. The management buyout provides more incentive to top executives than common profit-sharing plans or options to purchase company stock can. It is evident that there is an opportunity to become wealthier than a salaried executive; however, this may be outweighed by the risk of financial loss. Managers will feel more responsible and put a greater amount of effort in their daily work, if they are actually participating in the ownership of their firm.

REASONS BEHIND THE INCREASE IN MBOs

There are several specific reasons behind the increase in management buyouts using leveraged financing. These include the recent decline in interest rates as well as reduced inflation. In previous years many firms had practiced diversification strategies only to find later that these businesses did not fit into their strategic plans. Also, buyouts have given financial service companies, banks, pension funds, and insurance companies a new market. These firms are seeking large profits by backing the buyouts; however, in becoming part-owners they also assume a large risk. An expert at Shearson Lehman Brothers commented in reference to the cash committed to buyout funds, "There's more money available than deals."[2] Backers can make huge profits—as much as 50 percent on the equity portion of these deals. Also, when a company goes private there is an opportunity for spinoffs, where management and backers can benefit from the revenues generated.[3]

CHARACTERISTICS OF MBOs

A company that is being considered for a mangement buyout should have the following characteristics:

1. In a mature stage of the business life-cycle
2. An established cash flow
3. A heavy asset base (i.e., manufacturing equipment fully depreciated)
4. Stable and strong product line
5. Strong management with entrepreneurial tendencies
6. Low current and long-term debt
7. No legal problems (creditors)
8. Dominant market position (niche)
9. Decent growth prospects

Although there are similar characteristics associated with management buyouts, the objectives of management teams differ depending on each situation. Some management teams undertake buyouts in order to gain control and keep the company intact. Other buyouts are initiated to prevent hostile takeovers; after such a transaction, parts of the company are quickly liquidated.

The following companies were chosen to illustrate management buyouts. Each has many of the necessary characteristics for a management buyout, but they all have unique goals and objectives.

R. H. Macy and Company, Inc.

In October 1985, the senior executives of R. H. Macy and Company, Inc. proposed a leveraged buyout of the company for $3.7 billion. President Edward S. Finklestein claimed the purpose of the buyout was to free the company's management from the pressures of the short-term financial gains that are typically imposed on a publically owned company.[4] As a privately owned company, Macy's would not be required to report its financial status or pay dividends to its public stockholders. Taking the company private would have many benefits for the management. Although more than one hundred managers would be involved, each would be increasing his share of ownership. This would provide incentive and motivation for improved performance. In the past Macy's had lost several top managers to competitors; this management buyout would keep the talented executives in the company.

Approximately $600 million in financing for this buyout was provided by the managers and the remainder came from backers such as Citibank, Manufacturer's Hanover Trust Company, and General Electric Credit Corporation. Finklestein said that the company would continue its long-term strategies of geographical expansion, improving the quality of service, and selling more private label merchandise.[5] As a private company, Macy's would be able to budget their funds more freely in order to generate greater customer satisfaction and gain an edge in a highly competitive industry. However, the burden of a large debt would make geographical expansion and increased budgets very difficult to finance. Also, the management had to realize that they would not be totally independent as they would have to answer to at least one equity partner who would undoubtedly be keeping a close eye on them.

Some changes that have taken place since the management buyout are the following: As of October 5, 1986, Macy's subsidiary, Bamberger's, would now be known as Macy's. This change reflects the new top management's desire for a more centralized operation. Bamberger's corporate division was renamed Macy's of New Jersey. Also, the new management decided to sell off nine of its shopping malls for approximately $500 million. These nine shopping malls contain Macy's stores which would continue to operate after the malls were sold. Macy's would use the money obtained from the sales to help finance the debt incurred in the $43.7-billion buyout.

Levi Strauss & Co.

Unlike many firms which go from public to private, Levi Strauss first went from private to public seventeen years ago. This move was undertaken to finance their aggressive growth strategy. The growth strategy was necessary at the time in order to keep up with the growing market. The principal objectives were expansion and capturing additional market shares. The company began to experience financial difficulties when the environment changed and their strategy for growth was no longer the "best" strategy. The market was declining and Levi Strauss was having problems successfully introducing new product lines into the market. One of the results of this was that "in 1984 the company recorded one of its worst years ever. Earnings were down 80 percent, to just $41 million on sales of $2.5 billion."[6]

Levi Strauss's President, Robert D. Haas, announced on July 31, 1985, that the company was going private again. Haas led the buyout bid with members of the management and other Strauss descendants. The original proposal was presented to the board of directors in early July. A committee of four board members, who were not involved in the buyout, were appointed to analyze the proposal (four out of the seventeen board members were family members). Since the board was so strongly in favor of the buyout, it was unanimously approved. The buyout was part of the new strategic plan for the company's revitalization. The shares were bought back from common stockholders for $50 per share, an excellent price for a stock which was going for only about $30 a share when it was announced. The private owners of the stock were family members and/or members of the management. The company (with one exception) has always been headed by a family member, even when the company was public. Therefore, the members of the family are automatically affiliated with the company.

Strauss's new strategy involved drastically cutting overhead from its large number of holdings. This was accomplished by closing plants, laying off workers, and cutting other production costs in the producing plants. The strategy has been very successful: "now, despite a sales drop of 7 percent for the first six months of 1985, earnings are up a stunning 165 percent."[7] Obviously going private has been the right move for Levi Strauss. It has pared down its operations and become more profitable, enabling it to pay off the debt it incurred to buy back its stocks and also to expand in the market which is seeing a turn-around recently.

After the buyout was completed the subsidiaries, which were not directly related to the "main" jean company, were divested. The large amount of debt incurred through the leveraged financing coupled with the new thrust of the company caused Standard and Poor's Corp. to drop Levi and Strauss from its index of "500 stocks." Though some workers lost their jobs during the transition, the change allows the company to concentrate on a more "people-oriented" approach. This marks a return to the original strategy of Levi Strauss—something which the public shareholders would not have tolerated because it does not generate additional profits.

Dodd, Mead & Co.

Thomas Nelson Inc. sold its Dodd, Mead subsidiary to Gamut Publishing Company. Gamut was a partnership formed to acquire Dodd, Mead through a management buyout, along with other book companies. This transaction returned the book publishing firm to private ownership. The two top executives who organized the buyout were J. B. Harder, a corporate financial consultant, and Lynne A. Lumsden, Dodd, Mead's new executive vice president. The distinguishing factor of this buyout was management's desire to keep the business intact as an independent company.

The parent company, Thomas Nelson, Inc., had been suffering losses up to the end of March 1985, and the first quarter of 1986. A turn-around by September 1986 showed sales were up 3.5 percent. Even though Dodd, Mead accounted for less than 10 percent of Nelson's sales, 1985 was their most profitable year.[8] Dodd, Mead's management was encouraged by the firm's recent success, but also reported difficulty with the parent company. Thomas Nelson Inc. publishes books which reflect religious principles and beliefs. This conflict between Bible publishing and trade publishing may have been the main contributing factor to the buyout.

The board for Thomas Nelson, Inc., the parent company of Dodd, Mead, was actively involved in the sale to the partnership formed by management. The board felt that Dodd, Mead's publishing business interfered with the scope of Nelson's business.

Two members of top management organized the buyout (Harden and Lumsden). This buyout was organized to keep Dodd, Mead intact, and to provide employees with an opportunity to participate in the ownership of the company.[9] So in this buyout employees did not sacrifice a thing. In effect, they may have gained more freedom and partial interest in the company.

Uniroyal Inc.

In another recent management buyout, Uniroyal Inc. went private in a leveraged buyout to escape a takeover bid by Carl C. Icahn. This transaction took place under the direction of Chairman Joseph P. Flannery. In this particular buyout, however, the company was dismembered to pay off $900 million in debt incurred during the leveraged purchase. Proceeds from the assets totaled approximately $1.1 billion. The top managers at Uniroyal, including Flannery, split $6.9 million which the company received after the buyout.[10]

In this case, again the firm was experiencing financial problems. In fact, in 1980 the tire and chemical manufacturer almost went bankrupt. Flannery, however, began to cut costs and pension liabilities attracting several takeover raiders, such as Carl Icahn. After the buyout Uniroyal sold its chemical business to Avery Inc. for $760 milliion and their $1-billion tire business merged with B. F. Goodrich Co. It is evident this buyout took place for the purpose of avoiding a takeover. The management had no intention of keeping the firm intact. All businesses were subsequently sold or merged with other companies.

In this case as well, the board had an active role in the buyout. The chairman of the board in fact arranged the buyout to ecape a hostile takeover. It is also reported that members of top management as well as Flannery split the profits from the sale of assets after the buyout. So in this manner, upper-level management and especially the CEO of Uniroyal had a very dominant role in the buyout.

In this buyout, employees lost jobs and sacrificed many benefits they were expecting to receive after retirement. Other sacrifices made by employees at Uniroyal included hourly workers who made wage concessions to keep Uniroyal afloat during the company's financially troubled times.[11]

First National Supermarkets

In 1985, First National Supermarkets was involved in a $52.6-million leveraged buyout, by a twelve-member management group. Their decision to go private was prompted by the repeated offers to buy their company. In March a foreign investment group which was not involved in the food industry made an attempt to take over the company. The privatization of the company was initiated by the confusion that was created within the company, due to these offers and related rumors among the employees.[12]

Raymond International Inc.

Raymond International Inc.'s board approved a leveraged buyout in 1983 by the company's employees for approximately $165 million. Under the buyout agreement, the newly formed company will be primarily owned by the 3,500 salaried employees through a stock ownership plan. Raymond was considered a likely candidate for a buyout because of its decreasing prices of stock. In 1981, Raymond earned $15.8 million and their stock was $2.66 a share. However, in 1982, their earnings severely decreased to $12.2 million or $1.94 per share of stock. The recessionary pressures on the industry it serves, which includes oil and gas production, mining, and heavy manufacturers, proved to be the major cause of their declining earnings.[13]

ARA Services Inc.

ARA Services Inc. provides a variety of services, including food, transportation, cleaning, and health and child care. Plans for a management buyout apparently came about from an unsolicited leveraged buyout bid in July. Even though ARA's executives would have been given the opportunity for ownership in the company, they were decidedly against the plan because they wanted to remain independent. Due to this ARA's senior management proposed a leveraged buyout in 1984. Under this proposal, sixty to eighty-five executives and various investors would be participating in the buyout. After much conflict, the completed buyout proposal was for $882.5 million or $62.50 per share.[14]

In conclusion, management buyouts have positive and negative repercussions. As seen in the Levi Strauss example, a firm may go private just so it is not forced to report all strategic and financial maneuvers to the public. Strauss has undergone the full cycle from private to public and back to private family ownership. In the Macy's example, managers risked their own assets in an effort to finance the transaction. These risks may have been worthwhile because management now has control over their own business. These executives have struggled their way up the corporate ladder and see buyouts as resulting in tangible rewards through ownership. This entrepreneurial spirit has enabled management to sometimes outperform their original expectations.

It is the opinion of this writer that management buyouts which keep the current employee base and the company intact usually benefit all parties involved. This is in contrast to those buyouts which are organized in an effort to dodge hostile takeovers. These buyouts often result in rapid divestitures in order for managers to collect large profits while the employees are losing their jobs. One must question the integrity of management's motives in these deals. It is also apparent that the management buyout may be subject to impending lawsuits from shareholders who are reluctant to give up their interest in the company. Lawsuits may be brought about by employees who fear losing their salaries and/or benefits from an unscrupulous buyout.

At this point in time, management buyouts have been generally profitable and successful. However, the test of this form of ownership will come when the economic tides change. Economic changes such as interest rate fluctuations and the availability of capital affect many aspects of a company's external environment. Though this current trend may be profitable, investors know that financial fads may fizzle out.

SUMMARY

1. Management buyouts have come a long way from the joint ventures, spinoffs, and franchising of the past.

Table 19.1
Case Comparisons

Companies Status	R.H. Macy & Co., Inc.	Levi Strauss & Co.	Dodd, Mead & Co.	Uniroyal, Inc.
Public to Private	X	Private to Public to Private	X	X
Purposes/ Reasons for Buyout	-Management wants control -To free management from pressures of short-term financial gains	-Do not want to report all strategic and financial maneuvers to the public -Want to concentrate on long-term earnings	-Want to keep business intact -Conflict between Bible publishing and trade publishing	To escape a takeover bid
Financial Status	No financial problems	Earnings were substantially decreasing	Financial problems	Severe financial problems- almost went bankrupt
Stage of Life Cycle	Mature	Mature	Mature	Mature
Market Position	Dominant market position	Good market position but discontinued growth	Good market position	Good market position
Source of Buyout	Mgt. risked their own personal assets and received outside funds	Not only mgt. but also family	Management	Management Leverage
After Buyout: Strategies and Company Status	-Will continue long-term strategies of geographical expansion -Improve quality of service -Sell more private label merchandise -Earnings are presently increasing	-Divested -Laying off workers -Cutting production costs -Earnings are presently increasing	Parent co. is now increasing in sales	Parts of co. were quickly liquidated sold assets to pay some of the debts
Other Unique characteristics	Largest mgt. buyout of a retail firm as of 1985			

2. MBOs occur when existing management of a subsidiary, usually with other investors, purchase the company from the owner.

3. Buyouts can be accomplished by a cash purchase, using personal assets in conjunction with business assets as collateral for the loan and leveraged financing.

4. There is an increased popularity of management buyouts due to a more aggressive style in upper and middle management.

5. Specific reasons behind the increase in management buyouts are a decline in interest rates and inflation, diversification strategies that have failed, and the new market of financial service companies.

6. Although there are similar characteristics associated with management buyouts, the objectives of management teams differ. Some management teams undertake buyouts in order to gain control and keep the company intact. Other buyouts are initiated to prevent hostile takeovers; after such a transaction, parts of the company are quickly liquidated.

NOTES

1. Sue Birley, "Success and Failure in Management Buyouts," *Long Range Planning* 17, no. 3 (March 1983): 32–39.

2. Ellyn E. Spragins, "Leveraged Buyouts Aren't Just for Daredevils Anymore," *Business Week* (August 11, 1986): 50–51.

3. Marilyn Much, "Leverging Your Life," *Industry Week* (July 9, 1984): 42.

4. "Top Executives Offer to Buy Macy's," *New York Times* (October 22, 1985): sec. 1, p. A1.

5. Ibid.

6. Joan O'C. Hamilton, "Levi Strauss Wants to be a Family Again," *Business Week* (July 29, 1985): 28–29.

7. Ibid.

8. Madalynne Reuter and Marianne Yen, eds., "Thomas Nelson Plans to Sell Dodd, Mead to Its Management," *Publishers Weekly* (January 17, 1986): 14.

9. Ibid.

10. Zachary Schiller, "Uniroyal: The Road From Giant to Corporate Shell," *Business Week* (July 14, 1986): 29.

11. Ibid.

12. "First National Supermarkets," *Wall Street Journal* (September 13, 1985): 58.

13. "Board of Raymond International Sets Buyout by Workers," *Wall Street Journal* (June 22, 1983): 58.

14. "Buyout of ARA by Management is Proposed," *Wall Street Journal* (September 13, 1984): 4.

20

Employee Stock Ownership Plans

INTRODUCTION

In 1974 there were only about three hundred ESOPs; as of 1984 there were over seven thousand with nearly two thousand more plans underway. What explains this sudden increase in employee buyouts? Employees began to realize the advantages along with the economic self-interest gained by sharing in company ownership. Employee ownership gives employees access to credit with which they can become co-owners with the means of production, thus giving them a significant role in the organization. Although employee buyout is not flawless and does not overcome all labor-management problems, it is an alternative to the conventional business and perhaps this is why it has become more and more popular in the United States today.

EMPLOYEE STOCK OWNERSHIP PLANS

There are many ways to achieve employee ownership. The most common way is the employee stock ownership plan. There is no single correct definition of employee ownership. In general it means a plan in which most of the company's employees own at least some of the stock in their company, even if they cannot vote and even if they cannot sell it until they leave the company or retire. ESOPs work only in incorporated businesses which have stock equal to the value of the company. A company sets up a special trust and then gives it cash to buy from the present owners or gives shares of its own stock. The value of these contributions are tax deductible from the company's income up to a certain point.[1] The stock in the trust is put into accounts for individual employees based on compensation or a formula that is more beneficial to lower-paid employees. The stock remains in the trust until either the employee leaves the company or retires. As employees accumulate seniority they gain the right to the stock in their account by a process called "vesting." The employee does not have to pay tax on the stock until they are distributed and when they are distributed, the employee has many ways to reduce the tax.[2]

Companies have several different uses for ESOPs. They are used as an employee benefit plan, as a market for departing owners, as a way to raise capital, as part of participatory management philosophy, as a way to save companies, as a leveraged buyout, and as a return for worker concessions. Each will be briefly discussed.

First, companies can use ESOPs as an employee benefit plan. An ESOP is a tax-favored way for a company to give its employees extra benefits. A company does this by issuing new shares of its own stock to an ESOP. Then these new issues are given to individual employee trusts. These contributions from the company are tax-deductible for the market value of the stock for up to a quarter of the payroll of ESOP participants. The Economic Recovery Tax Act (1981) permits tax deductions for corporations who contribute up to 25 percent of the employees' payroll annually to the plan.

Second, a company may use an ESOP as a market for departing owners, This is done by setting up a plan and making tax-deductible contributions to it. The departing owner then sells back the shares to the company which pays for them with the contributions. An owner can sell to an ESOP to get the same tax deferral by reinvesting the proceeds from the sale in the stock to other companies. An ESOP is the most favored way to sell a business.

Third, a company may use an ESOP to raise capital with less cost. This is done by a company having its ESOP borrow the needed capital, with the company guaranteeing the lender that it will give enough cash to the ESOP to repay the loan. These contributions are tax-deductible up to a limit allowing the company to deduct both the interest and the principal on the loan instead of just the interest. The ESOP would use the loan to buy company stock, giving the company proceeds to the loan and the ESOP stock. The company gets better tax treatment with regard to the repayment of the loan. The same dollar used to repay the loan also creates an employee benefit plan.

Fourth, a company can use an ESOP as part of a participatory management philosophy. The idea behind this is to involve the employees in the company.

Fifth, an ESOP can be used to help save a company. This is the most publicized use of an ESOP even though it is one of the least used ways. Employees must first find out if a buyout is feasible. If it is found to be feasible, funds must then be found. Employees do not buy shares out of their savings, nor do they have personal liability for any bad debts to the company. Sometimes though, employees agree to wage concessions.

Sixth, a company may use ESOPs in a leveraged buyout. This is when management or investors borrow money to buy a controlling interest in the firm. The debt taken on is repaid from the earnings of the firm putting a strain on the company. Borrowing through an ESOP reduces the company's taxable income and can reduce the interest rate on the loan. ESOPs have created a broader market for banks, as approximately 40 percent are leveraged and rely on bank loans. Such loans are perhaps safer than a regular corporate loan because the ESOP loan is being repaid with pretax dollars and less earnings are needed to pay the debt.[3]

Seventh, a company can use ESOPs in return for worker concessions. Employers match at least one part of the concessions workers take with stock. This enables the workers to make up for their lossses and also gain representation on the board of directors.

ADVANTAGES OF ESOPs

The advantages of an ESOP are numerous and benefit not only employees but the firm and society as well. Employees benefit as part-owners through workplace conditions and increased financial security. Workers receive the satisfaction of knowing that they play a significant role in their company. Although most companies are not actually controlled by the workers and do not allow workers to vote their shares, it has continued to be beneficial. A worker in an employee-owned company has a much better input channel than in a conventional company, where employee input is rarely, if ever, taken seriously. Recent research also shows that companies with employee ownership have begun to encourage and allow more employee input. The systems are becoming more and more democratic as management learns to adjust to this type of environment. Eventually these companies, ideally, will allow workers to vote their stock as well as have shopfloor participation programs.

Employees also benefit financially from employee-owned companies. A typical plan provides employees with 10 to 15 percent of annual pay in stock. An employee who earns an average of $20,000 per year, for twenty years (assuming the stock value grows 10 percent) would be able to retire with at least $100,000 in his or her account. Employees constantly feel that their self-worth is increasing, which provides incentives for continued work for that company. Employees also realize that the better the company does in the long term, the more their stock is going to be worth at retirement. Consequently, the workers have a stake in the long-term achievement of the firm. This attitude of concern differs greatly from that of the average NYSE investors. Such investors are only interested in short-term profits.

Once employees begin to think of the company as "theirs" and treat work as a team effort to protect their investment, the company begins to reap the benefit of being employee-owned. Studies show that productivity in such companies has increased by as much as 300 percent. Most research shows increases at least in the 100 to 200 percent range.[4] Weirton Steel in West

Virginia is a good example of a company that has benefited from employee ownership. It was in 1982 that the management gave notice to employees of the plant it was no longer feasible to run the plant. The company planned to shut down the facility by 1987, leaving about 70 percent of the 8,800 employees out of work. Employee ownership was one of the alternatives suggested by management. Through an ESOP, the company was able to obtain low-interest state and federal loans to update the conditions of the plant with the addition of large tax write-offs on these loans. In order to buy the stock for the new employee-owned company, fringe benefits were reduced and workers took a pay cut. By doing this, Weirton was able to reduce labor costs to $18.25, giving Wierton an advantage over its competitors. Of the seven million shares of common stock the new company issued, 6.6 million were owned by the trust. Each year the company would make tax-deductible contributions to the trust, and the money would be turned back to the company in order to pay for the stock. After five years, the employees were to receive the distribution of the stock. At the first annual meeting in 1984 the company reported earnings of $48.3 million on sales of $845.5 million for the first nine months of the year. The use of employee participation teams and a new sales force team, productivity has increased and Weirton was able to increase its market share.[5]

The company's greatest benefit beyond increased productivity is probably the enormous tax advantages. Lenders are granted a 50 percent tax exemption on ESOP loans. The borrowing company is tax exempt when making payments into the ESOP trust and can deduct all interest and some principal on the trust/loan repayment from the pretax income. These tax savings are significant to say the least, and can amount to the difference between a shutdown and a successful recovery of a failing company.[6]

Finally, society benefits from employee-owned companies in two significant ways. First, employee-owned companies provide employment and could save thousands of jobs yearly. Also, employees, once retired, do not become a burden on the U.S. Social Security system. They have planned for the future, and instead of posing a detrimental threat to the country, they are involved with capital expenditures, investments, and savings.

Second, economists estimate that U.S. industry is going to spend between four and six trillion dollars in the next several decades in renovations in order to stay competitive. Employee-owned companies have extensive resources since they can borrow money through the ESOP. The company is also long-term-oriented since the employees are all concerned with job security. In order to ensure job security the company must look to long-term goals which require renovations and capital expenditures.

DISADVANTAGES OF ESOPs

Despite the advantages of employee ownership, numerous disadvantages and risks also exist. Employee ownership does not necessarily improve the relationship between labor and management, which is usually what is assumed. When subsidized credit runs out, the employees must work harder for less pay. This may lead to strikes. Owning a small part of the company is not the same as being a proprietor or owning a major part of the company. John Blasi states that "there is no direct, automatic relationship between employee ownership and improved economic performance."[7]

Employee ownership of a company does not always imply employee control. Here, a major risk exists for the employees, who may feel they are getting control, but end up having no voting rights. Only about 30 percent of ESOPs allow employees to vote with their stock share. This implies ownership without control. Many companies set up employee ownership plans for the company's own tax or financial advantage. However, the company would rather get these benefits without sharing ownership with the employees. Employes, therefore, will not think of the company as "theirs," which results in a limited relationship between labor and management because of the separation between ownership and control.

Management may feel that they are being threatened or challenged by the employees and therefore may not want ESOPs. Also, management does not favor employee ownership because this is a relatively new and unknown concept. Many companies are not yet comfortable with ESOPs. Unions are not ready for employee ownership either; they are more comfortable with the adversarial role they take with management.[8]

There are financial disadvantages to employee buyouts, for the employees and the company in general. If new shares are issued in an ESOP, the current shareholders suffer dilution." If an employee leaves a private company, his shares must be repurchased by the company, which may be very costly. On more general terms, employee ownership plans are expensive to establish and to maintain in a company. Therefore, employee ownership plans can be financial risks.

An example of an employee-owned company whose success story turned out to be a myth is *U.S. News and World Report.* John Kirby, an employee of this company, stated that he quit because "nobody felt that he had a vital stake that was susceptible to enlargement."[9] The company later put itself up for sale, which was likely to be beneficial for the older employees.

Another employee-owned company, American Cast Iron Pipe Company (Acipco), was bequeathed to employees upon the death of its founder. These employees did not own stock directly and did not collect dividends. They received profit-sharing bonuses instead. However, the employees felt they, not management, should control the company. If the employees were to win this fight, they were to receive $24 million that was owed to them.

Some of the disadvantages of employee buyouts are likely to be alleviated after further research is done in this area. When more companies experiment with and implement employee ownership plans, more of the risks will be identified and companies will be able to accommodate their plans to minimize these risks.

OVERALL EVALUATION OF ESOPs

After having researched and analyzed employee ownership, including how ESOPs work, the advantages and disadvantages involved, along with examples of successful and unsuccessful employee-owned companies, it seems that ESOPs can be very advantageous to a company as long as the plan is well implemented. Because companies with ESOPs receive tremendous tax breaks, this is often the sole incentive for a company to implement an ESOP system. However, this is not the basis for a successful employee ownership culture, which must be derived for a company to remain successful in the long run. In order for an ESOP to be successful the company must offer more to the employees than just the fact that they are now "co-owners" of the organization; however, this is not always the situation of companies turning to ESOP management, especially for those doing it for the sole purpose of a tax decrease. Although the company itself may be gaining in terms of a higher profit margin or more revenues to afford greater capital expenditures due to these tax breaks, the employees themselves see no gain from becoming employee-owners and therefore are less productive (this is especially true amongst employees who have given up a pay cut or part of a pension plan in order to implement the ESOP originally). What the company needs to implement are programs to involve the employees in company decisions and plans; they must make employees feel as though they have some sort of stake in the company.

Each organization which presently has an ESOP or is considering becoming one must determine their own key to success. Of the some seven thousand ESOPs that presently exist there are no definite conditions of a firm which could become the "perfect" ESOP. In addition to this, studies done on a cross-section of present-day ESOPs have shown that although many of them implement similar programs, many have extremely different standards when it comes to employee voting rights, percent of company stock owned by the ESOP, and so on. The one characteristic that has come across as being relevant in all ESOPs is that "employees will act more like owners if they see more stock in their accounts each year" and that "unless employees get substantial amounts of stock ownership, it is unlikely that they will really think of themselves as owners."[10] However, this one characteristic does not guarantee a successful ESOP; providing substantial annual contributions is usually the only foundation according to Rosen, Klein, and Young. In order to keep up employees' morale and productivity the organization must develop programs to enhance employee ownership and make them feel that their individual efforts contribute to the total organization.

The American Recreations Center (ARC) devised the following programs to reinforce the idea of employee ownership: (1) discuss employee ownership in employee orientation; (2) decribe employee ownership in employee hand-outs; (3) regularly mention employee ownership in the company newsletter;

(4) hold group meetings about ESOPs; (5) hang posters around the company; (6) hold informal conversations with employees about the employee ownership plan. Most successful ESOPs exercise at last two or three of these programs, according to Rosen, Klein, and Young.

Overall, we can see the employee stock ownership program has many benefits to offer the company, the employee, and also society as long as the program is well implemented. The company may gain great tax advantages along with motivated employees; the employee gains a feeling of ownership; and society gains through the satisfaction of people.

SUMMARY

An ESOP is a plan in which employees own at least some of the stock in the company. While there is no absolute definition, there is a generally accepted definition.

Companies have several different uses for ESOPs: (1) employee benefit plans, (2) market for departing owners, (3) raising capital at a reduced price, (4) a tool in participatory management, (5) can be used to save a company, (6) used as a leveraged buyout, and (7) return workers concessions.

There are many advantages of an ESOP. Employees benefit from better workplace conditions, increased job satisfaction, and increased financial security. The company benefits from increased productivity and enormous tax advantages. Society benefits from the number of jobs saved and industry renovations.

There are few disadvantages to an ESOP. Employees do not always gain direct control, relations with management do not necessarily improve, and strikes can still occur. Management feels threatened by the employees and this concept is still fairly new. The financial disadvantages that occur are stock dilutions and the cost of maintaining an ESOP.

At least some of the following conditions should be met to have a successful ESOP: (1) discussing employee orientation, (2) describing employee ownership through handouts, (3) publicizing the ESOP through newsletters, (4) group meetings about ESOPs, (5) hanging posters around the workplace, and (6) having informal conversations with employees about ESOPs.

Whether ESOPs will be adopted in industry will depend on a number of factors. Two that come to mind are the current economics and the relationship of management and unions.

NOTES

1. Lawrence J. Tell, "ESOPs and LBOs: No KOs for Kelso in This Fight," *Barron's* (November 18, 1985): 77.

2. Stanley B. Block, "Buy-Sell Agreements for Privately Held Corporations," *Journal of Accounting* (September 1985): 114.

3. Shela C. Turpin-Forster, "ESOPs Mean Business," *ABA Banking Journal* (October 1985): 164.

4. Ibid.

5. Rogene Buchholz, *Business Environment and Public Policy: Implications for Management and Strategy Formulation* (Englewood Cliffs, N.J.: Prentice-Hall, 1986), p. 248.

6. Turpin-Forster, "ESOPs," p. 163.

7. William Baldwin, "The Myths of Employee Ownership," *Forbes* (April 1984): 108–11.

8. Corey M. Rosen, Katherine J. Klein, and Karen M. Young, *Employee Ownershp in America: The Equity Solution* (Lexington, Mass.: Lexington Books, 1986), p. 143.

9. Baldwin, "Myths," p. 111.

10. Rosen, Klein, and Young, *Employee Ownership,* p. 143.

21

International Acquisitions

INTRODUCTION

International business may be conducted in a variety of ways. The amount a firm commits to foreign operations differs depending on the amount of resources that are located at home versus those located abroad. When deciding which form of international business a firm should adopt, several factors must be taken into consideration. These include the legal environment, cost, experience, competition, risk, control, and the nature of the assets. After taking the above factors into consideration, the choice among licensing, joint ventures, and wholly-owned subsidiaries can be structured within a portfolio perspective. Because of the recent surge of international corporate takeovers in the United States, this chapter will concentrate on international acquisition activity.

International acquisition is a form of involvement which typically appeals only to the firm which has had prior international experience and which seeks to obtain a business that is related to the firm's core business. Few companies are willing to expend a large portion of their resources on foreign operations in the initial stages. They may not even have the sufficient resources to expand abroad rapidly. At the same time, it is rare for a company to seek international acquisition of an existing firm which does business in an unrelated or secondary product line. If a firm were to obtain control over such a firm, there is a strong chance that the results would prove to be undesirable.[1]

MOTIVES FOR ACQUISITION

A major motive for seeking an acquisition is that a potential investor may find it difficult either to transfer some resource to a foreign operation or to acquire the resource locally for a new facility. One such resource is that of personnel, especially if the labor market is tight.[2] An acquisition provides a firm with the resources necessary for overcoming the constraints imposed by personnel requirements. This is particularly important to the firm which has experienced a great deal of growth in a short period of time. The desire for greater growth in a shorter period of time is actually another factor that typically entices a firm to seek to buy an existing firm. Oligopoly considerations can also influence acquisition activity within highly concentrated industries.[3] For example, Ciba-Geigy purchased Funk International, an American agricultural seed company in 1974. Within one year, Sondor, another leading Swiss drug company, purchased a U.S. seed company. Other acquisitions of seed companies by drug companies followed quickly.[4]

Another reason for a firm seeking to acquire another stems from financial motivations. The first type of financial motive is cited by Alibar: The strong currency effect suggests that companies from countries with relatively low-cost capital will value foreign earnings from operations above financial markets within the host country.[5] The lower capital costs are reflected by lower discount rates which results in higher net present value estimates. Though a firm seeking such a goal could establish its own firm in that country, it is argued by Alibar that a company that looks to financial motivations would typically not be willing to spend the effort to formulate foreign affiliates. Another financially oriented motivation is based on the idea that it may save a firm money if it buys an existing firm because it possibly provides the company with the goodwill and brand identification which could be very costly to develop in a foreign country. Many firms also find that acquisitions reduce costs and risks as well as provide quicker results. It is also argued by many firms seeking to internationally acquire another firm that it is a way of becoming a part of a foreign market without adding capacity to that market.[6]

RISKS INVOLVED IN INTERNATIONAL ACQUISITION

Although these motivations are often present, the firm seeking to internationally acquire another should be aware of some of the difficulties and risks involved. One of the most important concerns deals with the management style which the acquiring firm practices. If the firm believes that it can assume a passive management style and the firm will basically maintain itself, often financial troubles will begin to surface. Under such conditions, it can be argued that incentives for the affiliate to match its former performance are reduced. Management may no longer have the same incentive to perform under the new arrangement as it did when the company was more independent. Replacing the management team could pose a large problem. Problems also arise when the foreign firm attempts to standardize the existing personnel, facilities, and systems to conform to global standards. This can be more costly, time-consuming, and problematic than starting anew. Another major

Table 21.1
International Acquisitions of U.S. Firms

Buyer	Seller	Price
ASEA (Sweden)	Brown Boveri (Switzerland)	$15.0 *
# British Petroleum (Britain)	Standard Oil (U.S.)	$7.40
Amoco (U.S.)	Dome Petroleum (Canada)	$4.18
# Unilever (Netherlands)	Chesebrough-Pond's (U.S.)	$3.10
# American Hoechst (W. Germany)	Celanese (U.S.)	$2.72
JMB Realty (U.S.)	Cadillac Fairview (Canada)	$2.00
# Hanson Trust (Britain)	Kidde (U.S.)	$1.80
Groupe Bruxelles & Tractebel (Belgium)	Imperial Continental Gas Association (Britain)	$1.62
Rupert Murdoch (U.S.)	Herald & Weekly Times (Australia)	$1.54
# Blue Arrow (Britain)	Manpower (U.S.)	$1.34

* Billion
# U.S. Acquisitions

Source: *U.S. News & World Report* (February 22, 1988).

flaw in acquiring a firm is that the implementation of information and control systems often can be a difficult process. Similarly, the management attitudes and incentives are often less constructive in an acquired company.[7]

At present, the United States is experiencing a major increase in the number of foreign firms seeking to acquire domestic firms. European corporations have flocked to the United States in order to purchase companies. During 1987 European acquisitions increased dramatically and experts believe it will increase even more in the upcoming year. Great Britain alone spent $29 billion in acquiring U.S. firms in 1987. These takeovers range from huge multinational corporations such as British Petroleum Co. to smaller firms such as Sweden's Pharmacia. Everyone, it seems, wants a piece of the action where U.S. business is concerned. Table 21.1 contains the highest-priced international acquisitions of 1987.

The recent economic recovery in Europe has left numerous companies ladened with cash and unable to invest at home. It is in the United States that these companies find the outlet for their cash flow and, therefore, they have begun to invest heavily.[8]

Another reason why European companies are expanding into the United States is because of the dollar's continued slide against foreign currency. Also, since the market crash in October 1987, stock prices have dropped roughly 30 percent. U.S. assets are now at a 50 percent discount of that of a year ago. These factors are causing U.S. corporate assets to become big bargains. As stated by financial consultant Dominique Mars, "The wave started with smarter European management and healthier corporate balance sheets. The dollar makes it a tidal wave."[9]

Many U.S. corporations, at the time the European firms began to acquire U.S. businesses, were attempting to sell out before the new tax laws went into effect. This allowed the Europeans to act as saviors in bailing out these U.S. businesses; and with the recent large cash flows at home, the European firms had little trouble in doing so. French and German companies have seen their profit margins more than double in the past year, with spare funds waiting to be invested.

Even without the extra cash, European businesses have been successful in their U.S. acquisitions. This has been made possible through risky debt financing. For example, L'Air Liquide was able to finance half of its purchase of Big Three industries through a new equity offering. In Britain alone, up to 3 billion dollars in equity has been raised for the sole purpose of U.S. acquisitions. The ability of these foreign businesses to sell stocks to their home country, across the Atlantic, and pay cash has played a large part in the European takeovers.

One of these European firms that has grown by acquiring U.S. businesses is Electrolux, Sweden's largest manufacturer of electrical household appliances. In its early international acquisitions, Electrolux mainly pursued larger economies of scale. By buying a U.S. vacuum cleaner company, Electrolux was able to mix additional sales. The United States provided a place for greater competition, larger investments in research and development, and further dilution of administrative costs. Later, Electrolux saw opportunities in areas besides the vacuum cleaner industry and expanded by purchasing existing firms in foreign countries that produced different lines of products. Increased profits allowed Electrolux to acquire other firms, complementing their existing appliance lines. This allowed their economies of scale to grow even larger.[10]

U.S. officials do not seem to be troubled by the large amount of takeovers by European corporations. They instead hope that it will displace the trade deficit. Foreign officials, however, see themselves as rescuing the ill-fated industry of America. Whatever the viewpoint, European companies seem to have learned from their past mistakes in the United States and feel they are now ready to move into the U.S. market.

U.S. ACQUISITIONS OF JAPANESE COMPANIES

Even though foreign companies are becoming more involved in acquisitions of U.S. firms, the same holds true for U.S. firms and their takeovers of foreign companies. One of the main countries where these acquisitions are on the rise is Japan. This is quite ironic because two years ago the word *acquisition* was viewed with disdain in Japan; today these perceptions are changing.[11] Many U.S. firms are becoming frustrated with their dull trading-partner representation, poor direct-sales efforts, and unstable joint ventures, and are looking for new opportunities elsewhere. Acquisitions appear to reduce the time and cost of market entry, which makes it easier for foreign companies to compete with competitors in Japan and worldwide. Such acquisitions have led to faster and deeper market penetration than acquiring firms could have achieved otherwise.[12]

However, these Japanese acquisitions are not smooth and easy. Japan purchases much more from the United States than U.S. companies purchase from the Orient. Huge deals, particularly if hostile, are extremely rare in Japan and large companies refuse to be bought by U.S. firms. The largest foreign purchase so far has been Merck and Co.'s 1983 takeover of Banyu Pharmaceutical Co. The main consideration in U.S. purchases is not the extreme price, but rather the "Japanese culture."[13] Prices do play a role, though, since Japanese companies appear overpriced by American standards. Most of the companies which trade on the Tokyo Stock Exchange sell far more than two times the book value compared with one-and-a-half for Standard and Poor's industrial companies.[14] Japanese culture is a major factor, which means that U.S. firms will have to be satisfied with buying small, private Japanese firms which often have poor prospects. Americans will also have to make such acquisitions in slow motion and use a go-between. They are considered to creep because they often begin with the purchase of a small share, which will rise over time. The Japanese are also very secretive about how many companies have been acquired by foreigners.[15]

Recently Japan appears to have relaxed its restrictions on acquisitions, and such deals are less likely to be stopped since most foreign investment prohibitions have been abandoned. In the United States, an entrepreneur would sell his successful company to turn assets into cash, but in Japan this is different. Japanese firms consist of extremely close aggregates of people, and to sell a firm would result in the feeling of ostracism. This fear is prevalent in all Japanese firms but has decreased from the past where most large healthy firms would refuse to be taken over. Today these firms, particularly smaller ones, would consider being bought by another Japanese firm or bank to keep their company growing and increase employee opportunities. However, being acquired by a U.S. firm would be the last choice for a takeover alternative if the Japanese company was in trouble. Japanese firms are currently facing severe competition with their own domestic rivals and their survival rate is falling. Thus, these Japanese firms would prefer to be acquired by a foreign company as opposed to being "killed" by a domestic firm. Those industries that are in this threatened position and thus pose the greatest opportunities for foreign acquirers include pharmaceutical, chemical, metal, food, consumer goods, and electronic companies. Other prospects for foreign acquisitions include bankrupt or failing companies which are positioned in the "dog quadrant" of the Boston Consulting Group matrix. Money and technology could turn these Japanese "dog" companies into profitable firms and U.S. buyers are willing to take these chances.[16]

To make a Japanese acquisition successful, many rules must be followed. The acquiring company must find a trusted go-between who helps with the purchase. The go-between must be convinced that money is not the only concern in the acquisition, but also that the acquirer will not threaten national security and can offer technology and access to another market. This persuasion may take years, but such Japanese acquisitions appear to be worth it.

Merck & Co., the fifth largest drug maker in the United States, spent $313.5 million to acquire Banyu Pharmaceutical Co. of Tokyo. This 1983 acquisition was the largest ever by a foreign firm in Japan. Merck intended to be the number one pharmaceutical company in Japan. The reason Merck wanted to enter Japan is because Japan was the second-largest consumer of drugs in the world with 1984 sales of $16 billion (which directly follows the $22-billion U.S. market). Merck needed this additional business to help offset its heavy expenditures on drug research and development.[17]

Competition was high in Japanese pharmaceuticals, with Banyu ranking fourteenth and having revenues of $331 million in 1983. Another complicating factor was that the Japanese drug industry was in terrible shape. Doctors not only prescribed drugs but also bought them from wholesalers at low prices and then sold them to patients, who paid what they could. The doctors received additional reimbursement from the national health insurance program. The large markup on drugs was the major source of doctors' income. To keep these health costs in line, the government reduced the amount that would be reimbursed and manufacturers were pressured to cut the prices they charged doctors. Manufacturers like Banyu, which depended heavily on cheaper generic antibiotics, were thus in great trouble.[18] Banyu's poor position posed a great opportunity to Merck. Banyu and Merck had been partners in an unstable joint venture since 1954. For Merck to break this relationship and establish its own sales force, too much time and money would be required. Thus Merck persuaded Banyu into being purchased and Banyu finally consented to having a 5 percent share purchased. In August 1983, Merck increased its holding in Banyu to 50.5 percent. Through this acquisition Merck hoped to better penetrate the Japanese pharmaceutical market, especially for new drugs that were being developed. Merck needed quick sales returns on these drugs, which was difficult in the United States due to the extreme competition and heavily saturated market.[19]

When Merck made this acquisition, it did not know exactly what shape Banyu was in. Banyu had $100 million in cash and liquid assets, but nothing in growth. They spent only $14 million in 1983 R&D compared to Merck's

$357 million R&D expenditures. Banyu's top management was also in turmoil since it was never aware of its operating costs. Banyu also had a poor sales force of only 450 detail people, who were incompetent. No market research was done, so detail people would call on doctors and know nothing about their practices. Straight salaries without commission caused these detail people to lack incentive to contact tough customers. However, Merck has implemented changes and the sales force now totals 900 people. A strong incentive program was also established, as well as more effective wholesaler relations. For Merck to bring new drugs to the economy, marketing organization was required.[20]

Problems still face Merck due to the changing pharmaceutical and governmental environment. However, Merck has no regrets about its Banyu acquisition. Merck continues to look to the future and is counting on the success of two new drugs it plans to introduce in Japan. For all the money that it has spent in Japan, Merck now realizes it has a long way to go before it can capture that number one position.

Although there are some notable success stories, acquisitions of foreign firms appear to give low payoffs in comparison with the other methods of market penetration. It appears that almost 50 percent of U.S. acquisitions of foreign firms fail for various reasons. One main reason is that U.S. firms gain interest in firms that are much less similar to the U.S. company than appear on the surface. Often this is due to different types of customers or unfamiliar technology. Another strong failure factor is that companies have tendencies to acquire unprofitable enterprises in the belief that they can turn the firm around with new management.[21] To conclude it would seem safe to compare an acquisition with an entrepreneur, because an entrepreneur is "one who undertakes a venture, organizes it, raises capital to finance it, and assumes all or a major portion of the risk"—with risk being the main theme of an international acquisition.[22]

SUMMARY

Some companies may choose foreign acquisitions as a means of expanding. A firm thereby gets an ongoing operation, capacity is not added to the market, and there may be a quick return in investment. These acquiring companies face many risks in adapting to foreign management, dealing with the foreign environment, and implementing an information and control system. One of the most difficult countries in which to acquire a firm is Japan. Japan's different culture and social structure makes it very difficult for other countries to make Japanese acquisitions. Currently, with the low dollar and stock prices, the United States is experiencing a high rate of foreign acquisitions of its own firms.

NOTES

1. William H. Davison, *Global Strategic Management* (New York: John Wiley & Sons, 1982), p. 60.

2. John D. Daniels and Lee H. Radebaugh, *International Business* (Reading, Mass.: Addison-Wesley Publishing Company, 1986), p. 526.

3. Davidson, *Global Strategic Management,* p. 60.

4. Ibid., p. 61.

5. Ibid., p. 64.

6. Ibid., p. 68.

7. Daniels and Radebaugh, *International Business,* p. 527.

8. "Europe Goes on a Shopping Spree in the States," *Business Week* (October 27, 1986): 54.

9. Ibid., p. 55.

10. Ibid., p. 54.

11. James B. Treece, "If You Can't Beat 'Em, Buy 'Em", *Business Week* (September 29, 1986): 80.

12. Ibid., p. 80.

13. Lee Smith, "Want to Buy a Japanese Company?" *Fortune* (June 27, 1983): 106.

14. Ibid.

15. Treece, "If You Can't Beat 'Em," p. 80.

16. Smith, "Want to Buy a Japanese Company?", p. 106.

17. "A Japanese Tonic for Merck," *Business Week* (August 22, 1983): 39.

18. Smith, "Want to Buy a Japanese Company?", p. 106.

19. "A Japanese Tonic for Merck," p. 39.

20. "Merck Has an Ache in Japan," *Fortune* (March 18, 1985): 48.

21. Daniels and Radebaugh, *International Business,* p. 527.

22. John G. Burch, *Entrepreneurship* (New York: John Wiley & Sons, 1986): p. 4.

PART FIVE

Corporate Governance and Strategic Management

22

Strategic Management

The purpose of this chapter is to discuss the concept of strategic management in both the domestic and international environments. Corporate culture and related governmental regulations will be assessed and reviewed, and the basic differences between domestic and international business operations will be cited.

The term *strategic management* is defined as "the process by which top management determines the long run direction and performance of the organization by ensuring that careful formulation, proper implementation, and continuous evaluation of the strategy takes place."[1]

strategic management = formulation + implementation + evaluation/control

To further the definition, each of the three major stages will be described. Strategic formulation is the stating of the corporate mission and objectives. Formulation also deals with the development of strategy, and the policies that are used to complete the strategy. Strategic implementation is the means used to achieve the organization's mission. Some methods of strategic implementation are the use of programs, budgets, and procedures. The concept of strategic evaluation and control deals with measurement analysis of standards and corrective actions. In more simple terms, management analyzes the implemented strategy and decides if it is effective. If the strategy proves to be ineffective, steps are taken to improve the strategy.

THE STRATEGIC MANAGEMENT PROCESS

The strategic management process involves decision making by people in the organization. The first step in the process is assessment of organization strengths, weaknesses, opportunities, and threats (SWOT). Strengths are the internal capabilities of the organization that help to promote the organization's objectives in the competitive industry. Weaknesses hinder the accomplishments of the organizational objectives. Opportunities are the external circumstances that provide the organization with an extra opportunity to achieve or exceed its objectives. Threats are external forces that could harm the organization and keep it from achieving its objectives. The organization's SWOTs may offer a change in the mission, objectives, or strategy used to achieve the objectives.

The second step, formulation of organization mission, should be taken after the management has viewed its potential SWOTs. The mission statement simply identifies which businesses management is involved in. The mission statement sets the organization's boundaries for its operations and prevents it from overlooking any related fields.

The third step, formulation of organization philosophy and policies, is important and much analysis should be given before they are formed. The philosophy sets forth the values and beliefs of the organization that guide the behavior of its members in all aspects of business activities. Most companies have a written "code of conduct" which reflects the organization's philosophy. Organization policies provide guidelines that define the area within which objectives are established and strategies are determined, implemented, and controlled. They provide managers with constraints. Policies are formulated by top management and therefore reflect their beliefs. They should directly reflect the mission statement.

The fourth step is determination of strategic objectives. Strategic objectives are the results that the organization wishes to attain during a given period. They should help lead to the achievement of the mission. Both internal and external factors affect the formulation of strategic objectives.

Fifth is the determination of the organization's strategy. A strategy is a means to an end. It describes the method by which the organization achieves its objectives. Alternatives should be established by top management. Evaluation of those alternatives should be applied and strong consideration given to each. The top four or five strategies are selected and more consideration is given to these selected few. There are four different levels of strategies: societal strategies, corporate strategies, business strategies, and functional strategies.

The sixth step is the implementing of the organization's strategy. The implementation process covers the entire range of managerial activities including motivation, compensation, management appraisal, and controlled processes. Implementation can be achieved through the structure, processes, and behavioral tools of the organization. Implementing involves executing the strategic game plan of the company.

The final step is control of the organization's strategy. This is concerned

Figure 22.1
Strategic Management Process

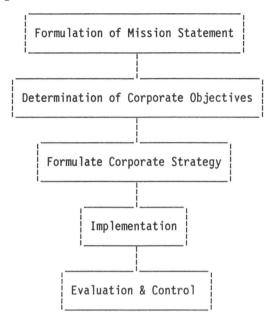

with measuring actual performance against planned performance. It is focused on the organization's actions to achieve the strategic objective.

INVOLVEMENT OF TOP MANAGEMENT IN STRATEGIC MANAGEMENT

The board of directors plays a major part in the functioning of an organization. A board of directors is a group of people elected by the stockholders of an organization that serves primarily to see that the organization is well managed. The board has the ultimate authority for deciding on strategies that may be implemented by management. Basically the board of directors is a body to whom the management of an organization is held accountable for its actions. Most publicly owned organizations have both inside and outside directors. Inside directors are employees of the organization while outside directors come from outside the organization's employment. Often, outside directors are executives of other firms. Also outside directors are usually paid for their role on the board. The board of directors is headed by the chairman of the board. The chairman may be and usually is the chief executive officer. The CEO is the "executive in charge." He is also accountable for the overall activities of the organization. The CEO provides direction by formulating a workable strategic plan that optimizes performance.

BENEFITS OF STRATEGIC MANAGEMENT

Studies have shown that strategic management has four benefits. First, it provides consistent standards for actions taken by management. It helps all parts of the organization focus on common goals. Second, strategic management helps managers to be cognizant of their environment. Third, all levels of management are given the opportunity to participate in the strategic management process. Finally, strategic management can have very positive effects on an organization's long-term performance.

ENVIRONMENT AND CULTURE

In terms of strategic management, there are two types of environments: broad and competitive. The broad environment is one in which many different organizations are affected by changes which cannot be traced to any particular one. There are five major sectors of the broad environment: economic sector, technological sector, political sector, social sector, and ecological sector. It is crucial for a manager to not only view each sector on a local or national level, but also to assess these trends on an international level.

The competitive environment is the environment in which individual organizations interact directly with the industry. In the competitive environment, the actions of all organizations within a specific industry affect the overall activity of a single organization. The effects caused by individual organizations can be advantageous for the industry as a whole, or for certain firms in the business. Conversely, if the caused effects are not expected, they can severely decrease the performance of some or all organizations in the industry.

Both broad and competitive environments have a major impact on the corporate culture of an organization. Corporate culture is defined as those characteristics which make an organization distinctive in its industry. The culture in a corporate environment is usually dictated by a set of values—a system established in accordance with the environment. The culture itself is an intangible asset. A corporate culture can be identified with some careful observation. It cannot be specifically defined because corporate behavior is contingent on an ever-changing environment.

There are several origins of culture. First, and most rare, is that a firm's culture stems from its founder—it conveys the values and beliefs of that individual. Second, the history of the operations of the firm often establish the way things are accomplished in the present environment. People hold strongly to their beliefs and values, while being resistant to any type of change. Third, individuals play a part in shaping corporate culture. Selecting a staff which maintains the present ideals of its personnel is a fourth possible origin. Finally, the process of socialization, which is helping a new employee to adapt and adopt the culture of the organization, is a strong source for setting the culture in an organization.

INTERNATIONAL CULTURE

Culture is defined as the sum total of beliefs, rules, techniques, institutions, and artifacts that characterize human populations.[2] The term *sociocultural* is often used to refer to aspects of culture because society consists of culture, sometimes various cultures. Knowing the cultures of foreign countries is a must for multinational corporation managers going abroad because the beliefs involved in the culture can have a significant effect on all areas of the business.

Sociocultural components include aesthetics, such as art, music, and folklore. Art and music differences in a foreign country have a heavy bearing on marketing internally. Attitudes and beliefs, specifically those toward time, promptness, achievement, work, and change, have a major impact on the business functions of the MNC and cause it to adapt. Religion is another sociocultural component. Religious conviction could cause workers to be absent from the job, or in extreme cases, cause them to suddenly stop work in midday, as in Pakistan and almost all Middle Eastern countries. Another component is material culture, which involves the technology and government of a foreign country, and how they interact, as well as economic aspects of the country. Levels of education are a vital knowledge point for MNC managers. Brain drain (when highly educated members of a poor foreign country leave to earn better salaries) and differences in educational levels for women must be considered. Finally, language is a key sociocultural component. Communication, obviously, must occur, and language differences must be dealt with in order to communicate. Also, words in the language can denote different things in different situations. Unspoken language is also important, as things people consider minor, such as closed office doors and conversational distance, can drastically affect worker-manager relations. Also, bribes are thought of differently abroad than in the United States. It is certain that in order for the manager of an MNC to be successful, he must be aware of and sensitive to the differences in cultures and societies. Aside from eliminating differences in communiction from the onset, the workers will tend to respect the manager for knowing their society, and for making an effort to cater to them.

DOMESTIC AND INTERNATIONAL ENVIRONMENT OF MNCs

The manager within a multinational organization must deal with three different environments: the domestic, the foreign, and the international environments (see model 22.1). Since the domestic environment is a constant factor affecting the dcisisons made within the MNC, the international environment encompasses both the domestic and foreign environments. This section will focus on these two realms. In particular, it will focus on the laws and regulations that affect the MNC, both domestically and internationally,

Model 22.1
The International Environment

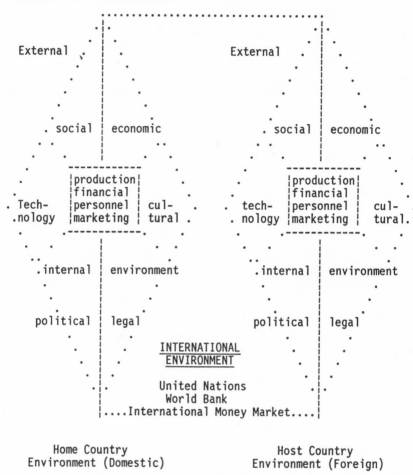

| Home Country | Host Country |
| Environment (Domestic) | Environment (Foreign) |

how and why they differ, and what the MNC can do to operate successfully within the bounds of these legal forces.

The Domestic Environment

Taxation is a prominent legal force. The type of taxation known to most is the income tax, where generally the higher the income is, the higher the tax levied. Another type is the capital gains tax, which is a tax for the selling of an asset at a greater amount than cost. Important aspects of taxation affecting the MNC include the complexity of the laws concerning taxes, the strictness of the government in the enforcement of tax laws, the source of the taxed income, and areas such as tax incentives, tax credits, and double taxation. An interesting aspect of taxation is that many countries have signed tax treaties, in which each nation outlines and defines its tax program. These treaties also provide for the tax authorities of both countries to exchange information.

A second legal force that affects the domestic arena is the antitrust restrictive trade practices of each nation. In this area, the United States differs from other countries in two ways: (1) it has a per se concept incorporated in its law; and (2) it attempts to apply its law extraterritorially.[3] The per se concept refers to the fact that if an action is illegal per se, it is illegal regardless of whether it does damage or harm. In applying laws extraterritorially, the United States has experienced criticism from foreign governments. It has taken foreign parties to U.S. court for violating U.S. law, which foreign governments see as out-of-line behavior.

Another national legal force that affects a firm is tariffs and quotas. Tariffs are designed to raise revenue and to protect domestic firms, while quotas are for the protection of the domestic producer. Aside from these, there are various other little tricks that a government can utilize to protect its domestic firms, such as packaging requirements, language requirements on product labels, and other trade barriers.

A national legal option that is open to certain countries is to seize foreign-owned property within its borders. This is known as expropriation or confiscation, and is legal as long as the country has it defined as a law. Any MNC would be wise to check into this before constructing a plant in any particular foreign country.

Domestication is a milder form of expropriation. Through the domestication process, the host country will try to persuade the MNC to sell a large percentage of its operations so that the host country will gain controlling interest. It will attempt this by pressuring the MNC.

The increased awareness of product liability has caused it to become a legal force. Stricter product safety laws are being passed, and in some countries managers can be found criminally liable for injuries or deaths of workers on the job. Despite concern expressed by the firms that this trend will stifle innovation and that increased insurance costs could wipe out the smaller producers, the pattern continues.[4]

Many governments have the power to control prices and wages set by firms operating in their country. It is believed that these controls would be relaxed if inflation were to decrease. There have been instances of lawsuits resulting from these government actions, especially against the U.S. government. Labor laws dealing with fringe benefits and protection of an employee's rights also play a major role.

The International Environment

In examining international legal forces, note that there are three groups: (1) contract enforcement; (2) solutions to jurisdiction, interpretation, and enforcement problems; and (3) patents, trademarks, copyrights, and trade secrets.

The problem of how to resolve a contract dispute between agencies of two different countries is difficult. An out-of-court settlement would be most desirable. However, within the past twenty years, contract enforcement in the international arena has not been much of a problem as evidenced by the smooth record of world trade in this time period. The growth rate of trade as well as the size achieved ($2 trillion in 1980) expose the point that international contracts are being carried out in good faith.

Of the possible solutions listed in "International Business: Introduction and Essentials" by Ball and McCullough, arbitration is the obvious favorite for many reasons.[5] In solving disputes involving jurisdiction, interpretation, and enforcement relating to contracts, arbitration is quicker. This is important as delays in court proceedings and appeals cost a firm valuable time, and time is money. Also, any evidence can be accepted by the arbitrator as long as he deems it relevant to the case and any rights to appeal the arbitrator's decision can be waived.

The third international force group consists of patents, trademarks, tradenames, copyrights, and trade secrets. Patents are rights of exclusivity granted the inventor of a new product or process. Patents are becoming somewhat easier to obtain in some countries, but in most cases, the inventor must submit a request to each country he desires a patent from in the language of that country. Some representatives of the developing nations are calling for shorter lives of patents, reducing it from fifteen or twenty years to five years. Naturally, inventors are resisting this, claiming that the major incentive to spend large amounts on inventions is to hold the patent for a while and make up the expenses incurred in developing the product or process.

Trademarks and tradenames are logos and names that designate specific products that differentiate them from similar products. Typical durations of trademarks are ten to twenty years. Tradenames are vital because they enforce and prevent counterfeiting. Counterfeiting has become so widespread that it threatens the health and safety of the public, as well as corporate profits. Copyrights are rights of exclusivity given to authors, publishers, artists, and composers, while trade secrets are information that a business wishes to keep secret. Since trade secret laws differ in each country in terms of duration and type of trade secret, an MNC must carefully review the laws of the country in which it is considering production. Industrial espionage, when one firm steals the trade secrets of another, is dealt with rather harshly and is not tolerated.

There are certain U.S. laws that affect international business. It is illegal for two U.S. firms to join efforts on a foreign project. This can put a major crimp on the international competitiveness of U.S. firms for exports. Taxation, in the U.S. laws, affects the international business scene in various ways, including the fact that Americans who live in foreign lands are taxed by two governments—the United States and the country in which the American lives. The Foreign Corrupt Practices Act has proven debilitating to U.S. MNCs. It outlaws certain types of bribes, but does not specify any in particular. It holds management responsible for keeping records on the MNC's behavior to make sure that no violations are occurring. It is felt by many executives that the FCPA puts U.S. MNCs at a serious competitive disadvantage. Others argue that no setbacks should occur, but the numbers show a one billion dollar loss due to the act.

The Antiboycott Law is also considered to be detrimental to U.S. MNCs' competitiveness. This law forbids a U.S. firm to do business with firms that are in a boycotting nation. This hurts the United States in the purchase of oil because many of the Arabian oil-rich nations boycott Israeli products, and want their buyers to do the same. The main constructive argument against the Antiboycott Law is that it hurts the U.S. firm but does no harm to the Arabians, who can sell or buy from any other nation, because no other nations have the Antiboycott Law. Finally, the U.S. government is waking up to the reality that U.S. MNCs are being hurt by these laws, and rectifications of these laws and regulations are beginning to take place.

INTERNATIONAL STRATEGIC MANAGEMENT MODEL

The composition of a unified model for international purposes would have to include the following:

1. Evaluation of international opportunities, threats, problems, and risks
2. Evaluation of company strengths and weaknesses in order to exploit foreign market opportunities
3. Defining company scope relative to international business involvement
4. Formulation of international corporate objectives
5. Development of specific corporate strategies for the company as a whole on international corporate strategy
6. Designing the procedure, budget, and process needed to implement the chosen strategy
7. Designing the control system (standards and motivation) needed to prevent a serious deviation from the expected strategy
8. Opening feedback channels from the first stage to the final stage
9. Reevaluating the implementation and making the necessary adjustments (see model 22.2).

STRATEGIC HUMAN RESOURCE MANAGEMENT

Through the changes in technology, economy, and social environment, organizations are depending more on their human resources to accomplish their objectives.

Model 22.2
International Corporate Strategy

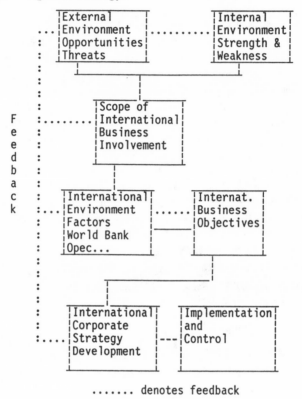

.... denotes feedback

Human resource specialists are faced with problems of equal employment. The Equal Employment Opportunity Commission, established in 1972, is the enforcement agency of the Title VI Civil Rights Act of 1964. The EEOC responds to a change of discrimination filed by the commissioners, an aggrieved person, or someone acting on behalf of the aggrieved person. As organizations have progressed in size, structure, and growth—both in the United States and in foreign countries—more cases concerning discrimination have increased.

There are social problems due to unemployment, segregation, and the judicial and penal systems. Due to some of these past cases, the number of regulatory agencies has increased.

Management is forced to use the human resource planning process to overcome these discriminatory obstacles in order to protect themselves. Organizations must allocate monies to improve working conditions, establish health programs, and provide facilities for the handicapped. These provisions are added expenses to the organization.

Human resource specialists face problems with international employment because of cultural differences. The strategic plan in another country will be different from the strategic plan in the United States. Human resource specialists must design the human resource planning process and strategy to fit the culture under consideration.

Human resources in the organization must be integrated with a strategic direction. They must work toward achieving the same goals and objectives. Affirmative Action outlines and enforces employee rights within organizations. If an employee feels his rights have been violated, he may file a complaint with Affirmative Action. Affirmative Action's purpose is to resolve problems within an organization so that cases will not reach the courts. Publicity, especially negative publicity, affects the overall outcome and performance of the organization. There needs to be special training, development, and activities programs established within the organization for specifically international assignments.

Expatriates are individuals who are not citizens of the country in which they are working. It is the responsibility of the organization to see that the employee and his or her family are prepared for the international assignment. Even more so, when the employee and his or her family return to their home country, they need training and counseling to adjust to the changes that may have occurred. During the process of repatriation, employees face anxiety with their personal finances, reacclimatization to the American life-style, and readjustment to the company.

CONCLUSION

This chapter has attempted to give an overview of strategic management and its importance in the domestic and international environments. An understanding of the culture and environment in the domestic and international arenas are important problems that need to be dealt with by MNCs management. Furthermore, MNCs must understand the regulations and laws within each of the environments with which they associate. Tax laws, antitrust laws, tariffs, and quotas are some examples of domestic regulations MNCs must be familiar with. Trademarks, patents, and copyrights are international legal forces which the MNC must know and understand.

NOTES

1. Leslie W. Rue and Phyllis G. Holland, *Strategic Management: Concepts and Experiences* (New York: McGraw-Hill, 1986), p. 5.
2. I. C. Brown, *Understanding Other Cultures.* (Englewood Cliffs, N.J.: Prentice-Hall, 1963), p. 4.

3. Donald A. Ball and Wendell H. McCullough, *International Business: Introduction and Essentials* (Plano, Tex.: Business Publication, 1985), p. 247.

4. Ibid., p. 251.

5. Ibid., pp. 254–255.

Select Bibliography

BOOKS

Ansoff, Igor. *Corporate Strategy: An Analytic Approach to Business Policy for Growth and Expansion.* New York: McGraw Hill, 1965.

Aram, John D. *Managing Business and Public Policy: Concepts, Issues, and Cases.* Marshfield, Mass.: Pitman Publishing, 1987.

Baker, John C. *Directors and Their Functions: A Preliminary Study.* Boston: Harvard University Press, 1945.

Ball, Donald A., and Wendell H. McCulloch, Jr. *International Business: Introduction and Essentials.* Plano, Tex.: Business Publication, 1985.

Beauchamp, Tom L. and Norman E. Bowie. *Ethical Theory and Business.* Englewood Cliffs, N.J.: 1979.

Berle, Adolf A., and Gardiner C. Means. *The Modern Corporation and Private Property.* New York: Macmillan, 1932.

Braybrooke, David. *Ethics in the World of Business.* Totowa, N.J.: Rowman-Allanheld, and Littlefield 1983.

Brown, I. C. *Understanding Other Cultures.* Englewood Cliffs, N.J.: Prentice-Hall, 1963.

Buchholz, Rogene A. *Business Environment and Public Policy: Implications for Management and Strategy Formulation.* Englewood Cliffs, N.J.: Prentice-Hall, 1986.

Burch, John G. *Entrepreneurship.* New York: John Wiley and Sons, 1986.

Carroll, Archie B. *Business and Society: Managing Corporate Social Performance.* Boston: Little, Brown and Company, 1981.

Cavanagh, F. *American Business Values in Transition.* Englewood Cliffs, N.J.: Prentice-Hall, 1976.

Chamberlain, Neil W. *The Union Challenge to Management Control.* New York: Archer Books, 1969.

Chambouline, Maitre Jean. *Directors and Board, Corporate Governance in the United States of America: Conclusion.* Translated by Alexander Reed and Carolyn B. Kilbourne. Spring 1980.

Clarkson, Kenneth, Roger Miller, and Gaylord Jantz. *West's Business Law*. New York: West Publishing Co., 1986.

Clegg, H. A. *A New Approach to Industrial Democracy*. New York: Blackwell and Mott, 1963.

Copeland, M., and A. Towl. *The Board of Directors and Business Management*. Boston: Harvard University Press, 1947.

Davis, John P. *Corporations*. New York: Capricorn Books, 1981.

De George, Richard T. "Can Corporations Have Moral Responsibility?" Cited in Tom L. Beauchamp and Norman E. Bowie, *Ethical Theory and Business*. Englewood Cliffs, N.J.: Prentice-Hall, 1983.

Diebold, John. *The Role of Business in Society*. AMACOM, a division of American Management Association, 1982.

Douglas, William O. *Democracy and Finance*. New Haven Conn.: Yale University Press, 1940.

Dunlop, John T., and Walter Gulenson. *Labor in the Twentieth Century*. New York: Academic Press, 1978.

Eisenberg, Melvin Aron. *The Structure of the Corporation: A Legal Analysis*. Boston: Little, Brown and Company, 1976.

Freeman, R. Edward. *Strategic Management: A Stakeholders Approach*. Boston: Pitman Publishing, 1984.

Friedman, Milton. *Capitalism and Freedom*. Chicago: University of Chicago Press, 1962.

Furlong, James. *Labor in the Board Room: The Peaceful Revolution*. New Jersey: Dow Jones, 1977.

Heidrick and Struggles, Inc. *The Changing Board: 1980 Update*. New York: 1980.

———. *Profile of the Board of Directors*. New York: 1971.

King, William R., and David I. Cleland. *Strategic Planning and Policy*. New York: Van Nostrand Reinhold, 1978.

Koontz, Harold. *The Board of Directors and Effective Management*. New York: McGraw-Hill, 1967.

Kuhne, Robert J. *Co-determination in Business: Worker's Representatives in the Board Room*. New York: Praeger Publishers, 1980.

Larner, Robert J. *Management Control and the Large Corporation*. New York: Dunellen, 1971.

Ledvinka, James. *Federal Regulation of Personnel and Human Resource Management*. Boston: Kent Publishing Co., 1982.

Louden, J. Keith. *The Effective Director in Action*. New York: AMACOM, 1975.

Mace, Myles L. *Director: Myth and Reality*. Boston: Harvard College, 1971.

Marx, Thomas G. *Business and Society: Economic, Moral and Political Foundations*. Englewood Cliffs, N.J.: Prentice-Hall, 1985.

Nader, Ralph, and Mark Green, eds. *Corporate Power in America*. New York: Grossman Publishers, 1973.

Nader, Ralph, Mark Green, and Joel Seligman. *Taming the Giant Corporation*. New York: W. W. Norton and Company, 1976.

Owen, Bruce M., and Ronald Braeutigum. *The Regulation Game*. Cambridge, Mass.: Ballinger Publishing Company, 1978.

Pegrin, Dudley F. *Public Regulation of Business*. Homewood, Ill.: Richard D. Irwin, 1967.

Pennings, Johannes M. *Interlocking Directorate*. San Francisco: Jossey-Bass Publishers, 1980.

Rhenman, Eric. *Industrial Democracy and Industrial Management*. London: Tavistock Publications, 1968.

Rosen, Corey M., Katherine J. Klein, and Karen M. Young. *Employee Ownership in America: The Equity Solution*. Lexington, Mass.: Lexington Books, 1986.

Rosenberg, Jerry M. *Dictionary of Business and Management*. New York: John Wiley and Sons, 1983.

Rue, Leslie W., and Phyllis G. Holland. *Strategic Management: Concepts and Experiences*. New York: McGraw-Hill, 1986.

Sawyer, Malcom C. *Theories of the Firm*. New York: St. Martin's Press, 1979.

Shapiro, Irving S. "Corporate Governance." In Irving Shapiro and Harold Williams, *Power and Accountability: The Changing Role of the Corporate Board of Directors* (Pittsburgh, Pa.: Carnegie Mellon University Press, 1979).

Steckmest, Francis W. *Corporate Performance: The Key to Public Trust*. New York: McGraw-Hill, 1982.

Stein, Jessy. *Random House College Dictionary*. New York: Random House, 1982.

Stein, Leon. *Big Business*. New York: Arno Press, 1978.

Stone, Christopher C. *Where the Law Ends: The Social Control of Corporate Behavior*. New York: Harper and Row, 1975.

Tricker, R. I. *Corporate Governance: Practices, Procedures and Powers in British Companies and Their Board of Directors*. England: Gower Publishing Company, 1984.

Vance, Stanley C. *Corporate Leadership*. New York: McGraw-Hill, 1983.

Wilson, James Q. *The Politics of Regulation*. New York: Basic Books, 1980.

JOURNALS

Alaberson, William B., and William J. Powell, Jr. "A Landmark Ruling That Puts Board Members in Peril." *Business Week* (March 18, 1987).

Ali, A., and D. Horne. "Problems and Skills in International Business: Tri-city Executives' Perspectives." *SVSC Economic and Business Review* 7, no. 1 (1986).

Alkhafaji, Abbass, Jeff Dubois, Patty Hunter, and Jim Mogan. "A Current Perspective on Leveraged Buyouts." *Industrial Management Magazine* (September–October 1987).

Anders, George. "Boesky Insider-Trading Case May Hurt Confidence in Markets, Spur Regulation." *Wall Street Journal* (November 17, 1986), p. 29.

Andrews, Kenneth R. "Rigid Rules Will Not Make a Good Board." *Harvard Business Review* (November–December 1982).

Baldwin, William. "The Myths of Employee Ownership." *Forbes* (April 1984).

Bandow, Doug. "Are Hostile Takeovers Good for the Economy?" *Business and Society Review* (Fall 1987).

Baruch, Hurd. "The Foreign Corrupt Practices Act of 1977." *Harvard Business Reivew* (January–February 1979).

Baum, Laurie. "The Job Nobody Wants." *Business Week* (September 8, 1986).

Bernstein, Aaron. "A Union's Novel Attempt at Shaping a Buyout." *Business Week* (September 8, 1986).

Bianco, Anthony. "Deal Mania—The Tempo Is Frantic and the Prosperity of the U.S. Is at Stake." *Business Week* (November 24, 1986).

Birely, Sue. "Success and Failure in Management Buyouts." *Long Range Planning* 17, no. 3 (1985).

Black, Robert F., Ron A. Taylor, Clemens P. Work, Patricia Scherscheb, Manuel Schiffres, and Cindy Skrzyeri. "How Deregulation Puts Competition Back in Business." *U.S. News and World Report* (November 25, 1984).

Block, Stanley B. "Buy-Sell Agreements for Privately Held Corporations." *Journal of Accounting* (September 1985).

Boulanger, Robert, and Donald Wayland. "Ethical Management: A Growing Corporate Responsibility—Part 2." *CA Magazine* (April 1985).

Braham, James. "An Inside Look at Outside Directors." *Industrial Week* (September 3, 1984).

Buchholz, Rogene A. "Social Responsibility Revisited." *Journal of Enterprise Management* (1982).

Burrough, Brian. "Back in Action." *Wall Street Journal* (January 25, 1988).

Byran, Christopher. "Big Profits in Big Bribery." *Time* (March 16, 1981).

Cook, Michael J., and Thomas P. Kelly. "The Foreign Corrupt Practices Act Has Made the Internal Accounting Controls of Public Companies a Matter of Law." *Journal of Accountancy* (January 1979).

Dill, W. "Public Participation in Corporation Planning: Strategic Management in a Kibitzer's World." *Long Range Planning* (1975).

Dunn, D. J. "Directors Aren't Doing Their Job." *Fortune* (March 16, 1987).

Edgerton, Jerry. "What the Boesky Scandal Means to You and Your Money." *Money* (January 1987).

Farrell, Christopher. "If Directors Are Doing Their Jobs, They Don't Need Insurance." *Business Week* (September 8, 1986).

Friedman, Milton. "The Social Responsibility of Business Is to Increase Its Profits." *New York Times Magazine* (September 13, 1970).

Geneen, Harold S. "Why Directors Can't Protect the Shareholders." *Fortune* (September 17, 1984).

Gest, Ted, Kenneth Sheets, and Ron Taylor. "As Lawyers Move in on India's Tragedy." *U.S. News and World Report* (December 24, 1984).

Glaberson, William B., and William Powell. "India's Bhopal Suit Could Change All the Rules." *Business Week* (April 22, 1985).

Greenwald, John. "The Popular Game of Going Private." *Time* (November 4, 1985), p. 54.

Hamilton, Joan O'C. "Levi Strauss Wants to Be a Family Affair Again." *Business Week* (July 29, 1985).

Hays, Laurie. "Pickens Impels Blitz to Topple Measure on Hostile Bids." *Wall Street Journal* (January 14, 1988).

"How the New Merger Boom Will Benefit the Economy." *Business Week* (February 6, 1984).

Ingersoll, Bruce. "Shad Defends SEC Move to Allow Boesky to Sell Holdings Before Probe Disclosure." *Wall Street Journal* (November 24, 1986).

Jackson, Stuart. "Union Carbide's Good Name Takes a Beating." *Business Week* (December 31, 1984).

Kim, Suk H. "On Repealing the Foreign Corrupt Practices Act: Survey and Assessment." *Columbia Journal of World Business* (Fall 1981).

Lewin, Tamar. "The Corporate Reform Furor." *New York Times* (June 10, 1982).

Lewis, Ralph F. "What Should Audit Committees Do?" *Harvard Business Review* (May–June 1978).

Loving, Rush, Jr., "How the Airlines Will Cope with Deregulation." *Fortune* (November 20, 1978).

Mace, Myles L. "The President and the Board of Directors." *Harvard Business Review* (March–April 1972).

Maisonrouge, J. "The Education of Modern International Managers." *Journal of International Business Studies* (Spring 1984).

Martz, Larry. "True Greed." *Newsweek* (December 12, 1986).

Mauro, Tony. "Liability in the Board Room." *Nation's Business* (May 1986).

McComas, Maggie. "Life Isn't Easy." *Fortune* (December 9, 1985).

Mercer, Robert. "Raiders Might Be After Your Company Next." *Industrial Week* (June 29, 1987).

Miller, Ken. "Westinghouse Makes Clean-Up Profitable." *Business Week* (June 3, 1985).

Miller, Michael W. "Boesky Case Expected to Bring Windfall for Lawyers from Suits Claiming Losses." *Wall Street Journal* (November 21, 1986).

Murray, Thomas. "Here Comes the 'Tin' Parachute." *Dun's Business Month* (January 1987).

Nelson, Joani-Horchler. "A Catchall Parachute." *Industry Week* (February 9, 1987).

Newcomb, Peter. "No One Is Safe." *Forbes* (July 13, 1987).

Noah, Timothy. "The Business Ethics Debate." *Newsweek* (May 25, 1987).

O'Conell, Joan M. "Do Mergers Really Work?" *Business Week* (June 3, 1985).

Pauly, David. "The SEC Bags Ivan Boesky." *Newsweek* (November 24, 1986).

Powell, Ben. "Is It Safe to Go Back into the Board Room?" *Newsweek* (March 18, 1985).

Powers, Ron. "Businessmen Wear Black Hats." *Business Month* (December 1987).

Proxmire, William. "The Foreign Payoff Law Is a Necessity." *New York Times* (February 5, 1978).

Ricklefs, Roger. "Executives and General Public Say Ethical Behavior Is Declining in the United States." *Wall Street Journal* (October 21, 1985).

———. "On Many Ethical Issues, Executives Apply Stiffer Standards Than Public." *Wall Street Journal* (November 1, 1985).

Russell, George. "Going After the Crooks." *Time* (December 1, 1986).

Samuelson, Robert J. "The Super Bowl of Scandal." *Newsweek* (December 1, 1986).

Scott, William A., and Terrence R. Mitchell. "The Moral Failure of Management Education." *Chronicle of Higher Education* (December 11, 1985), p. 35.

Sethi, S. Prakash. "A Conceptual Framework for Environmental Analysis of Social Issues and Evaluation of Business Response Patterns." *Academy of Management Review* (Janaury 1979).

Shiller, Zachary. "Uniroyal: The Road from Giant to Corporate Shell." *Business Week* (July 14, 1986), p. 29.

Shiller, Zachary, and Amy Dunkin. "New? Improved? The Brand Name Mergers." *Business Week* (October 21, 1985).

Sigler, Andrew. "Takeovers: The Economic Cost." *Corporate Board* (September–October 1985).

Simon, Ruth. "Of Pots and Paintbrushes." *Forbes* (November 3, 1986).

Typgos, Manuel A. "Compliance with the Foreign Corrupt Practices Act." *Financial Executive* (August 1981).

Smith, Ephraim P. "Interlocking Directors Among the Fortune 500." *Anti-Trust Law and Economics Review* (Summer 1970).

Soloman, Lewis. "Restructuring the Corporate Board of Directors: Fond Hope—Faint Promise?" *Michigan Law Review* (1978).

Sommer, A. A. "Corporate Governance: Its Impact on the Profession." *Journal of Accountancy* (July 1980).

Spragins, Ellyn E. "Leverged Buyouts Aren't Just for Daredevils Anymore." *Business Week* (August 11, 1986).

Stone, Christopher D. "Why Shouldn't Corporations Be Socially Responsible?" *Business Ethics* (1984).

Tell, Lawrrence J. "ESOPs and LBOs: No KOs for Kelso in This Fight." *Barron's* (November 18, 1985).

Turpin-Forster, C. Sheila. "ESOPs Mean Business." *ABA Banking Journal* (October 1985).

Weidenbaum, Murray. "The Best Defense Against the Raiders." *Business Week* (September 23, 1985).

Weigner Kathleen. "To Make Your Company Raider-proof, Run It Right." *Forbes* (November 3, 1986).

Weiss, Gary. "ABC's of LBOs: What Makes Leveraged Buyouts Popular." *Barron's* (August 19, 1985).

Work, Clemens P. and Manuel Schiffres. "Leveraged Buyouts—Are They Growing Too Risky?" *U.S. News and World Report* (November 18, 1985).

Yang, C., and J. Weber. "Is Delaware About to Harpoon the Sharks?" *Business Week* (January 25, 1988), p. 34.

"Assuring America's Competition Preeminence." *Business America* (March 23, 1987).

Daenis, H. *The Rise of the Modern Industrial Enterprise.* Chicago: Dryden, 1976.

"Deregulating America." *Business Week* (November 28, 1983).

Wildstrom, Stephen H. "A Risky Tack for Democrats." *Business Week* (July 20, 1987).

"Praise the Lord and Pass the Loot." *Economist* (May 16, 1987).

"TV Ministries Enveloped in Infighting." *Broadcasting* (May 30, 1987).

Powell, Bill, and Rich Thomas. "The Raiders: A Quick Fall from Grace." *Newsweek* (December 8, 1986).

Mitchell, Russell, and Pete Engardio. "But Can He Handle An Ax?" *Business Week* (January 25, 1988).

"Business Must Tell Holders More or Face Tougher U.S. Controls, SEC Chief Warns." *Wall Street Journal* (September 30, 1977).

"Management Should Fill Only One Seat on a Firm's Board, SEC Chairman Urges," *Wall Street Journal* (January 19, 1978).

"AICPA Executive Committee Statement on Audit Committees of Boards of Directors," *Journal of Accountancy* (September 1967).

Securities and Exchange Commission, Accounting Series, No. 123 (March 23, 1971).

"Corporate Governance Faulted in a Study by SEC Staff." *Wall Street Journal* (January 28, 1980).

"Shareholders Communications: Shareholders Participation in the Corporate Governance Generally, Final Rules" (Securities and Exchange Commission Release No. 34–15384). *Federal Securities Law Reporter* (Para. 81, 766, December 6, 1978).

Miles, Gregory A., and Matt Rothman. "No More Rubber Stamps in the Board Room." *Business Week* (December 1, 1986).

"The State in the Market: Public Sector Enterprise." *Economist* (December 30, 1978).

"Anderson Reflects on Managing Bhopal." *Industry Week* (October 13, 1986).

Comes, Frank S., Richard A. Melcher, and Jonathan Kapstein. "Europe Goes on a Shopping Spree in the States." *Business Week* (October 27, 1986).

Treece, James B., "If You Can't Beat 'Em, Buy 'Em." *Business Week* (September 29, 1986).

Smith, Lee. "Want to Buy a Japanese Company?" *Fortune* (June 27, 1983).

"A Japanese Tonic for Merck." *Business Week* (August 22, 1983).

"Top Executives Offer to Buy Macy's." *New York Times* (October 22, 1985).

Index

About the Author

ABBASS F. ALKHAFAJI is Associate Professor of Management at Slippery Rock University. His articles on corporate governance have been published for several professional academic meetings and journals.